The Stupidity Problem

AND OTHER HARASSMENTS

THE

Books by John Fischer

THE STUPIDITY PROBLEM

MASTER PLAN U.S.A.

WHY THEY BEHAVE LIKE RUSSIANS

JOHN FISCHER

STUPIDITY PROBLEM

AND OTHER HARASSMENTS

HARPER & ROW, PUBLISHERS

NEW YORK, EVANSTON,

AND LONDON

917.3
F52s

48,908
feb., 1965

For Bernard DeVoto,
a man hard to follow
and impossible to emulate

Contents

Foreword

The material in this book originally was published in *Harper's Magazine*—nearly all of it in a column with the peculiarly unfitting title of "The Editor's Easy Chair." I began writing this column in 1955, unexpectedly, unwillingly, under tragic circumstances and (as I then thought) on a strictly temporary emergency basis. I have been at it ever since; and not a moment has been easy for me.

Nor was it for my predecessors, except in the very early days. The first "Easy Chair" column appeared in the October, 1851, issue of *Harper's* about a year after the magazine was started. It was a leisurely, graceful essay, of a type then in high literary fashion and now virtually unknown. It is noteworthy only because it launched the column which has become the oldest editorial feature in American journalism and, so far as I can discover, in the English language.

In its century-plus lifetime it has been conducted by only six men: Donald G. Mitchell, George William Curtis, William Dean Howells, Edward S. Martin, Bernard DeVoto, and me. None of the first five was, in fact, the editor of the magazine. Each of them expressed his own views, without interference from the editors. Yet it came to be regarded over the course of years as the editorial voice of the magazine.

When Bernard DeVoto died of a heart attack on November

13, 1955, he had been writing "The Easy Chair" for twenty years. (His last manuscript reached what are still called The Editorial Rooms at Harper's the day after his death, as the editors had known it would; he never missed a deadline.) Under his ministry the name of the column was almost ludicrously inappropriate. Like most professional writers, he did not write easily. Into each manuscript of about three thousand words he put many days of legwork, research, and profane labor at his typewriter, as he revised each line over and over again until it said precisely what he meant it to say. Nor was the end product, in most cases, meant to ease anybody's soul. DeVoto loved America profoundly —he never went overseas because he said he still hadn't learned enough about this country—and he was impatient with its imperfections. Moreover, he was a turbulent man, of strong opinions, usually expressed at the top of his voice. As a consequence, he found himself in a good many fights. He described his job as the writing of cultural criticism; and since his criticism always had a bite, he wasn't surprised when the culture sometimes bit back.

"I suppose," one of his readers once remarked, "that DeVoto is so interested in conservation because he feels that the more he sees of people the more he wants to preserve the grizzly bear." Along with a lot of others who knew him only from his writing, this lady thought of DeVoto as a professional curmudgeon, who woke up with a growl every morning and promptly looked around for somebody's leg to chew off.

She was wrong. In fact, DeVoto was a sentimentalist with a coronary melting point fourteen degrees lower than maple sugar. He was incapable of saying no to anybody who looked either needy or put-upon. The upshot was that he spent a large part of his time helping people to find a job, a publisher, a sound whisky, an elusive fact, a comfortable motel, a sense of prose style, justice, or a reliable psychiatrist—all the while emitting roars of exasperation. For he was a shy man, and any creature that suffers both from shyness and a soft interior has to grow some kind of protective armament: witness the porcupine and the armadillo. (He also devoted an inordinate amount of thought, energy, and profanity to counseling the young—including, for example, Arthur Schlesinger, Jr., and me—and trying, despairingly, to teach them how to write, think, and conduct their lives, which he regarded as all the same thing.)

Benny's unexpected death put The Editorial Rooms in a first-rate crisis. Over two decades he had established a unique pattern and a passionately loyal readership. Clearly it wasn't going to be easy to find a replacement.

At the time I had been editor-in-chief of the magazine for a little over two years, and had been writing for it fairly often for about twenty. While my associates and I sought a writer to take DeVoto's place, I took on, by default, the job of filling "The Easy Chair" temporarily. Some three months later we still hadn't found another DeVoto, and it was becoming apparent that we never could; but I found that I was enjoying the column. I've been writing it ever since, with occasional help from guest contributors.

It is of course very different from what it was in DeVoto's time, just as his column differed from his predecessors'. Yet its purpose remains what it has always been: to attempt some kind of appraisal of the society we live in. To me, as to DeVoto, Americans have always seemed endlessly surprising, entertaining, and sometimes inexplicable. Trying to figure out what they are up to, and why, and what might come of it, has been for me—as it was for him—a chief preoccupation.

The resulting columns have been part reporting, part commentary. Naturally many of them dealt with current topics, which are no longer at issue. Others attempted to examine subjects which are, it seems to me, of continuing interest. Thirty-eight have been assembled in the following pages—not in chronological order but according to a rough grouping of subject matter. A few originally appeared not in "The Easy Chair" but elsewhere in *Harper's* before I took over the column. Some have been cut, and several passages have been slightly amended to take account of subsequent developments.

I am indebted to the other editors of *Harper's*—especially Miss Catharine Meyer—for their brutal and unfeeling comments on these pieces when they were first submitted in manuscript. Often they made me revise sentences which they deemed unclear, and cut or subdue passages which seemed to me particularly splendid. Though I screamed and stomped my feet at the time, I had to admit eventually that they were always right. I am also indebted to Cass Canfield, who urged me to put this material together in book form; to Miss Genevieve Young, who did the preliminary selection and most of the labor of preparing the book for the press; and to my family, for almost supernatural patience with me during the many weekends and evenings when I was working on these columns.

—JOHN FISCHER

January 4, 1964

PART I

UNFINISHED BUSINESS

1 : What Women Can Do for Peace

AT A DINNER PARTY a few nights ago, a charming and intelligent woman remarked that her main concern right now is to decide what she can best do to help the search for peace. She suspects that the present activities of the women's peace organizations—picketing, mass demonstrations, and such—are largely irrelevant, and sometimes actually harmful to their cause.

"But," she says, "a great many women, including me, feel strongly that we have to do *something* to prevent another war. This is a primitive, powerful emotion. It has to find an outlet somewhere—and if it can't be channeled into some constructive direction, it is bound to boil up in irrational ways."

She has a point. The following suggestions are submitted, therefore, in hopes that they may help her and other concerned women to focus their considerable energies and talents in a more useful way.

So far these ladies have concentrated almost entirely on disarmament, and especially the abolition of atomic weapons. The results have been frustrating, because picketing cannot help in a delicate diplomatic negotiation any more than it can in a brain operation. Moreover, the ladies have no way to put effective pressure on the Kremlin, Peking, and de Gaulle, who are the chief obstacles to a disarmament agreement. Their basic mis-

3

take, however, is their assumption that arms are the main, if not the only, cause of war.

There is remarkably little evidence to support this assumption. I do not know of any case in which an arms race was the underlying cause of a war—though in the years before 1914 it certainly did something to inflame more deep-rooted rivalries. The most common historic reasons for conflict have been national ambitions, messianic ideologies (ranging from the Sword of Islam and the Crusades to modern fascism and communism), racial hatreds, a ruler's dreams of glory, or (as with the Vikings and Homeric Greeks) simple lust for loot. And when people bent on killing can get no better weapons, they do quite well with clubs and stones—as India's Hindus and Moslems demonstrated when their subcontinent was partitioned after World War II. In that flare-up of religious and racial passion, something like a million and a half men, women, and children were slaughtered without benefit of modern arms.

Nuclear weapons would of course make another war unimaginably worse than anything in human experience; but it is not clear that they make it more probable. On the contrary, there is a growing belief in Washington that at least for the moment the nuclear stalemate may be a positive, stabilizing force. It would be a fine thing, of course, if an arms-control agreement can eventually be achieved—if only for the enormous savings in money and resources. But it would not be a sure guarantee of peace.

In the future the chief danger of war seems likely to come not from an arms race or even from the classic causes but from an element new to history: the world-wide pressure of population. Indeed, if the earth's population continues to rise at the present rate for another forty years, major wars appear to be inevitable.

Local overpopulation has of course led to war in the past. It was, for example, a main reason why the ancient Greeks invaded Italy and Asia Minor to found colonies, and why the Goths, Mongols, and Huns flooded west from the Asian steppes in successive invasions of Europe. But never before has the pressure of population risen, all over the globe, so rapidly and steadily as it is rising today. If it keeps up, an explosion is inescapable—just as it is when the steam pressure in a boiler climbs above the bursting point.

A glance at the accompanying chart shows why this is so. For many centuries the number of human beings increased very

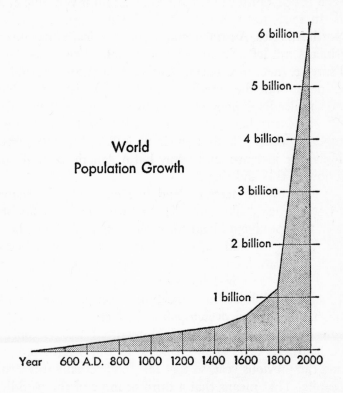

slowly. Then, about 1800, it began to shoot up like a rocket. In roughly a million years between the first appearance of man and that date, the total reached about one billion. In the century and a half since then, it has leaped to nearly three billion. In the next forty years it seems certain to double again. The explanation has been documented in countless books: how modern medicine and sanitation sharply cut the death rate—

especially deaths among young children—while the birth rate kept right on.

So what? Up till now—so the Micawbers among us say—we have managed to take care of a trebled population pretty well. Maybe something will turn up before it trebles again. God will provide. . . .

Such happy optimism is hard to maintain if you look at a few facts. In 1800, fertile continents were still largely empty—most of North America, Australia, and Latin America. Today no empty continents are left. Small patches of not-yet-overcrowded land still survive, here, in Canada, Southeast Asia, Siberia, and a few other places; but they are filling up fast. Nor is it true that the world's multiplying population has fared reasonably well. While living standards have risen since 1800 in this country and Europe, in other places they have fallen. Most Indians and Chinese, for instance, and many Latin Americans don't eat as well now as they did then.

For it takes two acres of land to feed a person adequately. (Not well—just "adequately.") Yet we have only about one acre of food-producing land for each person on the globe—and we are adding 55 million hungry mouths every year. We can't possibly add farmland that fast. Every new acre now has to be won, at heavy cost in labor and investment, from the deserts and swamps; while at the same time other acres are being lost through erosion and overcropping. In fact the Food and Agriculture Organization of the UN reported last October that there had been little if any increase in world farm production during the previous year, so that less food actually was available per capita. That means that a third or more of the world's people already are hungry most of the time—but not as hungry as they are going to be.

Conceivably by heroic effort and yet-unimagined scientific breakthroughs—the creation of edible algae, perhaps, and the large-scale harvesting of seaweed—mankind could double food output in the next forty years, thus keeping barely even with population growth. But even if this improbable feat could be accomplished once, it obviously cannot be repeated indefinitely. Since the surface of the globe is strictly limited, the "Standing Room Only" sign will have to go up eventually—and much sooner than most of us realize.*

China, where such facts press the hardest, has now become the most dangerous nation. Already it has a fifth of all the people in the world, and it adds 22 per cent every decade. They are crammed inside a territory which is barely able to feed them in a good year; a bad year means famine. So they press outward as inexorably as a glacier—into Korea, Tibet, India, Southeast Asia, tomorrow perhaps into Outer Mongolia and Siberia. Their Communist faith gives an extra edge to their belligerence, but they would still be dangerous if they had never heard of Marx. For when a hungry man has to choose between starvation and grabbing his neighbor's garden, he is likely to grab. (It is noteworthy that Chiang Kai-shek's government-in-exile has not repudiated Red China's claims either in Tibet or in India.)

Indeed Mao may be speaking the literal truth when he proclaims that he does not shrink from a nuclear war. He may figure, in his icy way, that the extinction of some 200 million people is the only means of reducing China's population to manageable proportions; that it would still remain the most populous nation, even after such a holocaust; that more industrialized states would suffer still worse devastation; and that Chinese expansion thereafter would be all the easier.

So at least believes a veteran and levelheaded Polish diplomat, who has had long experience with the leaders of Red China. "The frightening thing about them," he told me recently, "is that they don't plan in years or decades. They think in terms of centuries. And they have no scruples whatever, so far as I can detect, about human life."

And Asia is not the only continent where population pressure has reached the bursting point. Too many people scrab-

---

* Other planets? No. None in our solar system will support human life, and not even the most imaginative scientist has ever suggested that we will ever be able to export people in substantial numbers to other solar systems.

bling for too little land has led to the tribal fighting in the Congo (where several little civil wars have spluttered along quite independently of the big fight over Katanga). The same thing lies behind the unrest in northeast Brazil, in Haiti, in Bolivia, in Chile and Peru.

Even in Mexico, which has carried out the most successful agrarian-reform program in Latin America, land hunger is again causing ominous rumblings throughout the countryside—as it must so long as the population continues to grow at 3 per cent a year.

Nor is this country exempt. For a long time we won't face a food problem, and it is hard to imagine our changing into a bellicose nation like China. But even now the pressures of population are threatening both our living standards and our foreign policy. As Adolph W. Schmidt of T. Mellon and Sons, a conservative and eminent financier, recently pointed out, within the next forty years "everything about us must double if our present living standard is to be maintained . . . houses, apartments, roads, office buildings, schools, the endowments of your colleges, universities, and hospitals." He added with some reluctance that "I do not believe that we in Pittsburgh will double everything around us during this relatively brief period. If we do not, a number of people will have to do with less in the year 2000 than they now have." Another equally respected economist and businessman, Marriner Eccles, has predicted that our problems of unemployment, rising taxes, urban congestion, and education are all insoluble unless our rapidly growing population is curbed.

For the past twenty years our foreign policy has been built on one key idea: if we can help the rest of the world to become prosperous, it will then become stable, peaceful, and maybe democratic as well. In Europe it worked; so it seemed reasonable to hope that some counterpart of the original Marshall Plan might work in other continents too. What we overlooked is the fact that population in the underdeveloped countries is growing three times as fast as it is in Europe. The result was summed up by Eugene Black, former president of the World Bank, in his 1961 annual report to the United Nations: "Unless population growth can be restrained, we may have to abandon for this generation our hopes of economic progress in the crowded lands of Asia and the Middle East."

He might have added Latin America; and he should have noted that in the next generation these hopes will be slimmer still.

Our obvious course, if we want to salvage our foreign-aid program and our hopes for peace, is to do all we can to bring the population explosion under control. (And not merely in distant and impoverished lands; until we control our own growth rate—which is higher than that of Europe, Japan, and some other countries—nobody is likely to take our advice seriously.)

This indeed is precisely what has been recommended by the Draper Committee on foreign aid, by Eugene Black, by Senator William Fulbright, Chairman of the Senate Foreign Relations Committee, and by scores of other responsible citizens who have learned the facts at first hand. Yet Washington does nothing. Most politicians are afraid even to mention the subject out loud. "Probably never in history," James Reston reported in the *New York Times*, "has so obvious and significant a fact been so widely evaded. . . ."

The reason, as we all know, is that our politicians are afraid of offending Catholic voters. But here, as in so many other matters, our politicians may be victims of a cultural lag; for Catholic opinion on population problems has been undergoing a remarkable change in the last few years.

As long ago as 1951 Pope Pius XII approved "the legality of the regulation of births" for "medical, eugenic, economic, and social reasons." Since then an increasing number of Catholic spokesmen—*Commonweal* magazine, Father Louis McKernan of *Catholic World*, Father John A. O'Brien of Notre Dame, to mention only a few—have published serious discussions of population problems. As Father O'Brien has pointed out, "substantial agreement" already exists "between Catholics and non-Catholics concerning the overall objectives of family planning." The chief remaining difference concerns methods of birth control.

The Church so far approves only two means: abstention and the rhythm method—the latter not yet altogether dependable. But Pope Pius XII expressed hope that "science will succeed in providing this licit method with a sufficiently secure basis"; and Father O'Brien has urged the federal government "to launch a crash research program to render the rhythm method 100 per cent effective." Moreover, an eminent Catholic physician, Dr. John Rock of Harvard, has been urging research into "entirely new approaches" to develop "a number of effective methods which all religious groups can accept."*

Perhaps, then, we already are within striking distance of the goal proclaimed by Father O'Brien: "to take the birth control issue out of politics."

Even now there seems to be no reason why women of every faith should not work together on the really basic peace issue: How can we check the world's population pressures before they explode into war?

It is an issue which they can attack with unique effectiveness, since children and family have always been primary feminine concerns. When women speak on these matters, they carry an authority greater than they can ever hope to have on questions of weaponry and arms control. In this field, moreover, they have before them specific, urgent tasks, which will yield concrete results much more quickly than any amount of "Ban the Bomb" agitation. For example:

1. The greatest need is to discover methods of birth control which will be effective, acceptable to all religions, and simple and cheap enough to be used by the poorest and most primitive

---

* Both the scientific and political aspects of the question are also explored in Dr. Rock's book, *The Time Has Come: A Catholic Doctor's Proposals to End the Battle Over Birth Control*, published by Knopf.

people. Many promising scientific leads have not yet been followed up, simply because not enough money is available to finance a crash research program. If Congress would authorize the National Institutes of Health to spend a mere one per cent of their budget on such research, "there is every reason" (to quote Father O'Brien again) "to believe that the problems of family planning and population control could be solved." Incidentally, this would be a tiny fraction of the cost of a single Polaris submarine.

2. Our foreign-aid people should be directed to supply help in population control to any foreign country requesting it.

3. The laws in a few of our states need changing so that birth-control information can be freely supplied to anyone wanting it. (A number of Catholic clergymen have endorsed such changes, as Father O'Brien noted in an article in the October 10, 1961, issue of *Look*. And the Gallup poll has found that they are favored by three out of four members of the general public.)

(4) Public hospitals, health services, and welfare agencies should be authorized to provide birth-control information, treatment, and materials to their clients upon request—in each case following the methods approved by the client's own religious doctrine.

(5) An immense amount of education is needed to bring home to the ordinary citizen, here and abroad, the desperate urgency of the population crisis. Many responsible, well-educated people who are vaguely aware of the population explosion apparently are unable to connect it with their own lives. How else to account for the college graduates who cheerfully—and with no sense of sin—produce four, five, and six children? What they do not grasp, evidently, is that the question is a moral one. To put it baldly, anyone who increases the total number of people in an overcrowded world adds to the likelihood of war.

Once this simple mathematical truth is widely understood, it may lead to the acceptance of a new commandment, ordained by natural law: Thou Shalt Not Produce More Than Two Children.

It might be called the Commandment of Survival—because

God does indeed provide, whenever any species outbreeds its environment; though not in the way the Micawbers have in mind. The Adirondack deer starve, the Australian rabbits are wiped out by myxomatosis, the Norwegian lemmings rush into the sea. Thus if human beings cannot find a rational way to control their numbers, Providence will do it for them in the immemorial way: by famine, pestilence, and war.

We shall have, therefore, only ourselves to blame if some future historian (assuming that one survives) records as an example of Divine Providence that nuclear weapons were invented just in time to keep the world's population from spurting entirely out of control.

April, 1963

2 : Conversation at Midnight

Schloss Leopoldskron,
Salzburg, Austria

THIS CASTLE IS SUPPOSED TO BE HAUNTED. A Nazi gauleiter shot his wife, his three children, and himself in the little lookout room on the top floor that morning when he saw the American tanks break into the valley; and other troubled spirits (I am told) have been mewling and clanking around the staircases for a good two hundred years. So it was only sensible to take precautions.

The best protection against ghosts, Father Florian said, was a bottle of the red wine put up by his fellow monks at the Peterskeller. It is not very good wine, but it is strong, and after a few glasses any apparition would hardly be noticeable. As my spiritual adviser (self-appointed) he had taken the liberty of bringing a liter with him.

"I detest being interrupted by spooks," he said as he pulled the cork. "Or, for that matter, by anyone else. Close the door. I have to reprove you, and I don't want those people wandering in with their silly questions."

This was unfair. "Those people" are fifty-eight young men and women who are, for the moment, living here; Father Florian is merely an occasional visitor, usually uninvited. They have come from sixteen European countries, because each of them has a professional interest in the United States, and because the Schloss is now occupied by a curious kind of school, known as The Seminar in American Studies. It is true that they often cross-examine the five Americans who serve as faculty until all hours of the night, but their questions are seldom silly. They are people of trained intelligence—diplomats, newspapermen, teachers, sociologists, civil servants—and their inquiries sometimes are uncomfortably sharp. Father Florian never asks questions; he gives answers, whether you want them or not. He is dogmatic, fat, and impertinent; and I am fond of him.

He filled two glasses and settled himself in the only comfortable chair in my study.

"The trouble with you Americans . . ." he said.

"Look," I interrupted, "let's get back to the ghosts. For the last month these people have been telling me what is wrong with Americans, and I am beginning to get the idea. We are a bunch of crude materialists. We've got no culture, no respect for tradition, no sense of history, no ideals, no palate. . . ."

"Nonsense," Father Florian said. "It is true that most Europeans believe those legends, but I am going to tell you what is *really* wrong with America. I traveled back and forth across your country for seven years, making a serious study of the American soul. And I don't think you understand yourselves any better than these youngsters who have been talking at you."

He loosened the rope he wore around the middle of his cassock and eased his throat with a little wine.

"The real trouble," he said, "is that you are a bunch of dreamy poets. You are besotted with culture. You spend more time and money on it than you can afford. Idealism is a fine thing, but you Americans have carried it too far—to the point where you can no longer bear to face a hard, material fact when you meet one. This is dangerous. You will have to learn to be practical, or you will perish.

"Now don't misunderstand me. We are grateful for your cultural leadership, though naturally we can't admit it. We have to snarl a little, to save our self-respect—but we are soaking up your culture like a parched field soaks up rain. We play your music, read your novels, and wear your clothes all over Europe. Look at all our girls in blue jeans and pony tails, and all our little boys in cowboy champs. Chaps? Ah, yes. Thank you.

"Even alcoholic Paris, thank Heaven, is being infiltrated with milk bars, and half the boys in my parish are trying to play the trumpet like Satchmo. My city of Vienna invented musical comedy, but *Kiss Me, Kate* is the biggest hit there since the war. This is embarrassing, because we haven't produced a good musical of our own for thirty years. And Germany, which is temporarily out of playwrights, is making a national hero out of Thornton Wilder.

"At this very minute there isn't a housewife east of the Danube who isn't scheming to get a vacuum cleaner, a washing machine, and an icebox. Wonderful aids to the spiritual life. When a woman doesn't have to spend all her waking hours in drudgery, she can find time for literature and art and even, sometimes, for the Church. If we Europeans have a religious revival we should give part of the thanks to the United States. We won't do it, of course."

A strangulated moan began to reverberate through the west wall. Father Florian cocked an ear and suggested that perhaps we should send for another bottle. No need, I explained. That was the normal voice of the neobaroque plumbing in the bathroom—the one with the three crystal chandeliers—which Max Reinhardt had installed when he lived here.

"Nevertheless I shall take another glass," the friar said, "for this castle and all its ghosts can bear testimony to the warning I am about to deliver. Schloss Leopoldskron is, in fact, a relic of a cultural spree, much like the one on which America is now embarking. And I must warn you that a nation can pay too high for such a flowering of the spirit.

"That is precisely the mistake we Austrians made a couple of centuries ago. Our Empire was then the first power on the Continent. We had recently won a terrible war. Our armies were invincible; our economy was thriving; our political system obviously was the soundest ever ordained by God. So we took all that for granted—indeed we affected a contempt for the material side of life—and for three generations we devoted our considerable energies to developing an extravagant and delightful civilization.

"Like yourselves, we were a religious people. We worshiped the Holy Trinity, instead of the automobile, but we lavished on it fully as much money, artistry, and sacrificial effort as you now devote to the products of Detroit's Big Three.

"Don't interrupt. I am not, at the moment, criticizing your faith. Other pagan countries have done worse. Your wheeled idol combines all the best features of Moloch, the Juggernaut, and the Golden Calf—and as a student of comparative religions I must admit that your consecration to it is impressive.

"How many lives do you offer up a year? Forty thousand? The Toltecs did no better for Quetzalcoatl, although their method of execution was less messy. How many priests in gray flannel habits sing its praises? How many farms and homes do you destroy to clear its path? What will you not sacrifice in toil, cash, and inconvenience in its service? I myself have watched your people at their Sunday afternoon devotions, standing bumper to bumper on the highway, their lips moving in silent prayer. And I have seen how your male children—acolytes, I presume—anoint their heads with oil and prostrate themselves for hours at a time beneath the sacred object. In its heathen way, such piety is admirable.

"But can you afford it? Austria couldn't—and I beg you to profit from our example while there is yet time.

"We, too, had no patience with anything old-fashioned. We tore down perfectly good Gothic churches and replaced them with bigger and fancier models. For our archbishops and their mistresses we built palaces by the dozen—like this one and Mirabell and Hellbrunn. Every inch we decorated with plaster curlicues and gold leaf, at immense expense, just as you encrust your rolling temples with chrome and fins and colored lights. Both you and we, it seems, have an insatiable taste for the rococo.

"Nor did we see anything wrong with combining our religious life with sensuality. Music and love and laughter were the leitmotifs of our eighteenth century. Our entertainment industry —like yours—grew enormous; our theaters and orchestras were the envy of the world. Mozart got as much homage as Dave Brubeck, and almost as much money. (Their work, as I am sure you have noticed, sounds oddly similar—two varieties, so to speak, of baroque chamber music.)

"And while we frivoled away our substance and brainpower in this joyous outburst of creativity, a glum little band of Frenchmen were incubating the revolution which—a few years later— was to destroy us. Nobody warned us, and perhaps we wouldn't have listened if they had. Who could believe that a ridiculous fat man named Bonaparte might one day stable his cavalry in our churches?

"He was a crude type, interested in cannon, not culture. Almost as crude as the Russians—who made the sputnik while you were designing more worshipful cars. Now I don't doubt that the auto is an icon of surpassing loveliness. But is it practical? At this moment in history can you really afford to go on spending a billion dollars every year to make purely cosmetic changes in your automobiles? A less poetic nation, I should think, might use its money and its talent in less romantic ways.

"No, no, I am not talking about rockets. You will get those, all right, because your pride has been wounded. But the contest between you and the Russians will not be decided with rockets. You will have to keep them in reserve, of course, but neither side will dare to use them; you may be dreamy, but I don't think you are suicidal.

"Meanwhile the contest will be fought with far subtler weapons—weapons which you apparently can't build, and haven't the faintest idea how to use. Know-how—isn't that the phrase? Well, you Americans just haven't got it.

"Take diplomacy, for example. Since war is no longer feasible, diplomacy obviously has become a decisive instrument. The Communists have known this for a long time, and they have built a formidable diplomatic machine. All of its parts are tooled and polished to mesh together—a corps of highly trained diplomats, a superb intelligence apparatus, an even better propaganda setup, military pressure where needed, and all the economic levers from trade pacts to bribery. They have been using it to win one thumping victory after another.

"You Americans, on the other hand, apparently don't even know what diplomacy is. You still think of it in terms of striped pants and tea-sippers, and you treat its practitioners with contempt, as if they were male ballet dancers.

"Your policies—if I may use the word loosely—never seem to mesh. Your President, Vice President, and Secretary of State sometimes issue three contradictory statements on three successive days. Any blabber-mouthed Congressman, general, or Faubus can destroy months of patient diplomatic effort in a single hour, and often does.

"You do have a few competent diplomats—Charles Bohlen and George Kennan probably know as much about Russia as any men in the West—but for some reason (which no foreigner can possibly understand) you refuse to use them.

"What you do use is a herd of amateurs. They are estimable gentlemen, no doubt, with a cultivated taste for race horses and convertible debentures—but in an embassy they are strictly greenhorns. You wouldn't dream of asking them to play first base for the Yankees, or to fix your carburetor, or to fill your teeth. For these jobs you insist on professionals. Yet when your survival as a nation is at issue, you call in any stray millionaire who happened to contribute to the right campaign fund.

"You see why we foreigners cannot believe that you are a serious people?"

With considerable difficulty, I managed to interrupt. Only millionaires, I pointed out, could afford to accept appointment to a major embassy. By ancient tradition the United States does not pay its foreign-service professionals enough to cover the running costs of such a post.

"Thank you," he said, "for reminding me of another American habit which has always baffled me. Why are you always unwilling to pay for what you need most?

"In helping others you are incredibly generous. For luxuries—from deodorants to mink stoles—you spend your money with childlike abandon. But when it comes to the real necessities, you are stingier than a Styrian peasant.

"For the price of one ballistic missile, for one-tenth of what your women spend on lipstick, you could staff all your embassies with well-trained professionals. And that is a comparatively petty example. Take a big one.

"All of you seem to be pretty well in agreement that you need schoolteachers. You have discovered, with alarm, that the Russians are way ahead of you in the kind of education that pays off. Their children get more hours of instruction in ten years than yours got in twelve—and better instruction, too, because they average seventeen pupils to a class, while you average twenty-seven. They turn out eighty thousand engineers a year; you turn out thirty thousand. All their high-school graduates have a good, stiff training in mathematics, physics, and chemistry; less than a third of yours can match them in any one of these fields.

"What is more important still, Russian students learn foreign languages. In their higher institutions, 65 per cent of them study English alone. How many Americans learn Russian? One per cent?

"This fact ought to scare you more than the sputnik. Because skill in languages—not just for a few people, but for millions—is the place where a successful foreign policy begins. When a Russian goes abroad for any purpose, he can talk to the local people in their own tongue—whether they are Arab villagers or Burmese guerrillas or French scientists. When Colonel Rudolph

Abel set up his spy center in Brooklyn he spoke Brooklynese like a Flatbush bartender. When Soviet technicians build a steel mill in India, their plans are drafted in Hindi.

"Yet of the half-million Americans who travel overseas every year, I don't think I have met a dozen who could manage even the simpler European languages with fluency. By the way, how well do you speak German?"

Father Florian had the tact not to wait for an answer. (I would have had to tell him that I can order a cup of coffee, and that—in a pinch—I can ask whether the train is on time. If the station-master speaks slowly enough, I can often understand his reply.)

"The Russians got ahead of you," he said, "because they are hardheaded businessmen who understand the law of supply and demand. When they wanted teachers they paid for them. Not just in cash—though I understand that their top professors do get the equivalent of about $50,000 a year. They also offered something more important: prestige. In any Soviet town a teacher is a Big Man. He enjoys as much standing in the community as a real-estate speculator in New York or an oil-lease broker in Dallas. He lives in the best suburb, gets the best table in restaurants, and is invited to the best parties. So their bright youngsters head for the teaching profession just as naturally as yours head for Wall Street or Madison Avenue.

"But you Americans have never learned to meet a payroll—not in your schools, anyhow. You offer teachers less than truck drivers, and then you wonder why you have 135,000 classroom jobs unfilled. I have even heard—but this I can't believe, it must be Communist propaganda—that some of your universities will pay more for a football coach than for a physics professor.

"With my own eyes, however, I have seen how you go out of your way to make your scholars feel disreputable. You ridicule them in TV shows and comic strips. Your politicians harass them. Their own pupils treat them with disrespect. You call them names. Incidentally, would you be good enough to explain precisely what you mean by the term 'egghead'? . . . I see. . . . Then tell me this: who but an egghead can make an intercontinental missile?

"Or, for that matter, a workable foreign policy. As I was saying a moment ago, this is where your impracticality shows up in its most embarrassing form. In other aspects of life you often behave with good sense; if a carpet sweeper or an adding machine breaks down, you get a new one. But when a foreign policy doesn't work, you cling to it all the tighter—out of sheer sentimentality, I suppose. Your China policy has been a farce for years; your German policy is stalled on dead center; your Middle East policy has failed beyond the Kremlin's wildest hopes. Yet you cherish them like heirlooms.

"Much as our beloved Emperor Franz Josef did. He was a well-meaning old gentleman who devoted most of his time to shooting rabbits—golf had not reached Austria in his day. He was not an intellectual and he suffered from a sentimental attachment to old mistresses and old doctrines. He never would let go of his Balkan policy, for example, even when it plainly was dragging him to disaster. He was, as you may remember, the last of our great emperors. . . .

"It is this same softhearted streak, apparently, which keeps you from using what strength you have. You may be slipping militarily, but your economic strength is still unmatched. Here is your obvious instrument for a diplomatic offensive which might still save the Western world.

"The Russians already have showed you how, and with a fraction of your resources. They have used a few million rubles' worth of trade agreements—deployed along with their other diplomatic weapons—to rope in Egypt and Syria, and they are moving fast in India, Burma, and Ceylon.

"Why do you let them get away with it? Because—correct me if I am wrong—you insist on tying your hands with a protective tariff. To protect what? A couple of watchmakers, a bicycle manufacturer, and a few clothespin factories in Vermont. Because these gentlemen do not believe in the competitive free-enterprise system, they have been weeping on the shoulders of

Congress—to such good effect that your trade negotiators have very little to bargain with.

"Only a nation of bleeding hearts would throw away its sharpest weapon, in the midst of dubious battle, for the sake of such a hard-luck story. Can a country so impractical, so muddle-headed, be trusted in a harsh material world? Do you understand why we Europeans hesitate to tie our fate to yours—however charming your culture may be?"

The bottle was empty. The clock was striking two, and even the bathroom ghost had given up for the night. I was relieved when Father Florian at last heaved himself out of the chair and waddled to the door. He had not, I felt, been altogether considerate. He had known that I still had to prepare my notes for tomorrow morning's reassuring lecture about the United States.

January, 1958

3 : House Party for Eleven Doctors

IT WAS A GOOD PLACE for the party—or for the trial by ordeal, depending on how you looked at it.

The man who built it had called it a mansion; Europeans would call it a palace; to historians, it is an instructive relic of that gilded age, around the turn of the century, when princes of industry took a childlike joy in showing off their untaxed millions. For a short generation, the family of a railroad magnate had reveled here in ducal splendor—waited on by forty-five liveried servants, boating on their private lake, billeting platoons of socially certified guests in the seventy frescoed bedrooms, cantering their thoroughbreds through nineteen thousand acres of family park and forest.

Today, of course, nobody can afford to keep up such an

establishment—or, even if he could, he would not care to attract
the attention of our jealous sovereign, The Common Man, by
such a garish display. So nearly all such baronies have passed into
the hands of five institutions: the Church, which uses them for
seminaries, monasteries, and retreats; private schools and universities; labor unions, whose members seem to get a special
relish out of vacationing on the playgrounds of vanished cap-
italists; the Soviet Union, which houses its diplomatic personnel
in the old Morgan mansion at Glen Cove (perhaps for a similar
reason); and foundations, which need suitable places for holding
the innumerable conferences in which they take such delight.

(The list is significant. It is always possible to get a rough
idea of where the power lies in any society by noting who owns
the big houses. Washington is a conspicuous example. A generation ago, its most flamboyant piles housed a few millionaires,
such as Leiter and McLean, plus the United States Chamber of
Commerce. Today's landmarks are the new marble-and-glass
palaces of the Teamsters Union and the AFL-CIO.)

This particular estate—Arden House, near Harriman, New
York—is now owned by Columbia University, which had rented
it for the occasion to the Markle Foundation. The occasion was
a four-day house party, planned with cruel ingenuity.

As the guests began to arrive, late on a winter afternoon, the
house looked much like an ocean liner stranded on top of a
mountain. Its lights, blazing through the chilly fog, gave it the
same eerie feeling of isolation from all the world. The incredible
interior, with its tapestries, its sweeping staircase, the old-fashioned statuary, the ornate furniture, conveyed the impression of
slightly unearthly luxury which you get in the first-class salons of
a big steamer.

The guests of honor were eleven young doctors. All taught
medicine; each had been chosen by his school as the most promising of its junior faculty members. All of them looked a little
tense.

Four other guests were older and, at the beginning, less
nervous. These men—a university president, a social scientist, an

editor, the head of a Canadian government agency—had only one thing in common: they earned their livings by making rapid judgments about other people. For the purpose of the present rite, they were labeled The Committee.

The remaining guests—two foundation officials and wives of committee members—were relaxed enough. Their only duties were to watch the ordeal, and from time to time to provide solacing conversation to the victims.

Something else was present, invisible but not forgotten for an instant: $150,000 in prize money.

The idea was that everybody would live under the same roof like one big, cheerful family—dining, drinking at the excellent bar, bowling, strolling in the woods, chatting in easy groups around the great fireplaces. Each committee member would find occasion for at least one private interview with each of the doctors. The entire group would assemble for one, maybe two, general discussions of some topic remotely connected with medicine. (How do the boys handle themselves in an argument?) On the last night there would be a formal banquet, followed by a late party with as much liquor available as anybody wanted. (How do they let down after prolonged tension?)

At the end, The Committee would rate all the doctors in order of merit, from one to eleven. Not on their professional qualifications—these were presumed to be first-class—but on certain intangible qualities: character, judgment, dedication, leadership, what Hemingway has called "grace under pressure."

Each of the five at the top of the list would get $30,000, to help finance his research and teaching project over a five-year period. He also would be awarded the title of Markle Scholar—a title which carries very considerable prestige in the medical and academic worlds. In terms of his future career, it might well be worth many times the cash grant.

From the first hour, the pressure began to build. Some of the young men were especially equipped by experience to carry it with poise—the pediatricians, for example, who work constantly with emotional parents, or the surgeon who had served in a

Korean field hospital and who had in the last year performed six hundred major operations. The researchers, used to the calm atmosphere of the laboratory, took it harder. Nobody, of course, was able to behave with complete naturalness.

In casual conversations, a few men tried to display their intellectual brilliance. Others seized upon that side of an argument which, they thought, might appeal to the committeeman present at that moment. One or two made obvious efforts to be agreeable to the committeemen's wives. Another lapsed into resentful silence. On the whole, however, the candidates handled themselves remarkably well. Nobody made a complete fool of himself; nobody got drunk.

"None of us," as one of them remarked afterward, "actually collapsed into hysterics."

Neither did the committee members; but the burden of choice soon was wearing heavily on their nerves and consciences.

On the final morning, when the committee members gathered to compare notes, a strange thing happened. All of them, independently, jotted down almost identical lists. In all of the ratings, the four names at the top and the four at the bottom were exactly the same. Concerning the three in the middle there were minor arguments; but half an hour of discussion resulted in a unanimously agreed list.

(Even more remarkable was the reaction of the women. Unlike the committee members, they had not studied the candidates' dossiers, nor had they been present at the semiformal interviews. Yet, on the basis of a casual acquaintanceship, they reached conclusions almost precisely the same as The Committee's.)

How good were these judgments?

Nobody, of course, can say for sure. Obviously there is a danger that genius might be skipped over because it is concealed beneath an opaque personality. Markle Scholars selected in earlier years, however, have chalked up an impressive record of achievement, particularly in the administration of research and of medical education. (Deans of medical schools and directors of important research projects are being increasingly drawn from their ranks.)

No overlooked genius has yet turned up among the rejects; and the foundation trustees apparently feel that the system is the best they can devise. For what it is worth, so do most of the people who have served on the selection committees.

The point of all this is that the House Party Method might prove to be a valuable new tool both for government and for industry.

So far, it is almost unknown in this country. The British use it to pick foreign-service officers. (If they had used it earlier, when Burgess and Maclean first applied for diplomatic jobs, both very probably would have been rejected; it seems to uncover unstable personalities more surely than any other form of examination.) During the war our Office of Strategic Services employed a variant on the system to choose agents for particularly trying assignments in enemy territory. Some corporations have evolved (almost unconsciously) a faintly similar tactic—John P. Marquand described it in his *Point of No Return*—to help winnow out their junior executives. Aside from the Markle Foundation, however, no institution in America (so far as I can discover) is now applying it systematically.

What evidence is available indicates that it might be especially valuable in selecting one small but peculiarly important group of men—that is, trainees for top managerial positions in business and government. For nearly all big organizations, this problem is now acute. They find it essential to spot men in their early thirties who will be capable, twenty years later, of running the show; unless such men are discovered early, there is no way to give them the varied training and experience necessary to equip them for high command.

Yet the qualities which make a good leader cannot be easily detected by written examination, or by scanning efficiency reports and achievement records. The specialist, who often shows up best by such conventional measurements, may lack the peculiar skills (and traits of character) which make a good generalist. But these qualities do seem to show up quickly under the somewhat brutal system of scrutiny-under-pressure which is the essence of the House Party Method.

It would be interesting to watch the results of a few experiments along these lines by such institutions as, say, Standard Oil of New Jersey, the Episcopal Church, the Ford Motor Company, the State Department, and the Public Health Service. The upshot might be the development of an instrument as valuable to the science of management as the electronic microscope is to the physical sciences.

April, 1956

4 : Recipe for a Fast Million

"Take your last look," Elmer said, "at the poor but earnest scholar. Next time you see me I will be a millionaire."

I looked. Twelve years of teaching Social Psychology at a fashionable woman's college is enough to unhinge even as sturdy a man as Dr. Elmer Hammacker; but so far as I could tell he was sane enough.

"In six months," he said, "Detroit and Hollywood will be stuffing checks under my office door. Every account executive on Madison Avenue will make pilgrimages to beg a word from The New Oracle. No, I don't mean Dr. Dichter. I mean me. I've got a deal that makes motivational research look primitive. It's big, son, real big."

So is Elmer, who once played tackle for Iowa State. He never had fitted comfortably into his cubicle on the third floor of the Agnes R. Appleton Memorial Hall for Behavioral Science, and now that he was pacing around the room—all aglow with avarice and enthusiasm—he looked a good deal like an excited bull in a box stall.

"The name alone is worth a million," he said. "I'm going to

call it the Hammacker Institute for Status Symbol Prediction. Dignified but irresistible. What this country is bleeding for is a scientific way to predict coming changes in its status symbols. And I'm the man who can do it.

"Why is the automobile industry in such terrible shape? Simply because the symbols it is trying to sell have gone out of fashion. Everybody knows, of course, that for the last thirty years every automobile has been sold primarily as a badge of rank. As mere transportation, one car wasn't much different from another; but as marks of status in the social hierarchy there were enormous and subtle differences. This pecking order, as it existed till quite recently, was best codified by that distinguished social scientist William H. Whyte, Jr.; he explained why one make of car was suitable for a rising young executive, another for his boss, and yet others for physicians, band leaders, and college boys.

"The Cadillac, obviously, stood at the top. A man bought one, when he could, because it made him feel superior to all those creeps who drove Chevrolets. It served, roughly, the same purpose as a knighthood in England—to inform the world that he had arrived. And he bought a new one every year, if possible, to demonstrate that only the latest and best was good enough for him.

"Then all of a sudden the symbolism changed. Lots of people began to discover that nobody they really wanted to impress was much impressed by *any* automobile, no matter how big and shiny.

"Detroit spends king-size money on market research—but this disastrous shift took the industry entirely by surprise. Some of the big wheels out there won't believe it yet. My Institute could have told them what was coming at least five years in advance.

"In part Detroit can blame itself. It blurred its own symbols.

"Twenty years ago any schoolboy could identify most makes at a glance. But now that *all* of them have become oversized, overpowered, overpriced, and overdecorated, so that you can scarcely see the car for the chrome, there isn't much point in trying to inch up the status ladder from a Ford to a Buick to a Cadillac. The caste marks got to looking too much alike.

"But it probably would have happened anyway."

By this time Elmer was so wrapped up in his dream of glory that he was lapsing into the lecture-room manner which had intimidated so many generations of undergraduates.

"You must remember," he said, "that this country has always changed its status symbols at fairly regular intervals—simply because ours is the kind of mobile society which refuses to put up with any permanent certificates of class standing. The process always works about the same.

"The cultural elite—the people whom Russell Lynes has called The Tastemakers—adopt a certain insignia to set themselves apart from the common herd. It can be almost anything— an article of clothing, a residential address, a favored group of restaurants, a holiday resort, a hobby, a habit of speech, or a combination of several such items.

"Pretty soon, however, the common herd catches on. Usually, in fact, it is tipped off by the advertising men, who point out that anybody who aspires to real class had better drink Olde Doghair, vacation in Miami Beach, and buy himself an Ivy League suit. Since the herd in America is not inhibited by anything like the British tradition and the elaborate mechanism of The Establishment, which keep most Englishmen neatly fixed in the niches where God placed them, our common man—with his ineradicable instinct for social climbing—begins to latch onto the symbols which he hopes will make him a member of the elite.

"They don't, of course. As soon as the herd moves in, the elite moves out. It promptly abandons its old status symbols, and begins the mysterious process of manufacturing an entirely different set.

"For example, by the time that mobsters, movie stars, Texas millionaires, and other crass types were riding in Cadillacs, the people who create new styles of living had decided that they wouldn't be caught dead in one. They moved on to Jaguars—or, more often, to the Volkswagen. The VW is, in effect, a device for thumbing a lofty nose at the whole idea of the auto as a measure of status. It is also, I suspect, the Tastemaker's gesture of hostility toward the men who run the automobile industry. He feels that they have never been properly respectful of his role (and his power) in our society; and now he is demonstrating that Detroit's designers and advertising men, for all their millions, can't do a thing about public taste without his help. Detroit is finding the lesson both painful and expensive.

"My Institute," he said, "is designed to prevent this sort of corporate blindness. What we will do—for a suitable fee—is to inform businessmen when one set of caste marks is wearing out, and to predict the new ones which will take their place. My clients rarely will be able to do anything to prevent the change-over, but they will be able to get ready for it well in advance.

"Take the hotel men. I could have predicted two years ago that some of them were bound to lose their shirts on those rhinestone Taj Mahals they have been building in such profusion along Miami Beach. By 1956 the place already was being overrun by plumbers and used-car salesmen—and the people who set the trend in these matters were vacationing elsewhere.

"My charts indicate that a winter tan will remain an okay status symbol for at least another decade; but the elite groups will no longer get it anywhere near Miami. At the moment they are going to Phoenix and the Antilles; Bermuda is still all right if you have a cottage, but not if you stay at a hotel; even a hotel is permissible, however, at Tobago and Caneel Bay. Their next wintering place will be the Greek islands, and within eight years I forecast a strong migration to the South Coast of Turkey— perhaps the finest unspoiled riviera left anywhere in the world.

"Real-estate operators, obviously, will be among my leading clients, since they can be ruined by just one failure to foresee a trend. Zeckendorf ought to pay me handsomely for predicting just when the Upper East Side of New York is likely to lose its cachet, as Riverside Drive did about a quarter of a century ago; and he might even like to know why I expect a replica of Greenwich Village to develop near the Bowery.

"The entertainment industry needs me even more. Why, it seems like only yesterday when any man with pretensions to sophistication made a point of being seen in the right night clubs with the right blonde at least one a week. Now the head-waiters are getting snow-blind from looking at their empty tables. For the Institute it would be mere routine to predict when that particular form of ostentation—or any other—is about to go out of fashion.

"My method, like all strokes of genius, is basically simple," Elmer said. "I plan to place the American tastemaking groups, for the first time in history, under continuous scientific observation.

"The techniques are well established; anthropologists have been using them for years on Papuans, Eskimos, Manus Islanders, and a few American towns such as Muncie and Newburyport. My staff—headed, I hope, by Margaret Mead—will simply apply the same detailed scrutiny to a few key segments of our own society. It will report the first symptoms of change in their habits, costumes, pastimes, and snobberies. We can then be sure, on the basis of past experience, that the herd will follow their lead about five years later—though in some cases this crucial time interval may be a trifle more or less.

"The only hard part is to decide what groups to watch; and I think I've already got that licked.

"I shall set up three Field Observation Teams. The first will be assigned to the Ivy League universities. Their potency as style-setters is pretty obvious; what they did for the Brooks Brothers suit, the motoring cap, and chino slacks is already history. Perhaps it is less well known generally that they also incubated the sports-car fad and the skiing boom. Today the dirty-white buck shoe—until recently the private badge of a rather small in-group at Yale—is spreading fast across the country. When it reaches the West Coast, about three months from now, its day will be over. Trends in taste don't originate in Hollywood; they go there to die.

"The reason why so many trends get started on the Ivy League campuses is now being explored by one of my graduate students. Her tentative findings indicate that a significant number of the men at Princeton, Harvard, Yale, Amherst, Dartmouth, and a few other colleges share four key characteristics: (1) enough money to indulge their whims; (2) enough self-assurance to liberate them from the usual undergraduate fear of appearing different; (3) at least the rudiments of taste; (4) enough snob status to insure that their behavior will be widely imitated in the hinterland. Elsewhere this combination is rare.

"My second team of observers—I will thank you not to refer to them as snoops—will be stationed in Fairfield County, Connecticut. This area has a unique concentration of people in the communications industries: writers, TV executives, advertising men, publishers, and the like. A lot of them exhibit the same syndrome we discovered in the Ivy League universities—where, in fact, many of them were graduated, or expelled. In addition they are fearsomely articulate, and have ready access to channels for publicizing their own tastes throughout the country.

"Finally, they have a low boredom threshold; they change wives, hobbies, breeds of pets, and jobs more frequently than anybody else. An ideal culture medium, in short, for the rapid growth of status-symbol mutations.

"The third research team will have a different kind of assignment. Its job will be to keep tabs on a carefully selected panel of fifty persons, chosen from all sections of the country, who have proven ability to create new behavioral trends. Our tentative list includes at least two nonpolitical Rockefellers; David Ogilvy; a Japanese architect; Jacqueline Kennedy; John Gardner of the Carnegie Corporation; William Shawn of *The New Yorker*; David Reisman; Alfred Barr of the Museum of Modern Art; Just Lunning, the impresario of Scandinavian taste; Lincoln Kirstein; Mrs. Edison Dick; Arthur A. Houghton, Jr., of Steuben Glass; Mrs. Ronald Tree; and a representative selection of artists, novelists, and poets. These last are indispensable, because they are traditionally bellwethers in matters of taste. As Cleveland Amory pointed out in *The Last Resorts*, most of the fashionable playgrounds—from Bar Harbor and Provincetown to Taos —were first settled by intellectuals, who were followed in due course by the social climbers. A good many other movements—in art, drinks, city residential areas, furniture, and social attitudes—get started the same way.

"Wealth, you understand, does not by itself qualify anybody for inclusion on my panel. A good many of the members do have money, but they all have things that are more important—a sense of style, for instance, confidence (verging on arrogance) about their own tastes, and an instinct for nonconformity. These are traits which you might not, at first glance, associate with the Rockefeller family; but they are all there, concealed beneath that sedate Baptist veneer. The family's influence on American taste, by way of Williamsburg, the Museum of Modern Art, and similar ventures, has been incalculable; and Nelson Rockefeller right now may be establishing a new prestige symbol of enormous importance. He is making public service a prestigious activity for the rich.

"Any ordinary millionaire can display a yacht or a flock of chorus girls, but only a *very* wealthy man can afford to maintain a private staff of scholars for research into public issues, and in addition spend years of his own time on such chores as heading a commission to rewrite the New York state constitution. If you want to put it in Veblen's terms—which probably are over-cynical—you might say that this kind of disinterested public service is the ultimate form of conspicuous consumption.

"By way of contrast, look at the late Robert R. Young, a man who had practically no influence on the country's behavior patterns. He had money, but he lacked the leader's temperament. In fact, he not only was a natural-born follower, but one who followed fashions a whole generation out of date. He tried to be a tycoon when the Age of Tycoons was long past, and he was the only man of his time who thought it important to have big houses in both Newport and Palm Beach. He even curried the favor of dukes, a method of social escalation which had been abandoned by everybody else about 1917. Soon after he finally discovered that he was an anachronism whom nobody took seriously, he shot himself.

"It is of course unscientific for me to anticipate the reports of my Field Observation Teams, but I think I can already guess at a few of their findings—some trivial, others reasonably significant. For example:

"America's No. 1 status symbol—a place long held by the automobile—will again be the home, as it was fifty years ago. It will betoken the owner's social standing not by any measure so crude as price alone but by a whole set of more subtle indicators—the quality of its architecture, the layout of its garden, the pictures on the walls, the nature of its library and record collection. This phenomenon is of course closely related to the turning inward, the domestication—the withdrawal from gregarious activities, including night-clubbing and collegiate football —which are such pronounced characteristics of our younger generation.

"Incidentally, the automobile industry eventually will get over its present state of shock, and will start selling transportation instead of glamour. The company which will prosper will be the one that gets to the market first with a simple, sturdy, comfortable, economical, and unobtrusively good-looking car, which you can depend on not to get obsolescent for at least ten years —something like the Mercedes-Benz. As a matter of fact, the Rambler seems to be prospering on this formula already.

"Gentlemen farmers will raise Black Angus cattle rather than race horses. This will be a natural step in the trend away from gaudy ostentation, which started shortly after World War II. We have already seen its effect in men's clothes, office decoration, haircuts, domestic architecture, and the disappearance of such loud displays as the debutante ball. Today nobody, however wealthy, would dream of building a palace like Hearst's San Simeon. Instead of conferring prestige, it would make him look silly.

"Amateur painting will become increasingly respectable. Once rather suspect, it has now been sanctified by the two great war leaders, Churchill and Eisenhower. It will lead, in turn, to a steadily growing market for professional artists. Already more canvases—most of them bad—are being sold at higher prices to more people than at any time since the Medicis made painters into gentlemen and painting a lucrative profession.

"In Texas there are now only three approved ways for a rich man to spend his money. He can buy a ranch—a big one; a little bitty ranch won't do—he can finance a reactionary politician, or he can endow a Texas university. I predict that within the next ten years the opinion leaders in Texas will discover the rest of the United States, and that the most venturesome among them will make their first tentative contacts with the world overseas, and all the delightful possibilities it offers for spending money in unheard-of ways.

"But that's enough of this idle speculation. I have to go phone Margaret Mead. If I don't get the Institute under way pretty fast, those Bureau of Applied Social Research boys at Columbia might beat me to it."

Elmer went charging down the hall to borrow the dean's telephone; the college had never felt it could afford to give him one for his own office. It occurred to me that he hadn't said a word about the kind of status symbols which might be needed to keep ambitious men in the teaching profession.

July, 1958

5 : Running Barefoot Through a Hayloft Full of Ten-Dollar Bills

As A PRACTICING CHRISTIAN, I am always eager to relieve my fellow men of their burdens, especially cash. The following suggestions are offered in a spirit of pure helpfulness.

The fellow men in these parts who seem to be grunting under the heaviest burdens, and who certainly have the most cash, are the Philanthropoids. These are the people who make a profession of giving away other people's money. A sizable colony—employed by about a dozen foundations—has gathered in mid-Manhattan, handy to the banks; and during the last four years I have had some opportunity to observe their nesting habits, escape devices, recognition signals, protective coloration, and flock etiquette.

Whether they are small Philanthropoids, furtively peeking around for some place to bestow a few piddling millions, or the large Ford-size variety, their troubles are much the same. All day, and often far into the night, they crouch in their walnut-paneled sanctuaries, under a state of siege. Their predators are innumerable, cunning, relentless, and hungry. They swarm in the foundations' waiting rooms, equipped with sure-fire schemes to save the world and bushel baskets to carry away the money they need to get started. They lurk in the Scarsdale commuters' depot, hoping to bag an exhausted Philanthropoid on his way home. When a foundation man ventures out for lunch or for a quick restorative slug at the nearest bar, he is pounced upon by some character with froth on his lips and an urgent need for $27,000,-105.68.

Some of these vulturelike creatures—known in the trade as Philanthropees—have developed grant-wrangling into a Way of Life. I have noted several, mostly social scientists, who have lived quite comfortably for at least twenty years on loot snatched from one foundation or another; and since long practice has taught them how to outwit even the nimblest foundation executive, they probably will continue to batten on dead men's leavings until they pass to their Last Award.

A few forward-looking universities have, in fact, set up secret training programs to coach their faculty in the techniques of foundation-milking: How to Prepare a Plausible Application; Advance Plotting to Get a Grant Renewed; Stalking Philanthropoids with Cap and Gown; and similar basic courses in Grantmanship.*

---

* For the most useful advice, on the other hand, the would-be grantee should turn to *Fortune* magazine, which regards foundations with the same cool de-

So it is small wonder that foundation men tend to become morose, twitchy, and ulcerous. They quickly develop defensive tactics—a picket line of receptionists trained in judo, for example, and a rampart of memoranda stacked high around every desk. (A favorite device is to diffuse the decision-making power throughout the organization so that nobody can ever tell who finally passes on any application; thus the applicant never knows whose arm to twist.) Even if they succeed in beating off the crackpots and Messiahs, however, the Philanthropoids are virtually defenseless against Congressmen. Some of our more primitive lawmakers hate to see all that good money being spent without benefit of patronage—frequently on intellectuals, too, an obviously suspect lot—so they harry the foundations whenever they can't think of anything else to investigate.

But the saddest thing about the Philanthropoids is their lack of joy in their work. You might think that a man who does nothing but spend money—a man who could run around barefoot, any time he likes, in a hayloft full of ten-dollar bills—would pitch into his chores with a beaming eye and a carol in his throat. Alas, it isn't so. As Dwight Macdonald pointed out in his recent tome on the Ford Foundation, most of them approach their duties with the glum decorum of a Baptist missionary. They lack, in Kenneth Tynan's phrase, pizzicato of the spirit.

Why?

My own investigations have finally, I believe, turned up the answer. They were conducted without subsidy—a deplorable example of foundation shortsightedness—so my report is not as stately as it might have been if somebody had given me the trivial sum ($8,376,000.04) which I needed for secretarial help and other incidentals. Nevertheless, the essentials are here.

Clearly it is too late to save the Ford, Carnegie, Rockefeller, and other old-line foundations, so it seems wisest to start again

---

tachment as other forms of money. William H. Whyte, Jr., in his two articles on the subject (October and November, 1955), offers two hypothetical case histories in grant-getting—the Tyro and the Experienced Hand.

from scratch. What follows, therefore, is a prospectus for a new type of institution: The Haroun-al-Raschid Fund for Benevolent and Hell-Raising Purposes. Any oil millionaire is welcome to start it whenever his next well blows in; and I might even be persuaded to serve (regardless of personal sacrifice) as Executive Secretary and Purse Toter.

Organization obviously is the first step—and right here is where the old foundations went wrong. They set up a lot of vice presidents in charge of large, woolly abstractions, such as World Peace, Adult Education, and International Understanding. Nobody could have any fun with assignments like that. Our Fund will assign its officers to more specific and stimulating projects.

There will be, for instance, a Vice President in Charge of Love. Her first job will be to build a Primping Parlor in every large city. Such places have long been desperately needed. It just isn't feasible for a stenographer to leave her job in, say, Manhattan at 5:00 P.M., go home to the Bronx, and then get back to Greenwich Village in time for a dinner date. What she needs is a quiet, homey building near her office, containing about two hundred boudoirs. She could rent one of these for 25 cents an hour; there she could take a bath, fluff her hair, fix up her nail polish, change her clothes, and maybe nap for a few minutes between the close of work and a big evening on the town. Such an establishment would relieve the subway jam, increase the marriage rate, enhance the enjoyment of a good many young men, and add half an hour to every secretary's working day, since she wouldn't have to sneak off to the ladies' room at 4:30 to put on lipstick and paint her nails.

The same Vice President would seek to remedy another long-felt need: the lack of private and romantic places where young folks can do their courting. Drive-in theaters of course serve this purpose in rural areas; porch swings are still available in small towns; but kids in the metropolis have to make do with doorways, drugstore booths, and similar dreary makeshifts. Our Fund will finance a series of small parks—open only to couples —equipped with benches in hedge-girt nooks and an artificial moon for cloudy nights. For winter use we plan a chain of Hideaway Houses. Their interiors will be subdivided into a maze of curtained alcoves, furnished with snug sofas and piped for Muzak recordings of "Liebestraum" and the Venusberg theme. (If our Founder turns out to be stuffy, we might hire a passel of deaf, elderly widows to patrol the corridors as chaperons; but their hearing aids would be confiscated each night as they report for duty.)

We shall also have a Vice President in Charge of Scenery. His job will be to make the country look less messy.

He will offer a $50 bounty to anybody who chops down a roadside billboard. Whenever one of these public-spirited citizens is caught in the act, the Fund will pay his fine and court costs. He will buy up the ugliest building in every city over 50,000 in population, raze it, and plant the liberated ground in sycamores.

He will supply hot-rod cars and baseball bats to gangs of juvenile delinquents, and pay them to bust up every Bar-B-Q Drive In and Bideawee Tourist Court on Highway 66. This will discourage eyesores and keep the boys off the streets.

He will maintain a skyscraper full of criminal lawyers to defend arsonists, and any impulsive soul who happens to kill a slum landlord in a fit of well-justified rage. As Veblen once noted, the two essentials of progress are fires and funerals.

But won't Congress run us ragged with investigations? No, sir. Our charter provides that the first time a Congressman lays a hand on us we shall give all our remaining money to the rival candidate in his district, and then go out of business. We fear no evil.

We shall waste no money on museums, or the encouragement of creative writers. Instead we plan to buy paintings from young artists—maybe 5,000 a year—and hang them in schools, bars, comfort stations, courthouses, and barbershops. In every factory we aim to install a long shelf of books near the door, as Yale & Towne already is doing in some of its plants. Any employee can borrow whatever book he likes. (There will be no librarians, cards, or red tape. If anybody wants a book bad enough to steal it, he ought to have it.) After a while people will get so used to good pictures and books that they may start buying them for their own homes. Artists and writers don't need grants; they need customers.

(We shall, however, award annual prizes for the best historical novel without a female character, and for the best short story about the harsh world of children as seen through the eyes of a sensitive adult.)

Neither shall we have a Research Department. Other foundations support too much research already. But there will be a Department of Mysteries—a commodity in short supply nearly everywhere these days. It will look into certain interesting questions which more august institutions have neglected.

Such as the case of Katherine Fitzgerald, Countess of Desmond, born 1464. She broke a leg at the age of ninety when she fell out of a cherry tree. (It healed nicely and she lived for another fourteen years.) What was she doing up that cherry tree anyhow?

What did teen-age girls do before the invention of the telephone?

Is it true that every gambler who wins a pot with The Dead Man's hand—aces and eights*—eventually comes to a violent end?

Who lost Lee's battle order—after carelessly wrapping it around three cigars—at the beginning of the Antietam campaign? The records show who found it (still around the cigars) and how Lee's army was nearly destroyed as a result; but the name of the Confederate general who was guilty of this disastrous breach of security has been kept out of the history books to this very day.

Is there any evidence that the speeches at sales conventions ever increase sales by a single penny?

The list is practically endless, and a little inquiry into such

---

* So called because that was the two pair which Wild Bill Hickok held when Jack McCall shot him in the back at Deadwood in 1876.

mysteries ought to contribute at least as much to the gaiety of American life as the learned monographs now being ground out by the cord under foundation auspices. No Ph.D.s need apply; what our investigators will need is plenty of vagrant curiosity.

The Fund's most important executive will be the Vice President in Charge of Unworthy Causes and Petty Cash. He will have no office, since he will spend all his time on the road. He will carry a satchel full of $20 bills. These he will pass out to anybody who looks as if he could put the money to good use—and no nonsense about does-he-deserve-it. The old bum with a two-day beard and a hangover, the tired housewife who craves two weeks in Palm Springs without the children, the poet who has run out of bourbon, the politician who needs to climb a mountain and get reacquainted with his own soul, the poker player who holds a full house but no more chips, the bank clerk who has never taken a blonde to Atlantic City for a weekend in all his twenty-eight years of dull and faithful service—these are the clients our Number One Veep will seek.

Now and then he will hand $64,000 to a schoolteacher who is voted Best-in-the-School by secret ballot of the pupils. (They usually have an instinct both for justice and for teaching talent; which is more than you can say for all school boards.)

He will endow three caravans of Mohammedan missionaries to spread their gospel in Iowa, Mississippi, and Kansas. (Each convert is at once entitled to four wives, according to Islamic law; but he has to give up alcohol.) The result should be a sharpening of moral dilemmas, an enlivening of the daily gossip, and a broadening of spiritual horizons in our most pious states.

One day he will drop into a dime store in Milwaukee and present a mink coat to the homeliest sales girl. Next morning may find him in Baton Rouge or Atlanta, searching for the only restaurant proprietor in the South (if there is one) who has never served an order of fried chicken, the Curse of Dixie.

The Fund's procedures may not be exactly scientific, but they are at least personal. No other foundations can make this claim.

That, in fact, is their main trouble. They have become so antiseptic, so far removed from any sense of surprise and rapture, that they not only are not much fun; they are hardly human. To the ears of the typical Philanthropoid, the phrase "as cold as charity" sounds like a compliment. He has a heart of gold, mostly Rockefellers', but it is locked up tighter than Fort Knox; and the ordinary man who doesn't know how to draft an application, supported by a 128-page Project Justification, realizes that he will never smell a cent of that fragrant foundation moola.

Not so with the Haroun-al-Raschid Fund. Our manna will drop from heaven with the unpredictability of Arabian Nights largess. Every man will know that the shower might, just possibly, hit him next; so hope will glow forever in a hundred million hearts, and the nation will call our Founder blessed.

If this vision has touched you, and if you have a few millions to spare, we can start operations right away. I think I could pull a staff together in practically no time.

July, 1956

6 : How to Place Bets on Corporate Management

ONE OF THE COUNTRY'S SMARTEST and most venerable banks recently sent a question to the chief of its research department.

"Are there any earmarks," it asked, in effect, "which will tell us whether the management of a corporation is good or bad?"

The research people quickly found that this question is tougher than it looks. Profits alone are not a reliable guide. It is fairly easy for shortsighted executives to show good profits—for a few years—by letting their companies' plants run down, or by gutting reserves of raw material. On the other hand, a firm which has never earned a penny may be just on the doorsill of spectacular success, because years of developmental work and long-visioned management are finally ready to pay off.

In the end—after studying hundreds of corporations—the researchers discovered just one clue. It was totally unexpected; it apparently is still unknown to the business colleges or professional market analysis: and it has enabled the bank to place its financial bets with remarkably consistent results. (This, incidentally, is the first time it has ever been made public.)

Here, in effect, is what the research chief reported:

"If the top executive in a company gets a salary several times as large as the salaries paid to the Number Two, Three, and Four men, you can be pretty sure that firm is badly managed. But if the salary levels of the four or five men at the head of the ladder are all close together, then the performance and morale of the entire management group is likely to be high.

"The *size* of the salaries doesn't seem to make much difference," the report continued. "Whether the president of the corporation gets $20,000 a year or $100,000 isn't important—so long as his vice presidents get something like 75 to 90 per cent as much. But when the president pulls down $100,000, and his main subordinates get only $25,000 to $50,000, it is time to look for trouble."

A full explanation for this curious fact no doubt would require months of digging into psychology, office politics, the history of institutions, and the folkways of American industry. It is not the sort of fact which could be uncovered with a comptometer or a time-motion study, or any of the other tools of "scientific management." It is one of those things which the ablest businessmen discover intuitively—and which make Top Management not a science or profession, but an art.

April, 1954

7 : A First-Class Citizens' Council

WHAT FOLLOWS may sound offensive to a good many Negroes and to some white people. Nevertheless it needs to be said.

This is a proposal for a new Negro organization—a First-Class Citizens' Council. Its purpose is the genuine integration of Negroes into the normal stream of American life.

So far the established Negro organizations—the NAACP, the Urban League, CORE, the Southern Regional Council, and all the rest—have made only limited headway toward this goal. With their ingrained patterns of thought and action, they probably can never go much further. Before the Negro community can make its next big forward step, it must find a new kind of leadership, a new type of organization, and a radically different method of attack.

The old organizations have, of course, performed an invaluable service—not only for the Negro, but for all Americans. After two generations of hard fighting, they have finally broken down nearly all the legal barriers which had walled the Negro into a separate world. Much hard fighting is still ahead before desegregation—in schools, jobs, housing, eating places, and public facilities—is finally wiped out; but the decisive battles have been won. At last the law, the full force of the federal government, and the overwhelming weight of public opinion have all come over to the side of racial justice. No matter how stubbornly pockets of resistance in the Deep South (and some Northern cities) may hold out, the result is no longer in question. The rest is a mopping-up operation, like the war in Europe after Bastogne.

So now the American Negro faces an entirely new campaign. It may prove harder than the old one. Certainly it requires different weapons: lawsuits, sit-ins, and freedom rides—still indispensable in the remaining battles of the old campaign—will not work in the coming one.

For the next inevitable objective is full-scale participation, on easy and equal terms, in the ordinary operations of American society. It will be won only when the average Negro (not just the brilliant exception) is willingly accepted by the average white (not just the self-conscious "liberal") as a reliable neighbor, a good colleague to have in the office or plant, a welcome addition to the local political club, bowling league, trade association and PTA. This obviously will mean the erosion of a lot of white prejudices; but it also demands some big changes in the habits, character, and ambitions of a lot of Negroes.

The aim of the new Council would be to produce those changes. Its slogan: "Let's Make Every Negro a First-Class Citizen." Its goal: not merely to win the full rights which belong to every American, but to make sure that these rights are used —that the average Negro is both willing and able to carry the full responsibilities of good citizenship. Once he does, he may be surprised to see how fast white prejudice begins to melt away.

For this prejudice is not altogether baseless—as a few of the braver Negro leaders are now beginning to admit. It cannot be erased just by scolding white people, nor can it be touched by any sort of law or demonstration. It will disappear only when a considerable majority of whites are convinced that they have nothing to fear from close, daily association with Negroes in jobs, schools, and neighborhoods.

The first task of the First-Class Citizens' Council, therefore, will be to find honest answers to three questions:

1. What are these white people afraid of? Why do they begin to move out of a neighborhood as soon as any considerable number of Negroes move in? Why are so many desegregated schools becoming "resegregated," as white parents withdraw their children? (In Washington, for example, where desegregation was originally carried out with surprising success and good will, nearly 82 per cent of the students are now Negroes—although the population of the city is only 54 per cent colored. White families with

children of school age have either moved to the suburbs in large numbers, or have sent their youngsters to private schools.)

2. How much of this fear is rational, and how much is simply blind, unreasoning prejudice?

3. What can be done to remove the rational, valid reasons for such fear? Once they are gone, the purely irrational suspicions ought to be easier to cope with.

Nobody, so far as I can discover, has yet attempted a serious examination of these questions. White sociologists have shrunk away from them, for fear that they might be suspected of racism, or might give aid and comfort to the white-supremacy fanatics of the Deep South. Most Negroes have refused to look at them at all; it is easier—and more popular in the Negro community—to blame everything on white prejudice. (A few Negro leaders, as we shall note in a moment, are exceptions.)

A candid, careful investigation would show (I think) that many white people are afraid—with some reason—of four things:

1. CRIME

As the proportion of Negroes in a community increases, the crime rate usually rises sharply. The police chief of the District of Columbia has estimated that Negroes are responsible for 80 per cent of the serious crimes there, although they make up only a little over half the population. In Chicago, when Negroes were 17 per cent of the population, they accounted for 65 per cent of the jail inmates; in Philadelphia, the comparable figures were 21 and 80 per cent; in Detroit, 19 and 58.*

A few weeks ago a friend of mine—a middle-aged book editor—had to catch a train at the 125th Street station in Harlem. As he was walking up the stairs inside the station, he was slugged on the back of the head with a blackjack or some similar weapon. While he sprawled semiconscious on the steps,

---

* Cited by Theodore H. White, on page 235 of his *The Making of the President* (Atheneum, 1960); the figures are for 1955, the latest available to him at the time the book was written.

his assailant snatched his wallet, and then kicked him violently in the face. (If the kick had landed an inch higher, it would have destroyed his right eye.) None of the scores of people in the station, mostly Negroes, made any effort to catch the criminal. None made any effort to help the dazed and bleeding man. As it happens, this editor has always been a quiet, effective fighter for Negro rights. He has never had a trace of racial bias, and has none now. But he may think twice before he catches another night train at 125th Street; and he might feel a little uneasy if he had to live in a neighborhood with a large Negro population. Can you blame him if he wonders whether those bystanders in the station behaved like first-class citizens?

Such crimes—particularly the assault and robbery of taxi drivers—have become so common in Harlem that most New York taxi drivers avoid the area like a battle zone. (This works a real hardship on many law-abiding Negroes, who find it almost impossible to get a cab to stop for them after dark.)

In Washington recently a gang of young Negroes assaulted and robbed a white bus driver. The passengers, who happened to be all Negroes, watched passively—and not one of them was willing to help the police find the thugs.

In many Negro neighborhoods (and a few white ones, too) the bystanders not only refuse to help the police; they help the criminals. During the first six months of last year, 1,171 New York policemen were attacked while trying to make arrests; about a fifth of these were hurt so badly they needed medical attention. Last summer one such incident in Harlem flared into a near-riot, and three hundred policemen had to be called to get it under control. *Jet*, a Negro news weekly, blamed this trouble on "politics, poor Negro leadership," and "the street-corner rantings and ravings of a motley crew of soapbox speakers who fancy themselves 'black nationalists.'" It added that local Negro leaders "seemed content to turn their backs on it, hoping the problem will go away."

So long as this remains true, are the fears of the white community entirely illusory?

2. NEIGHBORHOOD DETERIORATION

The commonest fear among white families is that their neighborhood will go downhill if many Negroes move in.

Sometimes this fear is plainly unjustified. A number of my Negro friends are as house-proud as anybody I know; one of them has made his home and garden into a town showplace. Nor is this true merely of the relatively wealthy "black bourgeois." A Negro home I visit fairly often is a single room in a slum district, but it always is spotlessly clean, tidy, and comfortable.

Yet this is not always true. A neighborhood where I once lived in Washington is now occupied almost entirely by Negroes; it has indeed gone downhill, swiftly and unmistakably. In part this is due to overcrowding, and to incomes so low that the owners can't afford to keep their places up properly. But it is also partly due to plain old don't-care. Garbage, broken bottles, and old bedsprings accumulate in many a back yard; a loose porch board goes unfixed for weeks, though all it needs is one nail and two licks with a hammer; broken windowpanes get stuffed with rags. Moreover, the same families that can't find money for a bucket of paint or a pane of glass somehow manage, surprisingly often, to drive fancy cars and buy a fifth of whisky every weekend.

Similar examples can be cited in almost any American city. Still—nothing about this matter is simple—I know of communities in Atlanta, Chicago, and the San Francisco Bay area which have improved, rather than deteriorated, after an influx of Negro families. They prove a basic point: There is nothing inherently bad about Negro occupancy. Given ambition, energetic leadership, and a little elbow grease, it can result in neighborhoods as attractive as any. So the job of the First-Class Citizens' Council is by no means hopeless; it is just overdue.

3. CIVIC APATHY

A kindred fear is that Negro newcomers will not pull their weight in the community boat. Few of them seem willing to invest time and effort in the web of civic, political, and voluntary organizations which holds every American community together.

As a precinct captain in a district with a considerable Negro population, I learned at first hand how hard it is to persuade them to register and vote—and harder yet to get them to ring doorbells for either political party. Such indifference is at last beginning to cause some concern among Negro spokesmen. The *Michigan Chronicle,* a Negro paper in Detroit, recently pointed out that a third of that city's qualified Negro citizens never bothered to register—and that "at least 40 per cent" of those who did register failed to vote. And Louis Lomax, in his notably outspoken book, *The Negro Revolt,** noted that about 200,000 Negroes of voting age live in the Harlem district represented by Congressman Adam Clayton Powell, the most popular and flamboyant Negro politician in the country; yet he normally polls only about 40,000 votes, while his opponents seldom get more than 10,000.

"One reason why Negro leadership organizations think several times before launching highly publicized voter-registration drives," Lomax said, "is that they know Negroes simply will not go to the polls and register."

So, too, with many civic organizations. Negro parents are usually quick to complain (at least in Northern cities) about any covert—or even accidental—segregation in local schools. But how many attend the meetings of their Parent-Teacher Association? How many help collect for the Community Chest or offer to lead a Girl Scout troop?

4. Moral Irresponsibility

White people also are bothered by the casual attitude of many Negroes about sex, and about their family responsibilities.

Such worries are seldom discussed out loud—maybe because so many whites know that their own morals aren't exactly impeccable. But they do have some statistical justification. About 2 per cent of the white babies born each year are bastards; among Negroes the illegitimacy rate is above 20 per cent. And even

* Harper, 1962.

when they are married, Negro fathers tend to abandon their families with lighthearted frequency. About 8 per cent of the white families with children under eighteen are broken homes; for nonwhites, the comparable figure is 21 per cent.

One result is a heavy burden on the relief rolls, and a growing resentment among white taxpayers; nobody likes to support somebody else's bastards. Another result is that hundreds of thousands of Negro children grow up without a man in the family to provide discipline and example; which in turn means a steady rise in delinquency. A third is the reluctance of white parents to keep their children in schools with a high proportion of Negroes—not because they are afraid of intermarriage, but because they worry about the habits and attitudes their youngsters might pick up.

Is this blind prejudice? Can a man who won't support his children call himself a first-class citizen?

To all of these complaints, the traditional Negro leaders have a ready answer. The Negro's shortcomings, they argue, are the inevitable consequence of three hundred years of slavery and discrimination. When you hold a man down for that long, he can't spring upright overnight when the pressure is removed. He won't vote because he doesn't yet really believe that he can have any influence on government. He won't attend civic meetings because he has never been welcomed or listened to—and he is still afraid he will be insulted, or at best ignored. Broken families and promiscuity were forced on the Negro during slavery, and the resulting pattern takes a long time to change.

Crime, so the explanation continues, is largely a result of the Negro's low place on the economic totem pole. "Most Negroes would rather work than steal," as Lomax puts it. "By the same token they would rather steal than starve." And so long as many jobs are closed to them—by their educational handicaps, or by union or employer discrimination—those are the stark alternatives.

Moreover, the "frustration crimes"—dope addiction, drunkenness, sexual assaults, sometimes murder—often are (to quote

Lomax again) "rooted in the need to escape from the ugly reality of life in the Negro ghetto." Statistically they are closely correlated with overcrowding, slums, and—perhaps most important—the sense of hopelessness that afflicts so many young Negroes. Feeling that society has stacked its cards against them, they are likely to strike back at society. Especially white society. Much Negro crime, as Lomax points out, "has to do with getting back at white people."

These are valid explanations. For white people, they mean that Negroes need a great deal more help than they have yet had, to overcome the cultural lag that has been imposed upon them. They need—and deserve—the same concentration of money, talent, and organization that we are devoting to under-developed people in Asia, Africa, and Latin America. Given the best teachers, the best social workers, special attention to vocational education and job placement, an extra share of understanding and patience, most Negroes will be able to close the cultural gap surprisingly fast. The experimental Higher Horizons program in New York City's schools has already demonstrated how quickly they can move ahead, with a little encouragement and special attention.

For the Negroes, however, these same explanations can be dangerous. It is all too easy to use them as an excuse for despair. And they offer no solutions. So long as the Negro blames his plight entirely on circumstances, history, and the white man, he is going to stay in that plight. He will get out of it only when he begins to change his circumstances, make new history, and shoulder a bigger share of responsibility for the fix he is in.

For example, a Negro minister in a New York suburb recently called on his congregation to picket a dairy, on grounds that it had never hired a Negro deliveryman. The dairy replied that it had never had a Negro applicant.

"I'll have a half-dozen at your office tomorrow morning," the minister said. Not one showed up. The dairy then began a systematic effort to recruit Negro employees; after about six weeks it found one—just one—who was willing to take on the responsibilities of a milk route. A few months later he quit, apparently because the psychological burdens of the job were too much for him.*

Nor is this an isolated instance. For the last five years the National Urban League has been opening up more job opportunities for Negroes in "white" industries than it can find Negroes to fill. The industry I know best—publishing—has been open to qualified Negroes for many years; a substantial number have risen to positions of considerable responsibility. Many more would be welcome—particularly secretaries, bookkeepers, and computer operators—if qualified applicants could be found. Why they can't is something of a mystery, because the schools in New York and a dozen other big cities are presumably turning out thousands of Negro youngsters with the necessary training.

Maybe the answer lies in a parable frequently told by Dr. Benjamin E. Mays, president of Morehouse College in Atlanta. A zoo lion spent years pacing back and forth in his cage. Then one day somebody left the door of his cage open; but the lion still kept pacing back and forth.

So the job of the First-Class Citizens' Council will be to convince American Negroes that the door of their cage is at last open—not all the way yet, but wider than most of them realize. And each one who pushes through that door can help open it a little further for those who lag behind. Or, if he doesn't use his new opportunities well, he can make it harder for the next man to get through the door.

Take the case of five Negro drivers who worked for a taxi company in a Tidewater Virginia town. On the first day of the fishing season, not one of them showed up for work; nor did any of them let the manager know that they planned to take a day off—although they knew he had promised a half a dozen customers that he would get them to the airport early that morning.

---

* Nevertheless this story has a happy ending. The dairy refused to accept his resignation, and found another assignment for him inside a processing plant—not a menial job, but one requiring a fairly high degree of technical skill. He has learned to handle it to everybody's satisfaction, and the firm is continuing its efforts to recruit more Negro help.

Their irresponsible behavior is not the main point; what is really sad is that nobody in the local Negro community thought it worth mentioning. No Negro newspaper, no minister, no teacher, no official of the NAACP bothered to tell them that they were hurting *all* Negroes. That pan of fish will make at least seven people—the cab manager and his six disappointed passengers —hesitate a little before offering any Negro a job.

For constructive self-criticism is a rare, and much needed, commodity among American Negroes. The Negro press is loaded with criticism of white people—some of it justified, some of it as racist and intemperate as any utterance of Senator James Eastland; but it seldom condemns a Negro politician who takes bribes from a contractor, or a clergyman who makes out notoriously well with his women parishioners. Nobody pickets the Harlem numbers-game operators; nobody calls for social ostracism of the relief chiselers whom Lomax describes as "an abomination and an embarrassment."

Almost nobody, that is. Some of the more courageous Negro leaders are at last beginning to speak up—though not yet very loudly or often. The Reverend Martin Luther King has called on his followers "to admit that our standards do often fall short" and to do something about it. "Even the most poverty-stricken among us," he has written, "can purchase a ten-cent bar of soap; even the most uneducated among us can have high morals. . . . By improving our standards here and now we will go a long way toward breaking down the arguments of the segregationist."

Again, Whitney Young, the new executive secretary of the Urban League, is trying to reshape that organization for a new kind of attack on the Negro's problems. He is talking about mobilizing all sorts of community resources—from social workers to churches to the cop on the beat—in a concerted campaign against crime, broken families, and "social disorganization."

Curiously enough, the Black Muslims seem to be more effective than any other Negro organization so far in stimulating a sense of pride and self-reliance. Their doctrine springs from race hatred, and their political program is sheer fantasy; nevertheless,

in teaching thrift, hard work, business enterprise, decorous conduct and self-discipline, they can claim some notable accomplishments.

But these are thin beginnings. If a First-Class Citizens' Council, or something like it, tackles the job on a really big scale, I suspect that it will be led by new men, uncommitted to the rancors and tactics of the older organizations. Maybe by somebody like Bob Moses, a young man who gave up a bright career in New York to organize Negro voters in Mississippi. He is more like St. Paul than anybody I know; in spite of beatings, prison, and threats of death, he has plugged right ahead on his mission, setting a glowing example of selflessness, austerity, and honor. Maybe the leadership will come from men like Dr. Robert Weaver, who has risen to the highest post in government ever held by a Negro—not by demagoguery, but by long years of dedication to fair play and good housing for everybody, white and Negro alike.

Such men are not content just to demand their rights. They insist on carrying their responsibilities too. That's how you get to be a first-class citizen—as Crispus Attucks knew when he marched to his death in the Boston Massacre. The first man to die in the American Revolution, he was a Negro who knew that citizenship is earned, not given. He might well be the Permanent Honorary President of the new Council.

July, 1962

8 : A Small Band of Practical Heroes

THEY ARE QUIET PEOPLE. They do their work inconspicuously much of it by night. They seldom get involved in the kind of demonstrations that make headlines. To the outside eye, they haven't accomplished much. Some say they never will—not in

our lifetime anyhow. The local press and wire-service reporters try their best to ignore them. Besides, most of them—sixty-one out of sixty-seven—are in jail just now, and the remaining six have learned to expect arrest (or worse) at any minute.

For these reasons the outside world has not yet heard much about what this handful of students is trying to do in Mississippi. But in time it will. One day—perhaps sooner than now seems likely—our history books may add at least some of their names to the list of Americans who have done more than their share for their country, along with Ben Franklin, Nathan Hale, Clara Barton, Alvin York, Frank Merrill, Medgar Evers, John F. Kennedy, and the rest.

They call themselves field workers for the Student Nonviolent Coordinating Committee, or "Snick" for short. The mildest thing they are called by Mississippi whites is "outside agitators." Which they once were; nearly all came in the beginning from Northern universities, although about 80 per cent are now local recruits. Some, including a few girls, are white; most are Negroes. Their first goal is to win for Mississippi's Negro citizens the fundamental right of every American: the right to vote. But their ultimate purpose (though some of them may not fully understand it) is to bring the American Revolution to Mississippi, 187 years late. Until that happens—until the whole structure of its society is rebuilt on the American pattern—neither the right to vote, nor freedom of speech, nor the right to hold a job can ever be secure for either Negro or white.

No one who has not seen Mississippi with his own eyes can really comprehend how different it is from the rest of the United States, including its Southern neighbors. In many ways it is almost as remote as South Africa, which it somewhat resembles.

To begin with, it is the poorest state. Its per capita income in 1961—the latest year for which figures are available—was $1,229; and this includes all the contributions in the form of veterans' pensions, Social Security, relief, and farm subsidies from the hated federal government.

But not all Mississippians are poor. It is the only remaining

state dominated by a plantation economy—essentially unchanged since the first settlement—and the few hundred white families who own the big plantations and lumbering operations are often very comfortable indeed. Naturally enough, they don't aim to give up their way of life without a fight; and they are fighting men, as they have demonstrated in six wars.

Together with a few bankers and fewer industrialists, they make up the oligarchy which rules the state. They run it as they always have; for the Civil War—except during the brief hiatus of the Reconstruction—left their power structure intact. So did the Industrial Revolution, which hasn't really reached Mississippi yet. (Some of its leading citizens have told me that they hope it never will.) In one way or another, practically everybody else in the state—sharecroppers, tenant farmers, the thin middle class of filling-station operators, cotton gin owners, and little merchants—is beholden to the oligarchs. Anybody who gets out of line feels the weight of their wrath right now: a note is called at the bank, a lease is not renewed, credit dries up at the cross-roads store, an advertising contract is canceled, a college professor or a field hand may be fired with equal abruptness.

These are their gentler weapons. Violence is endemic in Mississippi, as anyone who has read its history, or William Faulkner, will remember. Virtually every male owns at least one gun* and knows how to use it, since hunting is the universal sport. Murder, mutilation, and arson have been used as means of political and social discipline for more than a century, against whites as well as Negroes. (See Will Percy's *Lanterns on the Levee* for an account of the ways such tactics were used in the twenties against independent-minded whites, including one or two plantation owners; and of how Percy—a hard man to scare—fought fire with fire.)

Against white dissenters a more common, and equally effective,

---

* Yes, most Negroes too. The wonder is that they haven't used them in self-defense. After the Evers assassination, Snick and NAACP workers and Negro ministers had to use all their powers of persuasion to restrain some Negroes who wanted to retaliate.

The best analysis of the reasons for the Southern tradition of violence is probably W. J. Cash's *The Mind of the South* (Doubleday, 1954).

sanction is social ostracism. A few years ago a Mississippi friend of mine dared to question the local credo out loud; he tells me that he "hasn't heard a friendly voice since," his wife has left him, and his business would be bankrupt if he hadn't been able to get outside help. At Ole Miss the handful of white students who showed hints of good will toward James Meredith have been forced to leave, not by the administration but by their fellow students. And Faulkner himself spent much of his later years outside the state, at least partly because the few neighbors who read his books suspected him of "moderate" leanings.

As a consequence of all this, Mississippi is not very different in essential characteristics from a Communist police state. (It may, indeed, be even more tightly controlled than Yugoslavia or Poland, where whispers of dissent—however muffled—can occasionally be heard.) It has an official ideology: Segregation and the Mississippi Way of Life. It has the usual single-party system—still labeled, ironically, Democratic, although it loathes democracy and almost every politician in the state denounced President Kennedy and his followers as The Enemy. Its ruling class is organized into an elite action group—the White Citizens' Council—which performs planning and disciplinary functions much like those handled by the Party hierarchy in Russia. It keeps its subjects in a constant state of alarm over the threat of intervention by a hostile power—in this case, the federal government. By a variety of devices, of which the poll tax is probably the least important, it disenfranchises about half its citizens—Negroes and poor whites—who are suspected of dangerous thoughts. As in other authoritarian states, terror (by police and by freelance brutalitarians) is an accepted instrument of government.

And, like the Communist countries, Mississippi loses many of its ablest people. An even larger percentage, in all likelihood, because Mississippi has not yet found a way to wall up its borders. As Willie Morris, an exile from the state, pointed out in this summer's issue of *Dissent*, "The occasional good student who graduates from Ole Miss usually leaves . . . never to come back." So do the better faculty members; the more spirited

Negroes; those of both races who nurse a hankering to speak their minds and to associate with whom they please; the men of conscience; and the ambitious. As a result, Mississippi has not produced a statesman since Jefferson Davis, nor a businessman of national stature, nor a scholar of the first rank. Its only intellectuals are a few writers—Faulkner and Eudora Welty, for example—who are tortured by a complex love-hate relationship with their own soil.

One result is a fatal lack of progressive leadership. Of all the Southern states, only Mississippi has so far failed to produce a single man with the courage, the imagination, and the political skill to show its people how they can (and must) learn to accommodate to the inevitable. Even South Carolina, even Alabama, eventually turned up leaders who were able to make a beginning on the tortuous process of desegregation. (Few people outside his own state yet appreciate the acumen and political deftness of President Frank Rose of the University of Alabama, who devised a way to admit Negro students peaceably despite the opposition of the Governor, the legislature, and probably a majority of the voters.) But in Mississippi all but a few of the moderate whites who remain are cowed into silence, and all the public figures have nailed the Confederate flag to their mast. Do they really believe they can win a return engagement?

My hunch is that the ablest leaders in Mississippi today are Negroes: the young men of the Student Nonviolent Coordinating Committee. Certainly they are the bravest, the hardest-working, the most indomitable, and probably the best educated. They or their successors may yet prove to be the salvation of the state. (If salvation is still possible—a question which Faulkner, among others, held in doubt.)

The one I know best is Robert Moses, an honor graduate of Hamilton College and of Harvard, where he took his M.A. degree in philosophy on a John Hay Whitney fellowship. After graduation from Harvard he taught for three years at Horace Mann—one of New York's better private preparatory schools—

while he worked on his Ph.D. He was well launched on a promising academic career (and a safe, comfortable life) when he decided in 1961 to put all that aside to work for SNCC; he is now working as director of its Voters Registration Project in Mississippi.

In the last two years he has been shot at, jailed, clubbed by police, and bitten by a police dog. Many days he has gone hungry—his salary, when it is paid at all, is $10 a week—and often he has not known where he could find shelter for the next night. Yet I have never heard him utter a word of regret, bitterness, hatred, or discouragement. He seems to regard persecution not as welcome, exactly, but as an honorable and inevitable part of the job.

Mr. Moses asked me to make it plain that he is in no way exceptional—that he has done nothing, taken no lumps, risked no more than every other member of the group. Some have been through worse. James Travis, for example, was seriously wounded by a shotgun blast fired into his car on February 28; Moses, riding with him, was unhit. Sixteen of the sixty-seven SNCC workers are, at this writing, in the state penitentiary under maximum security, while another forty-five are doing hard labor on the LeFlore County prison farm. White volunteers for the project, he says, often have the toughest time of all, because their very presence enrages the local whites. Let it be understood, then, that I mention Bob Moses only as an example, typical of all the rest.

This is the way he describes their work:

"When a representative of Snick comes into a Mississippi town, his first problem is to find someplace to live. Most Negro boarding-house keepers are afraid to take in somebody who might look like a troublemaker to the whites. They are afraid the lease might be canceled, or the taxes raised, or the house burned down. So in the beginning we often have to visit around for a long time, staying a few nights with one family and a few more with the next.

"The first job is to get some kind of organization started. We just talk to people in the streets, or call at their homes in the evening, going from door to door. After a while we may be able to call little meetings in a church. When I first came to Greenwood, the church people were all afraid to let us hold meetings. Now eight Negro churches are open to us. That is a real sign of progress; it shows that a lot of people aren't quite so scared any more.

"We talk mostly about how important it is for Negroes to register to vote. It takes a long time to persuade anybody to try. They tell us: 'I don't want to be bothered with that mess. I don't want those white folks shooting into my house at night.' They tell us what happened to Negroes who have tried to register— how they got beat up, or lost their jobs. Twenty-nine Greenwood people who attended a voter-registration meeting in a church were arrested and sent to the county prison farm for four months; rocks and a smoke bomb were thrown through the windows of the church. No, the whites didn't do that; they got a Negro to do it, by giving him thirty dollars and the promise of a job.

"But after six months in Greenwood, we got fifty people to try to register. Only two of them passed the test. They have to interpret a section of the Constitution to the satisfaction of the registrar, and of course he isn't easy to satisfy.

"By that time we had a little office in a room over a Negro store. In August of 1962 it was raided by two carloads of whites at 1:00 A.M. Three of our people who were there—Sam Block, Lawrence Guyot, and Lavaughn Brown—escaped by climbing out the window and running over the roofs, before the raiders broke in the door. But we had to give up the office, because of tax pressure against the owner and police charges brought against the man who leased the building. Most of that winter we had no office and no place to live. We just kept shifting from house to house. In December we managed to get another office, but it was burned in March.

"During this particular time we were trying to collect food and clothing from all over the country for destitute plantation hands and sharecroppers, because the county officials had stopped distribution of federal surplus food—which meant that about sixteen thousand Negroes had nothing to eat. Whenever we were able to get a little something to give to a hungry family, we also talked about how they ought to register. As a result, about a hundred marched down in a batch; they felt safer if they went together.

"It was soon after that Jimmy Travis got shot, and there were three more shootings in the following month. One time they fired into a Negro theater where a meeting was going on, and once into Sam Block's car while four people were riding in it, but nobody got hit. The shots were fired from cars without any license plates. The police paid no attention and when some of us protested, they put us in jail—I think the charge was disturbing the peace.

"About that time Dick Gregory, the entertainer, came down to help us with a demonstration and the Justice Department filed an injunction suit to stop intimidation. Soon we were able to rent a new and bigger office, and in the past five months, about 1,300 Negroes have tried to register. We don't know yet how many of them will be permitted to pass the tests—but maybe the situation is a little more hopeful, because the Justice Department is examining the records and it has filed a suit to abolish these tests as unconstitutional. It will take a long time, of course, for the case to work its way through the courts."*

Meanwhile, the SNCC staff is busy with other projects:

1. It is enlisting and training local Negroes to take charge, eventually, of the work in Mississippi—with considerable success.

2. With the help of researchers and technicians in New York,

---

* In 1960 only 163 Negroes—less than one per cent of the Negro population of voting age—registered in LeFlore County. By contrast, more than 50 per cent of the eligible whites registered. This year the SNCC workers hope that as many as four hundred Negroes may be able to get on the registration rolls. Usually only a small fraction of those registered dare to cast a ballot. This is easier to understand if you remember that this is the area where fourteen-year-old Emmett Till was murdered, and also is the home of the man charged with killing Medgar Evers.

it is trying to develop a simple, cheap teaching machine which Negroes can use to teach themselves to read—and thus to pass the voting tests. Throughout Mississippi, education for whites is poor; for Negroes it is negligible.

3. It is trying to set up a small library for Negroes in Greenwood, the LeFlore County seat. At present they have little access to books. LeFlore County has no bookstore—in fact, there are only a few in the whole state—and Negroes are of course barred from white libraries. So far, SNCC has collected about two thousand volumes, most of them contributed by students at Hamilton College in New York. Bob Moses tells me that they particularly need "a good set of reference books, children's books, and books written by Negroes"—though anything else of quality, including good periodicals and paperbacks, will be welcome.*

4. SNCC is conducting one-week seminars or workshops for high-school students in seven counties, to teach them a few basic facts about government—notably, how to overcome the many legal obstacles Mississippi has set up to keep Negroes from registering and voting. Major help in this enterprise is being provided by Northern law students—five from Harvard, two from Columbia, three (including a woman) from Yale—who are doing research on Mississippi's ingenious laws, and helping to prepare a Mississippi Political Handbook.

5. It is trying to line up as many volunteer workers as possible: white or Negro; local or from outside the state; for the school vacation months only, or for periods up to three years. The requirements are exacting. In addition to intelligence and the physical stamina for hard work on short rations, a volunteer has to have exceptional self-discipline and emotional maturity. He must be able to take insults and beatings without ever striking back.

"Hotheads are no help," Moses explained. "White volunteers

---

* This suggestion brought in more than 15,000 volumes—more than the SNCC Greenwood project could use immediately. The surplus was turned over to Negro colleges, many of which urgently need more good books for their libraries.

especially have to be able to keep their emotions under control. If they are too forward, too eager to gain acceptance, they just make the local Negroes suspicious. If they show fear, their fear is likely to infect others. If they lose their tempers or act defiant, they will cause unnecessary trouble with the local whites. We've had a few neurotics who have come down here—youngsters with a John Brown complex—but we've shifted them out fast.

"What we need most is people with teaching and organizing skills. Understand, this is like going into an underdeveloped country. What we really need is a Peace Corps."

Are the meager results worth all this effort and sacrifice?

I think so, if only for their by-products. Two of these may prove more important than the immediate results in voter registration.

1. A considerable number of Negroes are learning the art of leadership, in the hardest possible school. When he finishes a SNCC assignment in Mississippi, a man is bound to know something about the persuasion and management of people, and the carrying through of complex operations under fire. He also is likely to end up with a new (and well-earned) pride and self-confidence.

This generation of leaders will be very different from that of Adam Clayton Powell and Malcolm X. They aren't interested in demagoguery or self-aggrandizement. Nor do they have any use for demonstrations staged primarily for publicity or emotional release. They have specific, well-defined goals; they are driving toward them with relentless determination; they can't be frightened or bought off; they waste no energy on unfocused hatred; and they have a hard grasp on political reality. Unlike the Black Muslims, they don't dream of a separate Negro state in some utopian future; they want simple American justice, in Mississippi and now.

2. Harder to measure, but perhaps equally important, is their impact on the Southern mind. One thing that the average Mississippian does admire—however grudgingly—is courage. And he can't watch the SNCC people at work indefinitely with-

out beginning to wonder whether it is *really* true that all Negroes are innately inferior.

One of these days, when he is finally forced to deal with his Negro neighbors as human beings and American citizens, he will know, deep inside, that he has met an opponent worthy of respect. And because of that recognition (probably never voiced out loud) the inevitable adjustment to reality will come a little easier for most Mississippians. After all, only after Antietam did the Confederate troops begin to shed their contempt for the Union army. At the time, it looked like an indecisive and costly battle; but we now know that it was the actual turning point of the war.

October, 1963

9 : Money Bait

ALMOST BY ACCIDENT, a new method has been discovered for attracting wealth. It has never been publicly reported, so far as I can find—although one group of financiers is now quietly using it in an operation which promises to be highly profitable. Apparently they are the first to fully understand the formula, and to put it to deliberate use.

Earlier it had been tested successfully in two states—Massachusetts and California—but these demonstrations were inadvertent. Most of the people concerned did not quite grasp what was happening, or why. This isn't surprising, because the demonstrations occurred piecemeal, over a period of about fifteen years, without any conscious plan.

Once the formula is widely known, however, it should be possible to apply it more quickly in at least a dozen other places. The South, Puerto Rico, and the Pacific Northwest look like the best bets. All of them have one of the two vital ingredients, and probably can create the other if they really try. The result might well be a surprisingly rapid rise in new factories, skilled employment, and per capita income. In certain other states, however, it is never likely to work, for reasons to be noted in a moment.

Our poorer communities have, of course, been looking for just such a recipe for generations. They have tried many kinds of lures to attract new industries. The favorite has been tax concessions —sometimes, as in the case of Puerto Rico, complete tax exemption for as long as twenty years. Often they have put up new buildings and offered them at low rent (or none) to any factory that would move in. In addition they usually have promised cheap labor, and some Southern states have hinted loudly that newcomers wouldn't have to worry about trouble with labor unions.

All too frequently the catch has proved disappointing. For the kind of industry that will snap at such bait is hardly worth having. The South, for example, succeeded in enticing a good many textile mills away from New England—but the industry already was in decline, and its low wages certainly have bestowed no crescendo of prosperity on the Carolinas or Georgia.

On the other hand, the exciting growth industries—electronics, for instance—aren't interested in cheap labor. They need highly skilled men and are willing to pay almost any price to get them—as anyone can see by glancing at the help-wanted ads in *Scientific American* or the Sunday *New York Times*. Neither are they much interested in low taxes, because low taxes mean poor schools. Such schools can't turn out the kind of brains these industries need; moreover, the men they seek aren't willing to settle in communities where their children will be doomed to a second-rate education.

In fact, the major growth industries of the postwar era—the prizes any ambitious community would love to get—differ in six important characteristics from the old-fashioned industries such as steel, textiles, and automobiles:

1. They mostly produce items of small size but great value:

transistors, magnetic tape, automation-control instruments, micro-bearings, computers, missile-fuel pumps, pharmaceuticals, inertial-guidance systems, to mention a few.

2. They do not use huge tonnages of raw material and fuel.

3. Consequently they don't have to locate near ore bodies or coal mines. Nor are they dependent on river transport or rail lines. Indeed so far as physical requirements are concerned, they can locate practically anywhere they please.

4. Their plants usually operate without noise, smoke, or smell. Therefore they don't blight the surrounding neighborhoods as a steel mill or paper factory does. On the contrary, these new-type factories are often an enhancement to the community. The cluster of Johnson & Johnson plants near New Brunswick, New Jersey—each a handsome specimen of architecture in a campus-like setting—is a noteworthy example.

5. They aren't greatly concerned about unions. For one thing, their scientific and other white-collar workers are almost impossible to organize. For another, wage costs aren't decisive. What is decisive is the quality of the product—plus constant innovation of improved or entirely new items. If a production team can come up with a better silicon diode or a more efficient process for making antibiotics, management isn't inclined to haggle about salaries.

6. Their one critical requirement, therefore, is brain power. If they hope to stay ahead of the competition, they must at all costs attract (and hold) really first-rate scientists, technicians, and executives.

It is interesting to note the places where such industries have, in fact, chosen to locate. Although some are scattered in many parts of the country, they have tended to gravitate toward two great concentrations: one in Southern California, the other in the Boston area. In the latter, they have sprouted thickest along Route 128—the semicircular expressway built a few years ago through what was then open countryside to bypass the traffic-choked metropolitan area of Boston. According to Dr. F. Leroy Foster, director of the Division of Sponsored Research for Massachusetts Institute of Technology, more than four hundred plants are now turning out electronic components or associated products within a twenty-mile radius of the Charles River Basin, the center of the area. Virtually all of them have been established since the war, and most within the last ten years.

The comparable concentration in Southern California covers a wider area, and has been even more spectacular in its rate of growth. San Diego, for instance, increased its factory employment by 54 per cent between 1954 and 1959, while Los Angeles reported a 21 per cent gain.

Why have such plants sprung up in these two places—rather than in, say, Arkansas, Mississippi, or upstate New York, which need new industry much more desperately? Certainly not because California and Massachusetts did a better promotion job or offered bigger tax and wage incentives; their promotion has been negligible and their tax incentives nil.

By happenstance, however, both areas did offer two powerful attractions: (1) A pleasant environment to live in, and (2) Great universities.

These often turned out to be the decisive considerations for a management which was worrying about the recruitment of key personnel.

To begin with, many of the people they wanted already had their roots down in these communities. They were faculty members or graduate students at MIT, Harvard, Boston University, Brandeis, or at Caltech, Stanford, or one of the many campuses of the University of California. (Indeed such people frequently start a factory themselves. MIT alumni have organized seventy-five new companies in the Boston area since the war. And the firm which eventually grew into the Raytheon Company was originally founded by Dr. Vannevar Bush—wartime director of the Office of Scientific Research and Development—and two friends, who wanted to make a special kind of thermostat. Raytheon now employs 40,000 people—the great majority in twenty-five plants near Boston.)

Moreover, other scientists can easily be persuaded to move to an area which has a complex of good universities. There they can keep in touch with the research under way in the best laboratories. They can consult whenever necessary with the leading minds in their fields.*

Above all, they have company. In the evenings they can visit with friends who share their interests and talk their language. And not merely with other scientists. These people frequently are true intellectuals, with a wide range of interests. They like to live in a community of scholars—historians, writers, sociologists, even an occasional artist—and they enjoy being near good libraries, good orchestras, good art galleries. If you plunked them down in Spearfish, South Dakota, they would go out of their minds with boredom; no amount of money could persuade them to stay there.

Robert S. McNamara is a case in point. A Phi Beta Kappa and once an assistant professor at Harvard, he is typical of the new breed of corporate executive. And it is significant that even after he became president of the Ford Motor Company he continued to live in Ann Arbor—thirty-eight miles from his office—because, as *Time* reported, "it is a university town" and he had "a liking for the academic life." (Or, to put it less tactfully, no intellectual is likely to live in Detroit if he can avoid it.) Dr. Bush provides another object lesson. After his retirement as president of the Carnegie Institution, he returned to MIT because he enjoyed "the excitement of its intellectual ferment."

By coincidence, both Southern California and the Boston area offered not only intellectual ferment but also pleasant places to live. The charms of Southern California (for some people, anyhow) are well known. And the construction of Route 128 made it possible for a man to live in the Boston suburbs, or in the rolling, wooded hills beyond, and still drive to his plant in a few minutes.

It is no coincidence, of course, that these localities also had

* Dr. Wernher von Braun, the rocket scientist, recently made the same point in asking the Alabama legislature for money to expand a small research center near the state university. "It's not water, or real estate, or labor, or power, or cheap taxes which brings industry," he said. "It's brainpower. . . . What do you think attracted the aircraft industry to the Los Angeles area? The desert and smog? No, it was UCLA [and the other great universities there]."

good schools. Any area that abounds in first-rate universities is almost sure to have better-than-average primary and secondary schools, both public and private. For almost by definition, intellectuals are passionate about education, and insist on getting the best they can for their children.

Finally, such people are apt to be sensitive to their physical surroundings. Because they detest ugliness, they can sometimes muster enough public opinion to fight back the tide of billboards, juke joints, used-car lots, and Tastee-Freez stands which has overwhelmed so much of the American landscape. (Witness the civic uproar which saved Walden Pond.) Both Los Angeles and downtown Boston are hideous enough, God knows, but their outlying academic communities generally have managed to preserve little islands of green and ordered serenity.

Since the key men in a space-age factory also are likely to value these things, it is only sensible to locate the plant where they are already available. Provided, of course, that the universities are there too.

The business firm which first spotted this pattern of behavior, and tried to make a profit out of it, apparently was the City Investing Company of New York City.

It discovered one-half of the formula about eight years ago. Its original idea was to buy up a twenty-thousand-acre tract of woodland on the west side of the Hudson River, thirty miles from Manhattan, and to develop there a cluster of modern research establishments. Each plant could be set in its own tree-shaded campus, a comfortable distance away from any other. Each employee could have his own country estate—within walking distance of his work.

On paper, this idyllic planned community sounded irresistible to the new type of science-based industries and their egghead personnel. Moreover, the company spared nothing to make its Sterling Forest development into a sylvan paradise. It found a choice site—close to Tuxedo Park and West Point, within easy reach of the New York Thruway, endowed with a brook and three lakes—and it spent hundreds of thousands of dollars on landscaping, flowers, and shrubs.

But, alas, the scientists didn't swarm in with the expected alacrity. In 1957 the Union Carbide Nuclear Company did begin to do some research there, and has since opened a new center, while the Sterling Forest management put up an International Research Building of its own. But there was no stampede like the one Boston and California had enjoyed.

The trouble, it seems, was that the scientists were afraid they would be lonesome. Who could they talk to out there in those woods? Chipmunks? Gardeners? Their wives?

So in 1960 the City Investing people hit upon the missing half of the formula. What they needed, obviously, was a university.

Last December they got it. The company gave a thousand acres of land to New York University, on condition that it would establish there a major campus for its science departments. The school's president promptly announced plans for setting up an atomic-reactor laboratory, classrooms and quarters for graduate students, adult-education programs, and housing for faculty and research personnel. The development may take twenty years to complete, he explained, but eventually the new campus will be fit company for the six campuses which NYU already operates.

That evidently turned the trick. Four corporations made plans to install research units in the Sterling Forest area before the university got around to laying its first brick.

Few private financiers are likely to command the resources (or the foresight) to carry through similar schemes. But the technique seems made to order for states that are eager to attract modern industry. Some already have a good start, even though they don't realize it.

In North Carolina, for example, the area between Chapel Hill and Durham looks like a natural for such an enterprise. Both are pleasant towns. They are surrounded by unspoiled (well, all right, not *hopelessly* spoiled) countryside; it could be hand-

somely developed—at a profit—by public purchase and zoning.
The Blue Ridge Mountains are an easy drive to the west, the
Cape Hatteras beach about the same distance east. In sum, a
potential for The Good Life as promising as anything Massachusetts or California can offer.

And here are two of the best educational institutions in the
South: the University of North Carolina and Duke. Around this
nucleus the state could—if it made a determined effort—build
up a truly great intellectual center. It might become not just the
best in its region, but one of the best in America. Inevitably it
would give North Carolina the educational leadership of the
South—and, as a consequence, leadership in modern industry as
well.*

It would cost money of course. A doubling of teachers' salaries,
new buildings, urban renewal, parks and landscaping, a long-
range, well-thought-out regional plan: all of these would have to
be financed somehow. (The big national foundations and the
tobacco industry might both be eager to help.) But in the end
the investment ought to pay off bountifully. In New England
the factory sales of electronic equipment alone amounted to $749
million in 1959, and are expected to pass $2 billion by 1970. Al-
ready these factories have created jobs for nearly a hundred thousand people—almost as many as the payroll of the region's
entire textile industry.

Comparable opportunities would seem to be open to Puerto
Rico, with its climatic advantages and a university already growing rapidly in stature; to the Puget Sound region; to Wisconsin,
Michigan, and a few other areas which already have some of the
basic ingredients.

For certain states, however, this sort of development seems
out of the question. How could anybody create either a great
university or an enticing environment in Nebraska or North

* In fact, a modest but promising start has been made in the Research Tri-
angle project sponsored by three North Carolina universities. But meanwhile the
state is losing ground as an attractive place to live, because it lacks the zoning
laws—and, apparently, the public interest—to preserve its invaluable scenic
resources.

Dakota? The Deep South will continue to lose, rather than attract, educated people so long as it threatens to destroy its public-school system over the integration issue. (The North Carolinians, notoriously more commonsensical than most Southerners, seem likely to solve this problem without much uproar.) Texas, Arizona, Colorado, and Nevada—plus some others—have not yet demonstrated that respect for intellect and education which is necessary to the growth of great universities. Maine and Idaho probably couldn't raise the money.

Clearly the new recipe for industrialization will not work everywhere—but it does look too good to remain indefinitely the secret weapon of Massachusetts, California, and the City Investing Company. It will be entertaining to see what community first shows enough enterprise to try to break their monopoly.

September, 1961

10 : The Stupidity Problem

A WOMAN in Woods Hole, Massachusetts has chided me for being remiss in the first duty of every editorial writer: to tell the President and Congress how to run the country. She brushed aside my excuses—that (a) they were hired to do this job and (b) maybe they know more about it than most columnists. Nonsense, she said; such evasion is sheer cowardice, and besides, any columnist who doubts his own omniscience ought to turn in his uniform. Does David Lawrence flinch from instructing Congress in economics? Where would the Supreme Court be without Arthur Krock to interpret the Constitution? How could any Secretary of State conduct our foreign policy without the guidance of Joe Alsop?

At the moment, unfortunately, I can't lay my hands on a set of hydramatic, nonslip solutions to the country's fiscal and foreign problems. But since the Woods Hole lady insists, I am in a position to offer the President some advice on one matter that seems to be giving him plenty of trouble: unemployment. After all, I have held, and lost, more jobs than he has, even though mine weren't so classy.

It is perfectly clear, to me at least, why we haven't been able to find jobs for our three or four million unemployed. The human race—or anyhow that sample of it located in North America—no longer fits the kind of society it has to live in. Our society just doesn't have any jobs for certain types of people. If it continues to develop along its present course, the number of such unemployables seems likely to grow rather rapidly. Meanwhile, at the other end of the scale, an increasing number of important jobs will remain empty, because there aren't enough men and women able to fill them.

So the chief characteristic of The Overdeveloped Society (if that is the right label) will be a permanent surplus of some kinds of workers, together with a permanent shortage of others. For the assortment of jobs which need to be done is simply out of kilter with the natural distribution of brains.

A few figures show how this happened. According to the psychologists, intelligence seems to be parceled out among human beings in line with a fairly consistent pattern. If you should round up a hundred typical Americans off the street, getting a fair sample of our whole population, you would find that about forty-six of them would have something close to "normal" intelligence—that is, Intelligence Quotients between 90 and 109. Another twenty-nine would be quite bright, with IQs ranging from 110 to 139. And one or two would be really brilliant, with IQs of 140 or above.*

---

* These figures are quoted from Lee J. Cronbach's *Essentials of Psychological Testing*, second edition (Harper, 1960), p. 172, and are based on the standard Stanford-Binet tests. Similar tables can be found in most basic psychology texts.

Such figures probably should be taken with a moderate amount of salt. For example, some educators have suggested that the usual Stanford-Binet tests may

On the other hand, twenty people in this group would have to be classed as fairly stupid, since their IQs would fall between 70 and 89. And two or three, with ratings below 70, would barely have enough sense to come in out of the rain.

From the beginning of history until fairly recently—say, a couple of generations ago—every society in the world had plenty of jobs for low-IQ people. They could herd sheep, pick cotton, dig ditches (even the Erie Canal was made with spades), h'ist that bale and tote that load. Indeed, nearly all of the earth's work called for strong backs and weak minds—for drawers of water and hewers of wood. Jobs that demanded real intelligence, on the other hand, were strictly limited; most communities had room for only a few doctors, ministers, teachers, lawyers, and captains of industry. Scientists were practically unknown. (As Robert Oppenheimer once pointed out in these pages, quoting Professor Purcell of Harvard, 90 per cent of all the scientists that ever lived are living today.) Government administrators were almost as scarce; Alexander Hamilton could run the Treasury Department with five clerks. As a consequence, thousands of high-IQ people lived in frustration, because they could find no work equal to their talents. In many parts of the world this is still

---

exaggerate the native brainpower of people who come from comfortable middle-class backgrounds, while underestimating the intelligence of those from poor families and laboring-class traditions. Frequently tests are so poorly administered that they give inaccurate results. Moreover, recent experiments in the New York schools seem to indicate that an individual's IQ is not permanently fixed—that it can be raised quite a few points by special educational efforts and motivational stimuli. Conversely, anybody confined for too long in a dull, unchallenging environment may grow stupider. (From my own boyhood work on farms, I know that prolonged association with cattle and horses—two of the stupidest creatures God ever made—can have a numbing effect on the mind.)

Finally, the Stanford-Binet tests seem incapable of measuring some types of mind. They work best in testing one's ability to handle language, figures, and abstract concepts; but they tell little about one's capacity for handling colors, sounds, shapes, and human relationships. Consequently, a person of real talent and high social value—a painter, musician, sculptor, mechanic, or a woman with the warm empathy needed to run an orphanage or kindergarten—might score low on the conventional IQ scale.

If such limitations are kept in mind, however, the general conclusions pointed by the IQ figures seem sound enough: Some people are born a lot brighter than others, and will stay that way. No amount of special training and stimulus will convert a 70-IQ mind into an intellectual giant.

true. Some of the brightest people I ever met—in Greece and Yugoslavia—are hauling nets, throwing the shuttle on hand looms, sweeping streets, and winnowing grain with a hand basket.

But in the industrialized countries, as we all know, human muscle has now become almost obsolete. Anything it can lift, a machine can lift better. Practically any task involving repetition of the same motions can be done faster and cheaper by a mechanical or electronic device. So the muscle-worker is out of luck. He can still find a few things to do—collecting garbage, for example, unloading trucks, replacing railway ties—but these are mostly in minor or backward industries which have not yet got around to complete mechanization. And the number of such low-IQ chores is dwindling every day.

Farming perhaps offers the most vivid illustration of what is happening. As recently as my grandfather's day, farming was a set of inherited motions, not very different from those used by the Babylonians. As a boy in Ohio, he sowed wheat by hand-broadcasting and harvested it with a scythe. Since neither of these operations strains the cerebral cortex, a youngster who was too dumb for anything else could always make a living on the farm; the demand for field hands was virtually unlimited.

Today, however, a successful farmer has to be a combination geneticist, mechanical engineer, chemist, cost accountant, agronomist, tax expert, and economist; in all likelihood he is a college graduate. While he may still hire some unskilled migrant labor for a few weeks a year to harvest certain fruit and vegetable crops, he can very frequently operate a big farm without any help outside the family. If he does take on a full-time hand, he looks for a smart one; no farmer wants to entrust $40,000 worth of complex agricultural machinery to a dope.

It should be noted that this permanent dejobbing of the slow-witted is something different from the problem of technological unemployment. For example, the printers and flight engineers recently thrown out of work are mostly well above "normal" in intelligence; since they were smart enough to acquire fairly complicated skills—now made obsolescent by technological changes—they presumably are smart enough to do something else useful. But that 22 per cent of the population with IQs below 89 may in many cases never learn to do *any* useful job.

The youngsters who drop out of high school before graduation are a case in point. Most leave school not because of economic problems but because they can't keep up with the not-very-demanding work. The federal Bureau of Labor Statistics has reported that 80 per cent of the dropouts are lagging by at least one grade; and Dr. Cronbach notes that "the very dull tend to drop out as soon as they reach age sixteen . . . . By the end of high school, almost no one with IQ below 85 is still in school." This is one reason why the unemployment rate for sixteen- to nineteen-year-olds is twice as high as for adults. A few get jobs as messengers, gas-pump operators, or dishwashers. Many others drift straight from the classroom to the relief rolls, or to crime. For as our society is now organized, we can't find any use for most of these young dullards—a situation unjust and miserable to them, and to the rest of the community both costly and dangerous.

The counterpart of this situation is a severe and increasing shortage of people brainy enough to man the upper level jobs in our Overdeveloped Society. The design, supervision, and maintenance of automated equipment require a lot of smart, highly trained people—and even now industry can't find enough of them. Did you ever hear of a good computer-programer who was out of work?

So too with the rest of our society. All the professions which demand better-than-average minds—medicine, law, journalism, teaching, the sciences, advertising, the military—are moaning about their difficulties in attracting enough competent recruits. And as the structure of society grows in both complexity and size, the need for able managers (in business and government alike) grows in almost geometric ratio. Our inability to locate enough first-rate managerial talent in many fields—from college president to corporate comptroller, from regional planner to operations analyst—may yet prove to be the breakdown point in our civilization.

For we have apparently built ourselves, unintentionally and without quite realizing it, a society which calls for a distribution of intelligence entirely different from that which God provided. It remains to be seen whether we can make it work.

In order to do so, we probably will have to change some of our most cherished mental habits—not just those of the President and our Congressmen, but of all of us. For one thing, we'll have to face up to the fact that all men are *not* created equal, except in the limited political sense which Jefferson had in mind when he drafted the Declaration of Independence. Until we do that, it will be impossible for our public officials to find useful work for the 20-plus per cent of the population with below-normal intelligence, or to train them for jobs they are capable of handling. And it will remain almost equally hard to make the best use of our limited supply of high IQs.

Right now it is not only unfashionable, but almost indecent, to hint that such a problem even exists. Our educationists presumably know all about IQ distributions, and they are surely aware of the National Education Association's findings that about 25 per cent of Selective Service registrants fail the Army's mental tests.* Yet they keep on talking about "slow learners," "culturally deprived children," "underachievers"—almost any euphemism to avoid admitting that a lot of children are unable to absorb the kind of education we are trying to push down their throats at such expense.

This is not entirely the educationists' fault. It is true that the canonized educational doctrine still puts undue emphasis on protecting the little ego from the harsh facts of competitive life; but this is at least in part a reflection of community pressures. Just suppose that a school principal called a doting suburban mother into his office and told her:

---

* This figure is for registrants in New York State in the year 1959; but there is no reason to believe that it is consistently lower in other states.

"I am sorry to have to report that little Johnny does not have an inferiority complex, as you have always assumed. He is just inferior. He will never get into Yale. He doesn't even have enough brains to pass his final high-school examinations. With proper training, however, he might become an adequate bellhop or waiter. I suggest therefore that you remove him at once from high school, thus saving a great deal of the taxpayers' money and your own, and enroll him in the Hotel Employees Institute."

The resulting uproar, as we all know, would shake the walls of the Board of Education. And it is not only Johnny's parents who would be affronted. Many of us would feel that it was somehow undemocratic, or at least inhumane, to blurt out such unpleasant truths.

We are even a bit uneasy about giving special attention to especially talented pupils. In recent years there has been a good deal of talk about the gifted child, and the better school systems are experimenting with enriched curricula. Yet in the great majority of high schools, the really bright youngster is still bored, underworked, and educated far below his capacity.

The social and economic biases in American society are at least partly responsible for this failure to make the best use of our best brains—wherever they may turn up. Wealthier parents, quite naturally, try hard to protect their duller offspring from the consequences of their stupidity. As a result, prosperous communities are likely to spend an inordinate amount of their school money trying to cosset and prop up the mental laggards—to the neglect of the uncommonly able. At the same time, our poorer neighborhoods are likely to have poor schools, where the bright youngster may never be spotted and almost certainly will not get the intensive, top-caliber instruction he deserves. Americans are not yet ready, apparently, to search out the high-potential students —at whatever age their talent begins to show and anywhere they can be found, in slum or suburb—and to say:

"This 5 per cent have the possibility of becoming our future William Faulkners, Robert McNamaras, George Gershwins, and Alfred Sloans. They represent an invaluable asset. Therefore it is vital to the public interest to give them the very best teachers and equipment, and to push them to the limits of their capacity. The second-raters will have to get along with what is left."

Undemocratic? By our traditional habits, it may be. But in the not-so-distant future it may prove to be the only way possible to run the peculiar kind of society we are developing.

We might also profit if we could change our national attitude toward certain kinds of employment.

From the earliest days of the Republic, most Americans have regarded personal service as somehow degrading. Hardly anybody wanted to be a housekeeper or cook, and those hapless widows who were forced into such work to avoid starvation usually did it bitterly and with little pride. Butlers and valets were legendary creatures who belonged in British country homes or Wodehouse novels, but had no place in democratic America. Waiting tables was, and is, so unpopular that many restaurants have to import their help from Europe or Puerto Rico.

These prejudices evidently are peculiar to America, not to democracies in general. In Switzerland, the oldest democracy in Europe, the profession of waiter is both honorable and much sought after, while it is still possible to hire good-natured and efficient household help in Scandinavia, Ireland, and Greece. (In England, however, the Americanization of society has made the butler and the maid almost extinct; those few who still exist there are mostly imported from Sweden, Italy, and Eire.)

Whatever their origins, such attitudes are costly. Both the efficiency and the tone of American life would be vastly improved if personal service came to be regarded as an acceptable way to make a living. For we now have the curious spectacle of millions of people on relief, while at the same time millions of households are looking for desperately needed help—to care for elderly relatives, tend the children, and help with the heavier chores. If such help could be found, countless women—many of them highly educated—could be freed for teaching and other understaffed professions; innumerable old people would not have to be condemned to nursing homes; any number of businessmen could save the energy now dissipated in shoveling snow, putting up storm windows, and tinkering with balky plumbing. It might even become possible to get prompt and courteous service in the average hotel and restaurant—but no, that is carrying fantasy too far.

Such work demands no great intelligence and only a minimum of training. Yet it is scorned by nearly all the people on the unemployment rolls. That isn't our kind of work, they say— and relief officials ordinarily will not require their clients to accept any job opening outside their customary trade.

I have no idea how such ingrained attitudes might be changed. Perhaps it could be done by professionalizing service work, and thus removing the stigma of the servant. Already this is being attempted, with some success, by a few companies which send out crews of trained men and women to do spring housecleaning, household repair, and the like. Their workers wear snappy uniforms, they work for the company instead of the householder, and they put in a regular eight-hour day; as a consequence they seem to feel more independence and self-respect.

No doubt there are many other and better ways to find useful work for the low IQs, and to persuade them to do it. My main point is that nobody seems to be thinking about such things, because nobody is yet willing to admit publicly that the Stupidity Problem needs coping with. The steps recently taken by the government to fight unemployment—new factories for distressed areas, retraining for technologically displaced workers, general stimulus of the economy—may be fine for their own purposes; but they ignore the special problem of the dullard. This is not only expensive, but dangerous. When you condemn people indefinitely to idleness and public charity, you condemn them also to frustration and bitterness—to the kind of discontent which may have a lot to do with the crime rate, drug addiction, and political unrest.

It ought not to be beyond human ingenuity to create worthwhile jobs for these people, if we only set our minds to it. If we tended our forests, for example, as carefully as the Germans do, we would need millions of man-hours of not-very-skilled work—and we would increase enormously the value of a precious national asset. We could use a lot of muscle power in deferred maintenance of our dilapidated railways. We might even set a few hundred thousand men to work cleaning the litter off our streets and the beer cans out of our trash-clogged parks and streams. And we might start now to devise an educational system which will candidly train every youngster for a level of work that fits his intelligence, instead of pretending that each of them is potential college material.

I am pretty sure that the lady in Woods Hole, who is something of a sentimentalist, won't like any of these suggestions; but then she asked for it.

September, 1962

11 : George Villiers and Other Studs

A DREADFUL BOOK has recently been published in England.* God grant that it may never be published here.

It masquerades under an innocent-sounding title: *Uncommon People.* Its author, Paul Bloomfield, purports to be a decent citizen, with a negative Wasserman test and no record of subversive activity. Its subject looks harmless; it is advertised as the story of George Villiers, who died 330 years ago, and the history of his descendants and those of five other respectable Englishmen. The unwary might mistake it for another of those tedious volumes of genealogy which are read by old ladies in Boston and Richmond.

* By Hamish Hamilton, Ltd.

Actually it oozes poison of high virulence. Nothing Marx or Lenin ever wrote poses such a sneaky threat to the American Way of Life. Their ham-handed arguments can be immediately recognized, by most Americans, as preposterous; but Bloomfield's are so plausible and seductive that it is doubtful that even the Daughters of the American Revolution could hold out against them. (The Daughters may, in fact, be especially susceptible to his evil whisperings.)

So if the Bloomfield Heresy were widely circulated in this country it might, in time, undermine our political institutions, our habits of courtship and marriage, our school system, and the whole tone of our social life. We can feel safe only if the customs officers do their duty with relentless efficiency, burning every copy of this book they may discover in the luggage of smugglers and returning tourists.

Bloomfield opens his work with a deceptively simple tale. He tells how Sir George Villiers lived through the reign of Queen Elizabeth I in comfortable obscurity, marrying twice and raising nine children. In his lifetime no one remarked him as exceptional. Yet, as the story of his family unravels through the centuries, it becomes plain that this farmer was one of the most exceptional men who ever lived. He may, indeed, have been the all-time champion sire—a sort of human Man-O'-War.

For his stud-book record is thick with genius. Villiers' descendants—legitimate or otherwise—have run the affairs of England for much of the last three hundred years. Of those now living, the best known are Sir Winston Churchill and Queen Elizabeth II, but they are by no means unique. Other members of the clan—the great Duke of Marlborough, for example, and the two Pitts—saved England in their times of crisis just as brilliantly as Churchill did in his. Whenever the island is in mortal peril, an offspring of Villiers seems to turn up at the head of the government, or the armies, or both; and he wins. (Unlike most Englishmen, these people are not good losers; they like to win, and make a habit of it.)

They also make a habit of running the kingdom, in peacetime as well as in war. Ever since Sir George's day there has hardly been a cabinet—except during the Labour governments—which did not contain at least one of them. They collect responsibilities, honors, and titles the way a blue serge suit collects lint, so that even to American ears a list of their names sounds like a roll call of chieftains—Salisburys, Cecils, Pakenhams, Stanleys; the Dukes of Berwick, Manchester, Atholl, Hamilton, and Grafton; the Stanhopes, Granvilles, Cavendishes, Ponsonbys, Howards, Russells, and "the proud fighting Napiers"; the Earls of Sussex, Jersey, Portland, Clarendon, Desmond, Denbigh, and Lichfield; Melbourne, Charles James Fox, Castlereagh, and Eden; plus miscellaneous lords, knights, and Big Wheels by the dozen.

Nor is their genius limited to politics and fighting. The Villiers Connection (as Bloomfield calls it) also produces far more than its share of brilliant performers in other fields—Bertrand Russell in mathematics and philosophy, Henry Fielding in fiction, Lord David Cecil in history, to mention only a few. (Though so far as I can discover, it has yet to come up with a really good musician or painter.) Never has there been another bloodline like it anywhere.

But a few have come close. Bloomfield goes on to trace the records of five other uncommon families: (a) the Quaker dynasty, descended from Robert Barclay, which spawned a remarkable brood of bankers, reformers, abolitionists, scientists, and of course politicians; (b) the Salisbury Cecils, who tend to interbreed with Villiers, and who govern as naturally as they breathe; (c) the Wedgwood-Darwin clan, which runs heavily to scientists and industrialists; (d) the Macaulay-Trevelyan strain, which produces mostly historians, poets, critics, novelists, educators, and painters (Aldous Huxley and Rose Macaulay are recent samples); and (e) the Strachey-Pattle-Stephen connection, which specializes in empire builders, teachers, and writers (including Virginia Woolf and David Garnett).

Altogether these six clans, in all their generations, add up to a tiny fraction of the British population. Yet they have been responsible for a very large fraction of British civilization. An inordinate share of all that is good, enduring, wise, beautiful, or merely famous in contemporary England has sprung from this handful of uncommon men and women.

Among all of them it is noteworthy that five uncommon characteristics show up in generation after generation. Not every member of the Six Families has all five, by any means, but many have two or three, and the truly eminent display a full hand. They are:

1. Intelligence. The most universal of the five traits; a really stupid person is hard to find on any of these family trees. This is not surprising, since all of them began with a brainy sire, and the scions generally took care to mate with brains. Occasionally an impulsive male would pick a beautiful but flannel-headed wife; but the women—like females everywhere—were less romantic and more practical. They almost never took up with an inferior man.

2. Energy. These people seem able to work, make love, and fight harder than ordinary mortals. Their sheer vitality often carries them to extremes; many are nearly as famous for their drinking, wenching, roaming, and riotous behavior as for their more respectable achievements. When the first Duke of Buckingham—one of the handsomest men who ever pinched a thigh—made improper advances to a French queen, he wore for the occasion a bejeweled suit that cost 80,000 pounds; the Marlborough scandals were notorious: and Lady Hester Stanhope, after a series of tempestuous romances, finally ran off to an Arab sheik and lived happily ever afterward in his desert tent. Even Winston Churchill can scarcely be described as moderate in his drinking and working habits.

3. Charm. Most of them had it to burn. Again, Churchill and Buckingham are the obvious examples—but countless lesser members of the Six Families had (and still have) a curious power to fascinate other people. This is particularly true of the

Villiers women, who frequently became the mistresses of kings. But it is also true of such odd fish as Charles Darwin and Virginia Woolf, the unfortunate Cornwallis, and such swashbucklers as Colonel David Barclay and Sir Charles Napier.

4. Ruthlessness. These clans—even Barclay's gentle Quakers —specialize in driving straight ahead for whatever it is they want, and God help anybody who gets in the way. Their most famous members often were not "good" people in the Christian sense; they broke most of the Commandments whenever they seemed a nuisance, and left behind them a trail of broken hearts and heads. But they were effective. They got their own way, and they got things done.

5. Responsibility. However sharply they kept their eyes on the main chance, they also had a sense of duty. As Bloomfield points out, "the uncommonness that ran in the great families . . . went with solicitude either for the common people, or for the decent and efficient conduct of public business, or both."*

The horrid moral of this book is inescapable: A nation depends for most of its culture, for its government, and for its survival on a relatively few uncommon people—and these come from a still smaller number of blood strains. As in other species, from the influenza virus to thoroughbred horses and Santa Gertrudis cattle, these strains start with a mutation. Suddenly and unpredictably, an exceptional individual crops up in a family of no previous distinction. One of his unusual qualities is purely genetic; he is what the biologists call a prepotent sire— the founder of a line which breeds true—thus producing exceptional offspring for uncounted generations. Such an event is as rare as it is precious. It would seem to follow, then, that a nation would do well to cherish and foster these uncommon people; for on them rests its hope of greatness.

The hierarchical society of Britain, with its privileged ruling

---

* In passing he notes yet another odd trait. Many of the elite, especially in the Sidney line, "had a knack of dying interesting deaths and uttering memorable last words."

class, was well designed to accomplish precisely this. It gave to exceptional families—once they had broken into the privileged group—the money, leisure, education, and opportunities they needed to develop and use their creative talents. The system was far from perfect, as Bloomfield acknowledges. It also gave special privileges to many families of scant talent, at great cost in money and class hatred; and in the last two centuries before World War I it was increasingly hard for able men in the lower ranks to fight their way toward the top. (In the turbulent times when the Villiers, Cecil, and Barclay clans got their start, it was fairly easy for a shrewd and ruthless man to climb fast; the hierarchical structure had not yet frozen, and the chopping block created a rapid turnover in the aristocracy.) Nevertheless, Bloomfield's book is about the most persuasive defense of the aristocratic principle that has appeared since Edmund Burke.

No idea could be more subversive to mid-century America, dedicated as it is to The Common Man. Our whole way of life is now based on the theory that only the mediocre and ineffectual deserve to be especially cherished by society. The notion that exceptional people ought to get exceptional consideration—and that their abilities might be transmitted by heredity—is felt to be shockingly undemocratic and un-American.

So if a man is stupid, lazy, and feckless enough, there is nothing our society won't do for him—particularly if he comes from a long line of stupid, lazy, and feckless ancestors. When he has a job, the union sees to it that he is never fired for anything short of the most outrageous sloppiness and shirking. When he doesn't, a relief check is always waiting. If he absent-mindedly begets more children than he can support, the state takes care of them. For good measure, we ply him with subsidized housing, free medical care, and the tender ministrations of social workers; and we entertain him lavishly with free television programs carefully tailored to his sluggish wits.

His children become the darlings of the public schools, which are primarily designed to keep mediocre youngsters (and their parents) happy. Here little Willie Jukes is taught "life adjustment," including how to dance, play the clarinet, and drive a hot rod—but rarely does any teacher insist that he learn to read and spell properly, because the effort might bruise his fragile soul.* Here, moreover, he need fear no penalty for stupidity or laziness. If he can't pass his examinations, he gets a "social promotion" anyhow, because it might make Willie feel inferior if he were left behind his class. The fact that he *is* inferior is considered irrelevant.

Behind all this lies a double theory: (a) it is our Christian duty to help the unfortunate—and who can tell whether a man is unfortunate or just plain copeless? (b) if we give the Jukes family a better environment, they may in time become better people. There is something to be said for this, and for at least fifty years the liberals have been saying it at the top of their voices. But in our flurry of concern for The Common Man, it is only natural that we should come to believe that hardly anybody else matters.

So too in our public life. Ever since the Jacksonian revolt against government by the Rich-and-Wise, we have insisted that every man is just as good as any other, and suspicion of the Hamiltonian gentry still lies heavy on our racial memory. We make no effort, therefore, to attract superior people into either politics or the public service. On the contrary, we go to some lengths to discourage them. The top pay in these fields, for a man who reaches the peak of his profession—a Senator, Governor, or high-level civil servant—comes to about one-tenth the income of a second-rate TV comic. Moreover, even the best of them live in constant jeopardy of harassment and vilification; and they can hope for none of the honors, titles, and emoluments with which less democratic nations reward their outstanding public men. Small wonder, then, that we

---

* It is true that a few schools are beginning to experiment with special classes for bright children; but many professional educators—notably the powerful barons of the teachers' colleges—still seem to view these "undemocratic" experiments with distrust. As a consequence, any youngster with an IQ above 120 is likely to spend most of his school years in brain-numbing boredom, entangled (and ignored) in a machine geared to the dull and plodding.

sometimes find a very common type of common man in office. The real miracle is that we occasionally get a first-class public servant.

In view of all this, we might assume that the American mind is well fortified by habit and tradition against the aristocratical propaganda of Mr. Bloomfield. But can we afford to be so smug? Wasn't it precisely this kind of complacent thinking that led to Pearl Harbor, the Blennerhasset Plot, and the Pumpkin Papers? Is it possible that we may be in deadly danger of falling prey to Bloomfieldism without even knowing it?

It is, indeed. For, in the back of our skulls, every one of us already is half-convinced that there might be something in what the man says.

We all believe, for example, in the aristocracy of cattle. If you were planning to stock a ranch or a dairy farm, you would think nothing of paying $30,000 for a herd bull—provided that his pedigree demonstrates his ability to produce outstanding offspring. If you race thoroughbreds, you might pay up to $10,000 for the right to breed a single mare to a stallion with good bloodlines and a record of many victories. Moreover, the owner of such a stud will, quite sensibly, spare no expense to pamper the horse with everything that might help him give a good performance. With such examples constantly before us, it would be an easy step to conclude that similar attention to the heredity and conditioning of exceptional human beings might also pay off.

Some Americans already have taken this fateful step. One of them is Dr. William H. Sheldon, who has spent nearly thirty years in studying the effects of heredity on human physique, temperament, and intelligence. His findings, published in a series of carefully documented studies, go even further than Bloomfield's; they indicated that bad characteristics, as well as good, tend to run in families for many generations—pretty much regardless of how good or bad the families' environment may be.

Anyone who has spent much time around jails and penitentiaries, as I have, can bear out at least half of his conclusions. The fact that strikes a visitor most forcibly, as he looks at a crowd of convicts in a prison mess hall, is that these are sorry specimens of humanity. The great majority of them *look* inadequate—undersized, misshapen, slack-faced, and dim—and their records, in fact, suggest that most of them took to crime out of sheer stupidity, or because they could not compete in the normal fields of human endeavor. They are, in Sheldon's phrase, samples of "poor protoplasm poorly put together." And it is surprising how often the records show an ancestor who also fell afoul of the law. (The criminal master mind of fiction may exist in fact, though I doubt it; if so, he presumably is too smart to get caught.)

Other Americans, better known than Sheldon, have also been infected by the Bloomfield Heresy. The most eminent, perhaps, was Abraham Lincoln, ordinarily regarded as a man of the people. He did not so regard himself. His law partner and close friend, William H. Herndon, relates how Lincoln once told him that his mother was the illegitimate daughter of Lucy Hanks by "a well-bred but obscure Virginia farmer or planter." And Lincoln argued that from this nameless grandfather "came his power of analysis, his logic, his mental activity, his ambition, and all the qualities that distinguished him from the other members and descendants of the Hanks family." This passage, from the first chapter of Herndon's biography, is not very well known—perhaps because it is so hard to fit into the Lincoln legend, and into the equalitarian doctrine of our times.

No one has yet made a study of eminent American families comparable to Bloomfield's study of the British elite. When one is made, it probably will not show anything like the same concentration of talent in a very few blood lines. For one thing, our mobile and diverse society has offered no opportunity for the inbreeding which has characterized the relatively small, close-knit British ruling class; then, too, we have developed talent from many levels—including a Kansas City haberdashery —which the more rigid British system seldom tapped.

Nevertheless there are some clues which suggest that Bloomfield's main conclusions might hold nearly as true here as in England. Each of us can name offhand a dozen families which have contributed far more than their share to American life through a number of generations—the Adamses, above all, and the Lees, Tafts, Roosevelts, Van Dorens, La Farges, Mavericks, Lodges, Strausses, Blairs, and Saltonstalls, to mention a few at random.

But this is too dangerous a subject to pursue further. It could lead to the most upsetting kind of revolution in American thought and conduct—a genuine respect for, and effort to foster, the Uncommon Man.

August, 1957

PART II

THE WRITER'S TRADE

1 : Writers and Their Editors:
Notes on an Uneasy Marriage

SEVERAL YEARS AGO, when my main job was editing books, I began to wonder whether it might be possible to introduce at least a trace of scientific method into a wildly unscientific business.

Every day authors or their agents would come in to get money to finance the writing of a book. Usually they would have a couple of chapters finished and an outline of the rest. Sometimes they had nothing but an idea, in their heads or scribbled on the back of an old envelope. (One agent, whose effrontery I have always admired, didn't even have that. She said she represented a radio commentator, and she suggested that if a publisher would put up $10,000 so that he could lie on a Florida beach and think for a few weeks, he might bring back an outline for a possible book.)

On such tenuous security, publishers frequently advance sums ranging from $500 to several thousand dollars—to be repaid out of the author's royalty, if and when he delivers a manuscript which can be published and sold to a far-from-eager public. The decision is made almost entirely on the basis of sheer hunch— or what publishers prefer to describe, wistfully, as "editorial judgment." The editor takes a look at whatever the author has

93

down on paper; checks the sales and reviews of his previous books, if any; finds out what he can about any recent books on a similar theme; wonders whether the buying public will have any interest in the subject when the book is published, maybe two years later; makes a personal estimate of the writer's talent, responsibility, and character—and then takes a deep breath and decides how much of the firm's money to gamble. (Even when there is no advance to the author, publishing a book requires an investment of at least $5,000.)

If an editor guesses wrong too often, he and his firm will be out of business. Even the best make so many bad guesses that every publishing house has to write off thousands of dollars in unearned advances each year. And the mistake of being over-cautious can be equally serious; I remember with shame at least five authors whose demands I turned down as exorbitant, and who are now bringing in fat, green wads of money for rival firms.

So—like many another naïve young editor—I started to look for some clue which might help me to calculate on a less haphazard basis whether any given author would be likely to earn enough to repay the money he asked for. I made a careful study of the performance records of some two hundred writers, looking for common characteristics which would distinguish the good risks from the bad.

Two showed up. Nearly all the successful writers had them, while the failures did not. They were: (1) An abnormal supply of simple animal energy, and (2) An overcharged ego.

This discovery proved less than revolutionary, because there is another essential ingredient—talent—which I never did learn to spot with any certainty until the writer had demonstrated it on paper, and not always then. Plenty of would-be authors are endowed with Napoleonic ego and the energy of a terrier pup, but still can't write a lick. Yet it also seems to be generally true that the most luminous talent won't get very far when the other two qualities are missing.

As a scientific finding, this may not amount to much—but

for an editor it does have its uses. In addition to cutting down his bad-debt figures, it can help him in developing a working partnership with his authors. For, once they have entered into their curious alliance, the editor's main jobs are then: (a) to keep his writer churning out manuscripts and (b) to nourish, protect, and shepherd that all-important ego.

The first chore is relatively straightforward. If the writer possesses that overflowing vitality which has characterized such diverse specimens as Tolstoy, Edgar Wallace, Tom Wolfe, and Dickens, he will write as naturally as a fire burns. The publisher will have to sell enough books to stoke the auctorial flames with their necessary fuel: money. On occasion he may also need to offer advice about markets, syntax, and organization of subject matter, and to prune back the luxuriant prose which unbridled energy so often produces. But if the sheer physical drive isn't there, the case is hopeless. Writing is a punishing trade, and the feeble soon drop it.

But there is nothing simple about the editor's second duty. Ego-nursing will take a different form with every author—but, like baby-raising, it always ought to begin with affection and respect. If an editor doesn't like authors enough to put up with their tantrums and change their emotional diapers, he is in the wrong business.

And he must understand that if a writer's ego ever wilts, he is ruined. It is the only thing that can sustain him through those lonely months while he is trying to piece together a book out of one recalcitrant word after another. Every morning he has to persuade himself, all over again, that putting marks on paper is the most important thing in the world; that he has something to say which thousands of people not only will listen to, but pay for; that it has not been said already (or anyhow not so well) by his innumerable competitors, from Homer to O'Hara; and therefore that his personal statement of Eternal Truth has to be recorded at all costs—even if his children starve and his neglected wife takes up canasta.

Only an ego-maniac can believe these things, for they defy

all the evidence. Any rational man could see that far too many books already are being published; that only a small fraction of them can possibly be reviewed; that even these usually will encounter an invincible indifference; that most books are nearly as perishable as fresh vegetables, and soon doomed to be pushed off the store shelves by a fresh crop; that the odds therefore are overwhelmingly against any given writer making a ripple on the public consciousness. Or even making a living. The average novelist can rarely hope to earn as much per year as the linotypist who sets his books in type.

Yet if his ego is sturdy enough, an author can ignore these facts and turn again to his typewriter—confident that he is not like other men, and that *his* book will beat the odds. And sometimes he is right.

That is why one veteran editor, William Sloane, once described his work as a cross between playing the horses and practicing medicine without a license. It is a kind of psychotherapy—a process of reassuring the writer constantly that his genius is unique, that the last chapter was a gem, and that the world breathlessly awaits his message.

Nor is this hypocrisy. It is true than an editor has to view the literary facts of life more realistically than a writer dares to, and that sometimes he has to administer flattery in doses that would gag an opera star. But, allowing for this therapeutic hyperbole, the editor believes what he says. He thinks his boy has what it takes, and he is backing this conviction with a big piece of the firm's money.

Phony enthusiasm, in fact, just doesn't work. The writer will soon spot it—and so will the salesmen who eventually will have to try to persuade somebody to read the finished book. So a capacity for real (and soundly based) enthusiasm is perhaps the greatest asset an editor can have. For example, the way in which Alfred Knopf's unsquelchable enthusiasm for Joseph Conrad finally created an American market for his works is still a legend of the trade.

Yet the editor cannot afford to let his author's ego get completely out of hand. He has to nurture and restrain it, both at once—a task always delicate, and sometimes impossible. He has to sort out the writer's delusions—tolerating and even encouraging those which are useful, while at the same time trying to curb those which are destructive.

The editor of a publishing house which specializes in light fiction once told me that he had worked for years with a highly successful woman novelist. Rarely in all that time did she ever talk about anything except her dominant obsession: the shameful way in which she was neglected and abused by her husbands, children, reviewers, booksellers, publishers, and public. Actually, he said, she was a pampered old dragon who got her own way in nearly everything and tyrannized the lives of everybody within reach. But her illusion was indispensable for her work. All her novels dealt with the same theme—the piteous fate of woman in an unfeeling world—and since this appealed to the streak of self-pity in millions of female readers, her books sold very well indeed. If she had ever been forced to confront the truth, she probably could never have written another line.

Again, I was puzzled for a long time by the conviction of most unsuccessful writers that no publisher will read a manuscript unless it is thrust into his unwilling hands by a friend, a wealthy aunt, or the banker who holds the mortgage on the printing press. Repeatedly I tried to explain that reading manuscripts is a publisher's business—that he gives them careful attention, whether they are delivered by the postman, an agent,* or his own mother; that, in fact, publishers are constantly on the prowl for new talent. Hardly anybody was convinced.

---

* Nearly a hundred literary agencies are now operating in New York. Perhaps a dozen of these have earned the full confidence of most publishing houses, because they understand the problems of both authors and editors and never submit anything which is not a real possibility for a particular publisher's list. Consequently, manuscripts from them often get prompter attention; but no reputable firm ever declines a manuscript, from any source, without at least one responsible reading.

At last it dawned upon me that not-yet-successful writers need this myth, and that it is both useless and cruel to try to dispel it. Suppose you have labored for two years over The Great American Novel, investing in it all the passion and talent at your command. Then it is rejected in quick succession by eleven publishers. There can be two possible explanations:

1. Nobody ever read it—or at best it was skimmed by some callow, Coke-drinking junior reader, who couldn't recognize genius if it kicked him in the teeth.

2. The novel is no good.*

Which would you believe? Which would you *have* to believe, if you planned to embark on another novel?

This necessity for maintaining an unshakable faith in his own talent sometimes leads an author into fantasies which are less benign. It then becomes the editor's responsibility to disillusion him. However tactful the editor may be, the process is always painful; and it is this which so often makes their relationship a tense and unstable one.

For instance, when the sale of a book is disappointing, the author always knows who's to blame. If it had been advertised properly—with billboards, skywriting, and TV commercials—if only the publisher had seen to it that the New York Times reviewed this work, instead of wasting its space on Faulkner and Hemingway, then surely the public would have discovered it, in carload lots.

At this juncture the editor may try to explain that the firm already has spent far more on advertising than the book could hope to earn; that book reviewers can neither be pressured nor cajoled—and that any publisher who tries will soon regret it; that the public seems to be tiring of sensitive novels about the torments of adolescence; that a sale of 3,182 copies of a first novel really is pretty good; and that maybe we will all have better luck

---

* A third possibility is that eleven experienced editors read it—and all of them guessed wrong. This has happened, with the result that a twelfth publisher profited from their mistakes; but such cases are extremely rare.

with the next one, especially if the narrative pace is a little faster.

These home truths are no comfort to the author.* Quite possibly they will merely encourage him to look for another publisher.

The same thing may happen when the editor offers advice on a manuscript. It may be his plain duty to point out that the heroine sounds like a fifth carbon as Scarlett O'Hara, and that a thirty-thousand-word description of Terre Haute in 1890 might well be cut out of the opening chapter. The writer may recognize these hints as sound and accept them gratefully. Or—you never can tell—he may regard them as a vote of no-confidence and a Philistine assault upon the integrity of his work.

For this reason, it is never wise to show a reader's report to an author. Such reports are probably the best literary criticism being written anywhere. They often sum up the strengths, weaknesses, sales potential, and literary stature of a manuscript with remarkable precision. *The New Yorker* recently observed, in a memorial note about the late Wolcott Gibbs, that if his written editorial opinions "could be released to the world (as they most assuredly can't be), they would make probably a funnier and sounder critique of creative writing in the late 'twenties and early 'thirties than has ever been assembled." But such reports customarily are written with a succinct, pitiless candor which might easily wound an author to his very gizzard. Consequently a prudent editor keeps the original in a locked file, and transmits the gist of it to the author in gentler (not to say muffled) terms.

Another thing which some writers find hard to tolerate is the idea that an editor is not a private possession, like a one-man dog. This type (fortunately not very common) wants full-time,

---

* Nothing is—short of astronomical sales and undiluted acclaim. And nobody is immune to the pangs of authorship. Between stints of editing, I once wrote a couple of books myself. To my astonishment, I found that I developed all the standard symptoms, although I knew perfectly well that my expectations were silly and my demands unreasonable.

undivided attention—not only to his literary affairs, but also to his plane reservations, theater tickets, and romantic tangles. Any reminder that the editor now and then has to deal with the problems of other authors is likely to touch off a spasm of jealous anger, accompanied in extreme cases by accusations of neglect and disloyalty. This syndrome (at least in my experience) occurs most frequently among women; perhaps it has something to do with their innate prejudice against polygamy.

But the author's ego is not the only potential source of friction. Editors also have egos which can cause trouble—and with far less justification.

The main danger here is that the editor may try, consciously or unconsciously, to impose his own conceptions on the writer. This is most apt to happen if the editor is himself a frustrated author; he may then—usually without realizing it—attempt to influence a novelist to produce the epic *he* had wanted to create. The upshot almost surely will be a disaster for everybody.

Or an editor may grow dogmatic. If he ever begins to think that he knows exactly how every kind of book ought to be written, and that he can guess infallibly what the public wants, then he is coming down with that special form of *hubris* which is the occupational disease of his profession. It will make him miss both the truly original work of art and the good commercial item which—according to conventional rules—should be unsalable.

I hate to remember the time when James R. Newman first told me his scheme for a history of mathematics. We were working together on a wartime intelligence assignment which had taken us to London, and one evening while we were drinking beer in his room at the Athenaeum Court Hotel he outlined his project. He wanted to gather all the basic documents of mathematical thought and arrange them into an anthology which would trace the development of the science in the words of the masters themselves. It would be a big book—perhaps five hundred pages. What did I think of it?

I told him it was impossible. Nobody would buy it; its subject was too specialized—in fact to most people (including me) downright repellent—and it would be far too costly to manufacture. Why didn't he turn his energies to something practical, such as a book on chess—a subject on which he was equally expert? Jim said he was bored with chess.

A week or so later he said he had revised his plan. He now thought the book should be two volumes—a really comprehensive work. Did that make it sound more promising? I said no, it sounded worse. The next night I flew to North Africa.

We didn't meet again until the war was over. Jim then told me that he had been plugging away at his anthology, in spite of my advice; that it had grown to four volumes; and that Simon & Schuster was going to publish it. I was dumfounded: S & S, always known as a real shrewd outfit, must have lost their minds.

The rest is almost too humiliating for me to repeat. As everybody in the trade now knows, Newman's *The World of Mathematics* became a phenomenon of publishing. Priced at an impossible $25, it sold more than 120,000 sets—in addition to distribution by two book clubs—and is still selling a steady three thousand sets a year. It also shattered my confidence in my publishing judgment, probably for good.

But all this may be giving a wrong impression. In spite of such calamities, the editing of books is one of the more cheerful trades. It has all the excitement of gambling. (Before I got into it, I used to play poker quite a lot, though badly; afterward, I found I got enough action in the daytime.) Exasperating as they sometimes are, writers are seldom dull—and no two are alike; so the business has none of the monotony which must afflict a manufacturer of, say, canned milk. But the biggest psychic income is the editor's feeling that he often helps to bring to birth a talent or an idea. He can, in his better moments, think of himself as a midwife to the culture of his time—a part of the process by which civilization is created, preserved, and handed on from one generation to another.

In his bad moments, though, an editor may feel that his profession is almost as painful as an undertaker's. The really depressing part has nothing to do with the wrong guesses or the trying habits of authors. It is just the constant necessity of saying "No."

For he must spend most of his working hours in being mean to people. Every manuscript accepted must be winnowed out of a stack of hundreds which are hopeless. Many of those rejected can be sent back with a form letter—but, for a variety of reasons, a surprising number require an explanation from the editor. Either by mail or face-to-face, he must tell the author that his child was stillborn—that all his labor, ambition, and emotional investment have come to nothing.

This always hurts; or should hurt. I have a notion that any editor has only so many no's in his system. Some have a lot, others only a few. When they are all used up, he can't stand being mean any longer, and he dies. Or—what amounts to the same thing—he gets so calloused that he can say no without a twinge; when that happens he is dead and doesn't know it.

October, 1959

2 : Myths About Publishing

GEOFFREY WAGNER, a novelist and college English teacher, announced recently in an English magazine that "American publishing has become big business." In his view, this is a calamity. "Most small publishers of interest," he says, are being swallowed up by a few big firms. The survivors, he claims, are adopting a "blockbuster technique" which has "resulted in astronomical pre-publication deals, movie tie-ins, etc." Although "the killings are much bigger than they used to be," Mr. Wagner believes this is a bad thing, especially for novelists. It helps nobody but the insolent and materialistic publishers, "gloating over [their] stock exchange listings."

This lament is simply an echo of rumors which have been rustling around in the American (and British) literary world for several years. So long as they were confined to this milieu— notoriously flighty and gossip-prone—they could do little harm. About 1961, however, they reached Wall Street, which is even more susceptible to rumors, fads, and hunches. Soon a lot of supposedly hardheaded brokers, speculators, and investment counselors convinced themselves that publishing really *was* becoming a big business, with an extraordinary growth potential.

The upshot was that a good many people got badly burned. They started buying publishing stocks—the relatively few available to the public on the stock exchanges and over the counter —with no more discrimination than they had shown a little earlier, when they plunged into the so-called space-age and electronics industries. Prices shot up, in spite of warnings from several worried publishers that there was no rational basis for such enthusiasm. The boom was brief. In 1962 publishing stocks dropped as swiftly as they had risen, to an average of less than half of their previous highs.

At this writing, however, they are beginning to creep up again. Brokers are issuing surveys of the publishing industry; some investment funds are showing an interest; and even a few authors —inspired perhaps by accounts such as Mr. Wagner's—have recently bought into publishing firms. Consequently it might be of some use to try to sort out the facts from the myths about publishing; and to look at the various parts of the business—such as textbook, paperback, juvenile, and "trade" publishing—which operate in quite different ways. (It would be unfair to expect Mr. Wagner to do this. After all, he specializes in fiction.)

To begin with, is publishing actually Big Business?

In comparison with other industries—steel, chemicals, automobiles, airlines, or even the ladies' garment trade—it is quite small. The total sales of all American book publishers climbed above $1 billion a year only in 1960—and that includes all texts, encyclopedias, reference books, and paperbacks, as well as trade books: i.e., ordinary hardbound fiction and non-fiction sold through bookstores. For the last decade book sales have been growing at a steady but unspectacular rate of about 10 per cent a year; they may total close to $1.5 billion in 1963.

Do a few big firms dominate the industry?

Again, no. Publishing is one of the most competitive of all businesses. Nobody can be quite sure how many firms are engaged in it, since anybody can bring out a book now and then for only a modest investment. But if you count only those firms which published at least five books in 1962, you would find (according to *Publishers' Weekly*) 470 of them. Not one company published as much as 3 per cent of the total number of titles.

Are "most small publishers of interest" being swallowed up by their giant competitors?

Far from it. Every year some companies disappear, through bankruptcy or merger, but new ones constantly take their place. Today there are more firms in the business than ever before— and some of the liveliest and most "interesting" are only a few years old.

The representative firm—if one can speak of such a thing in so diverse an industry—probably has got bigger (in sales volume and number of titles published) in recent years. In part, this is due to the natural growth of population and of the whole economy. Then, too, rising costs of paper, printing, postage, and everything else have forced publishers to look for every possible economy; and some savings do result from large-scale operations. As a consequence, many houses have tried to round out their line with paperback, juvenile, and other departments, in addition to the traditional trade books.

This seems, however, to be a self-limiting process. Publishing is a peculiarly personal business. Whenever a firm gets so big that it can no longer give constant, intimate attention to each author—if it begins to turn out books like so many cans of beans

—then it probably is on the verge of a decline. Its writers will soon drift away to smaller, nimbler, more imaginative publishers. It is astonishing how quickly a publisher can gather a stable of first-rate authors, if he can show them that he is primarily interested in them and their work . . . in producing the best possible books, rather than the fastest possible buck. For this reason, every successful publisher has been editorial-minded—in some sense, a professional man. He must of course be a competent businessman as well; but if his business grows to the point where he has to worry more about management than about writing, he is in trouble. Hence it is most unlikely that any one company will ever dominate publishing, in the way that General Motors and U.S. Steel dominate their industries.

How about those financial killings?

Another myth. Publishers had a pretty good year in 1962, but on the average they probably earned only about 4 per cent on their sales after taxes. The best houses (not necessarily the largest) did somewhat better; many did worse. Indeed, any publisher considers himself lucky when he barely breaks even on the the bookstore sale of his general list; for any profit, he looks to subsidiary income from reprints and book clubs, and to specialized works such as juveniles and textbooks. Contrary to common belief, the publisher seldom gets a share of any film, TV, or magazine rights income; ordinarily all that goes to the author.

Those "astronomical pre-publication deals, movie tie-ins, etc." are exceedingly rare—much rarer than they were in Hollywood's heyday. In fact, most publishers refuse to make prepublication reprint deals, for an obvious business reason: if a book sells well in its original hardbound edition, it will fetch a better price from the reprint houses than it could when its sales potential was untested. The same thing holds for film rights—although occasionally an established popular novelist does make a movie sale before his new book is published, or even written.

Well, then, why is Wall Street taking over the publishing industry?

It isn't. Thirteen publishing companies are listed on the New York Stock Exchange. About two dozen more are publicly owned, with stock traded over the counter. The great majority of firms—more than four hundred of them, including some of the largest—are still privately owned, by individuals, families, or small groups operating in effect as partnerships.

Most of the houses that have "gone public" in recent years did so for one of three reasons:

1. To facilitate a merger—as, for example, when a trade publisher joins forces with a textbook firm, to offer a more complete line of books and more effective marketing than either could offer alone.

2. To raise capital for expansion.

3. To avoid destruction by inheritance taxes. If a firm is owned entirely or in large part by one man, his heirs might have to liquidate the business in order to pay the inheritance taxes. Consequently the founder of a publishing house may—as he gets on in years—convert it into a public company, in order to spread the ownership and to get cash in advance for the tax collector. Or, as in one recent case, he may prefer to merge with a company which already is publicly owned, and whose publishing policies he respects.

Is public ownership, even on a small scale, a bad thing for literature?

In theory, it could be. David Dempsey suggested a few weeks ago in the *Saturday Review* that "The fact that it is publicly held changes a company's viewpoint. The head of a firm can no longer afford to indulge quite so many of his personal whims. A very considerable number of great authors—Conrad is the supreme example—got their start on the poor business judgment of their publishers. With the old family-owned houses, this could be done, and we were all the richer. But when stockholders expect an operating profit, year in and year out, it becomes more difficult."

This apparently is what bothers Geoffrey Wagner. In his article he complained that "today, books are published, not authors . . . few younger novelists can count on being followed through a number of books in the way not only possible but probable a century ago." In other words, if a fledgling novelist writes two or three books which the public refuses to buy, his publisher may not be eager to bring out a fourth.

True enough. Most publishers now probably will not carry an unprofitable novelist at a loss for quite as long as they would have done before World War II. The reason, however, may be different from that cited by Mr. Dempsey and Mr. Wagner.

For fiction has been losing ground to nonfiction for at least forty years. Back in the twenties, readers bought roughly two novels in their original editions for every one nonfiction book; today the reverse is true.* So in those days, a publisher could afford a bigger gamble on a young novelist, because if he eventually turned out to be a Scott Fitzgerald, a Hemingway, or a Harold Bell Wright, the losses on the early, unsuccessful books would eventually be recouped. Today the chances of this happening are much smaller. For example, the *average* sale of Wright's nineteen novels was more than half a million copies each, while one of them reached 1,650,000. Nowadays a sale of 50,000 is often enough to put a novel at the top of the fiction best-seller list; and the author's next book cannot by any means be sure of an eager, automatic audience of the kind that Wright and scores of other novelists once commanded. Moreover, it cost less to gamble on a novelist in the old days; a publisher could then break even if he sold some 1,200 copies—while today he would have to sell at least five or six times as many.

Personally I have not yet seen any hard evidence that publicly owned publishing firms are becoming less venturesome—but they are now, I think, more likely to gamble on nonfiction projects than on novelists. So are privately held companies. And this change seems to be related to a shift in public taste, rather than to the financial structure of the industry.

---

* In paperback reprints the trend is in the same direction, but slower. *Bestsellers* Directory reports that in 1956 about 14 per cent of such reprints were nonfiction; by 1960 the figure had risen above 26 per cent.

Why are readers turning from novels to nonfiction?

Any answer is at best a guess; but these are the explanations heard most frequently around publishers' lunch tables:

1. The rising level of education and America's increasing involvement with the rest of the world have led to a growing interest in serious nonfiction—particularly history, biography, politics, and international affairs. This kind of subject matter, for the same reason, is attracting many of the best writers.

2. The real world has become more exciting, and sometimes more fantastic, than the world of fiction. When men are exploring sunken cities beneath the sea, preparing journeys to the moon, building mega-death weapons, creating new nations by the score, cruising under the polar icecap, and staging rebellions every other weekend, it is hard for a novelist—short of genius—to compete. As Philip Roth recently said: "The actuality is continually outdoing our talents, and the culture tosses up figures daily that are the envy of any novelist. . . . The world we have been given, the society and the community, has ceased to be as suitable or as manageable a subject for the novelist as it once may have been."

3. Many former buyers of light fiction—romance, Westerns, mysteries, adventure stories—now get the same commodity on television, free.

4. Among serious fiction writers, one large group now seem (in the words of a veteran publisher) to be "more concerned with self-expression than with entertaining the public." Wagner defines them as the poetic novelists. With them, and with most of the critics who make "serious" literary reputations, storytelling has become disreputable. Their main concern is with sensibility, with the inner drama of the psyche, not with the large events of the outside world. Often they are accomplished craftsmen. Their style is luminously burnished; they write on two levels, or even three; their work contains more symbols than a Chinese band; it may plumb the depths of the human soul; it may be (in Felicia Lamport's phrase) as deeply felt as a Borsalino hat. But all too often it just isn't much fun to read.

If such exercises in occupational therapy don't sell very well, the author has small grounds for complaint. He has written them, after all, primarily to massage his own ego and to harvest critico-academic bay leaves. Since he isn't interested in a mass audience, why should it be interested in him?

Does this mean that less fiction is published nowadays?

Strangely enough, it does not. Publishers remain incorrigibly hopeful; last year they brought out 1,787 new novels—an all-time high—even though they probably lost money on a majority of them. (A first novel, for example, is lucky to sell more than three thousand copies; while the publisher's break-even point is about seven thousand.) They keep trying because there is always a chance that the next unknown novelist will turn out to be a Richard McKenna. His first book, *The Sand Pebbles*, won a major prize novel contest, was serialized in the *Saturday Evening Post*, became a book-club selection, and stood for many weeks at or near the top of the best-seller list. Then, too, every good publisher brings out some novels every year which he knows will lose money, simply because he believes in the book's quality or the author's not-yet-fully-developed talent.

If he is a sensible businessman, why doesn't a publisher take on only best-sellers?

Some have tried; but they have been no more successful than the horseplayer who bets only on favorites. Nobody has yet figured out a system for predicting with certainty how a novel or general nonfiction book will sell, or whether it may be a book-club selection, or what appeal it may have for reprinters. The successful trade-book editor still has to operate on an indefinable mixture of taste, experience, hunch, and personal conviction.

Against such unpredictable odds, how can a publisher survive?

If he depended only on trade books, his chances would make an actuary blanch. But, although such books get most of the public attention and practically all of the review space, they make up only a small part of the book business—less than 8 per cent of total sales. Consequently the prudent publisher usually tries to hedge his bets by developing other lines. For example, textbooks or juveniles or paperbacks, each of which brings in more money for the industry as a whole than hardbound trade books do. (In the case of textbooks, nearly four times as much.) Moreover, juveniles and textbooks are the fastest growing segments of the business. Paperback sales seem to have leveled off—for the moment, at least—except for the higher-priced, more intellectual reprints. This is hardly surprising, since the reprinters have run through three thousand years of literature in twenty-five years, and now have to depend heavily on the current output of the original hardbound publishers.

In these lines, too, nobody has discovered how to pick a winner every time. But the odds are a bit less daunting with textbooks, juveniles, and reprints than with trade books, and the profit margins are not so thin. Therefore, the publisher who spreads his bets over the whole field is less likely to be wiped out by a few bad guesses.

Why should any investor put his money into such a chancy business?

A hard question. The enthusiasts point to the steady rise in total book sales—a growth somewhat faster than that of the American economy as a whole, and not much affected by business cycles. They argue that this growth is likely to continue, because the number of schoolchildren keeps increasing; so does their demand for textbooks, since new knowledge is developing rapidly in many fields; and every year more students go on to higher education. Moreover, better-educated people read more books, throughout their lives.

So long as you look only at the total figures, all this is true. But any individual book is a gamble—and sometimes a very expensive one. A publisher may invest several hundred thousand dollars in a textbook project, only to find that a competitor beats him to the market with a better one. Or, on his trade list, he may have a half-dozen best-sellers one year and none the next. Furthermore, a publisher's chief asset is his ability, and that of his editors, to find good manuscripts—a highly intangible asset, and one remarkably hard for an outside investor to judge. With this peculiar talent, the successful firm must also combine, somehow, a special kind of managerial ability; for each book published is a different product, requiring its own special treatment in editing, manufacturing, advertising, and marketing—through a distribution system which is still far from ideal.

Consequently an investment in publishing is not like an investment in the utilities industry, which provides a standard product to a predictable market. Nor is it like the electronics industry, which is likely to make spectacular profits from time to time by scientific breakthroughs. It is not the best place, therefore, either for the widow who wants maximum safety, a steady return, and a minimum of bother; or for the speculator looking for a quick killing. For the moderately venturesome, who will take the trouble to study the individual firms in the industry with considerable care, it may offer its rewards; and it does provide (for some of us, at least) a fascination which no other business can match. But before anyone even thinks seriously about putting his money into it, he would do well to forget the current myths about publishing, and to soak himself thoroughly in the prosaic facts.

July, 1963

3 : Death of a Giant

The View from the Fortieth Floor is, so far as I know, the second good novel ever written about the magazine business. At least the label on the jacket says it is "A Novel" and an author's note insists that the characters are "entirely imaginary."

In the weeks following its publication,* these statements may be questioned. A good many critics are likely to argue that it isn't a novel at all, or anyhow that it does not fit their canonical formula. And people in the magazine business will read it—with the most intent interest—as a nonfiction report on the vast upheaval which is now shaking their industry.

This is inescapable, since the author, Theodore H. White, was an internationally respected reporter long before he turned to fiction; he has, in his words, "witnessed from within the collapse of three great publishing enterprises"; and he was one of the editors of *Collier's* during the months of its death struggle. Moreover, the events in his story closely parallel the final catastrophe at *Collier's*—although it is true that his main characters do not much resemble the people involved in that tragedy.

What interests me most, however, is not that story, dramatic as it is. The book's real significance comes from its insights into certain major (though little noticed) changes now under way in American society—and in its foreshadowing of things likely to happen in the field of mass communications.

In this respect it might be described as old-fashioned. The novel which examines a broad stretch of the social landscape is rare these days—much rarer than the introspective novel which tries to probe the depths of a single soul. That Mr. White does not attempt. The souls of his characters lie pretty close to the surface, and in any case he is more interested in probing the workings of a publishing-advertising-financing machine.

In other ways, too, it is out of the main stream of contemporary fiction. It is carefully plotted, and the action moves fast. It has heroes and villains. It deals with ordinary, recognizable people, trying to cope with everyday problems; none of them are junkies, perverts, beatniks, or psychopaths. It isn't sexed up; readers who want erotic titillation had better stick to Metalious and O'Hara. Its scene is the business world, where most Americans spend their lives, but which all but a few novelists regard

---

* On May 20, 1960, by William Sloane Associates. An interesting earlier novel about magazines and their editors was John Brooks's *The Big Wheel*.

as unworthy of their attention. (Maybe that isn't quite fair; perhaps most novelists avoid the business world simply because they don't know much about it. Mr. White does. His considerable firsthand experience obviously has been backed up by thorough research into the habits, techniques, and mentalities of bankers, liquor manufacturers, printers, lawyers, big-time real-estate men, and that peculiar subtribe of businessmen who track down Special Situations. Like Melville, Dreiser, and Balzac, but unlike many of his contemporaries, Mr. White is willing to put a lot of leg work into getting his facts straight.)

As a reporter, using the tools of fiction, Mr. White has set out to explore two little-understood facts about the magazine business:

1. The mass-circulation magazines, which reached their peak during the first quarter of this century, began to slide about ten years ago; as a group, they are still slipping, in both profits and influence; and there is no reason to believe they will recover their old place of dominance.

2. Magazines are created by editors; they die in the hands of businessmen.

Mass magazines grew out of a strange combination of circumstances which converged during the final decades of the last century. Those were the years when American industry discovered the techniques of mass production. A factory was no longer limited to serving a local market; it could now turn out enough shirts, or stoves, or soap to supply customers all over the continent. Moreover, the railroad network was completed at about the same time, so that the goods could be delivered anywhere. For the first time, in the words of one of Mr. White's characters, "the whole country is one market, you can make one brand image for the whole nation and deliver—but only if you can find a way of talking to the whole country at once. They need a big horn . . . a horn that will reach everybody."

And just at that moment another constellation of events made it possible for imaginative editors to create such a horn. Printers were developing high-speed rotary presses, capable of spinning out millions of copies of a magazine in a few days. The railroads, again, were now ready to deliver them promptly to every village. Public schools were turning out the first mass audience, creating the first nation where practically everybody could read—at least a little. For those who couldn't, including a swelling stream of immigrants, there were pictures—which now, for the first time in history, could be reproduced cheaply and fast, because somebody had just invented half-tone engraving.

The result was a sudden flowering of a new kind of magazine —McClure's, Collier's, The Saturday Evening Post, Leslie's, The Ladies' Home Journal, Munsey's, Cosmopolitan, and a few others. They spoke not to an educated elite but to the barely literate millions; they reached everywhere, as no newspaper could; they carried a national message to a people who were beginning to feel the heady emotions of a new nationalism. At last the advertisers had their Big Horn; and they used it, to the enormous profit of themselves and the magazines, to create the first nation-wide system of mass marketing.

To run such a magazine, it was necessary (as Mr. White says) "to invent a new kind of person."

"It was the first time anybody except the President of the United States had to sit in an office and think about this whole damned country all at once. Some editor had to think not just what the local people in Chicago, or New York, or Charleston, or San Francisco might want to read, but what would hold an audience together across the whole land, from coast to coast. The first time somebody sat in this kind of office in New York and started to play with the mind of the country, things started to happen. . . .

"For the past fifty years anything this country has done, the magazines kicked them into doing—the magazines closed up the trusts, cleaned up the cities, put through the food-and-drug acts, amended the Constitution, closed off immigration. . . ." (The kind of people who created, and used, this unheard-of sort of power were indeed a special breed, as we shall note in a moment.)

All of this could last, of course, only until somebody invented a bigger horn. Which, in the first years of the new century, Guglielmo Marconi did. Within a generation his radio sets were in every household, and the magazine industry had lost its monopoly as The National Voice. By 1950 most Americans were spending more time looking at television than at the printed page—and the mass-circulation magazines were in real trouble. A recent survey indicates that some forty million people in this country no longer read any magazines at all.

For television offers much the same commodity as the big magazines—romance, light entertainment, pictures—and offers it to the same audience. Moreover, the pictures move, and they are free. (Or so the customers think. In fact, we all pay for TV, whether we watch it or not, every time we buy anything advertised on the air, since the sponsor has to include his program costs in the price of his product.)

Inevitably the biggest share of the mass-market advertising shifted to the air. Last year less than eight cents of the total advertising dollar went into magazines, while nearly twice that much went into TV. Obviously some of the popular magazines were bound to die of malnutrition. The weakest went first— Collier's, The Woman's Home Companion, The American, The Country Gentleman. The survivors—notably Life, Look, The Reader's Digest, The Saturday Evening Post, and the big women's publications—are now fighting desperately among themselves for readership and for the rump slice of the advertising budget. Whether all of them can survive is a nice question. The Post, for example, has lost advertising linage every year for the last decade.

Paradoxically, its income from advertising has gone up in at least some of those years, and so has that of its competitors. The explanation is higher rates, based on a rising circulation. A contradiction? Not at all. Although the readership of at least some of the mass magazines has grown, it has not kept pace with the growth in population and leisure time, while TV watching has grown even faster. Furthermore, the rise in circulation often has been unprofitable. Within wide limits, a magazine can acquire as many readers as it likes—if it is willing to pay for them. This means cutting subscription and newsstand prices and spending whopping sums on promotion. When the competition is using the same tactics, such warfare can become extremely costly. As a consequence, the average net profit of all the mass-circulation magazines probably was something less than 3 per cent last year —an ominous showing, in comparison with TV and with most other industries.

Meanwhile, magazines of a different type have been flourishing. These are the so-called special-audience publications. They make no effort to reach a mass readership, and therefore compete neither with TV nor the big-circulation magazines. Instead each of them speaks to its own small, well-defined group—an intellectual elite of one kind or another.

One example is *Scientific American,* perhaps the most spectacular success in postwar publishing. Its circulation totals only 245,000, a microscopic figure compared with the more than six million of *Life* and the *Post;* but its readers are all members of a group which is climbing fast in influence, prestige, and income. Another example is *The New Yorker,* which now carries more pages of advertising than any other magazine (except a few technical journals) because it is edited expressly for an audience far above the average in sophistication, taste, and wealth. Other such publications are *Fortune, Harper's, Holiday, The Saturday Review, The Atlantic Monthly, Forbes,* and a handful more; they differ widely in content and character, but they all have two things in common: (1) a readership which is relatively small, well educated, well off, and devoted; (2) a steadily rising volume of advertising.

The last fact is easy to explain. If you want to sell something that has, at most, a half million potential buyers—a turbine, a fine wine, a sports car, a Mediterranean cruise, an idea, a new fashion, a hand-tailored investment program—it would be silly for you to advertise it to TV's thirty million viewers or *Life's* six million picture-thumbers. For your purposes, such an audience is mostly irrelevant—perhaps entirely so, since the man who is able to buy these things isn't likely to waste much time looking at pictures. He is more apt to spend his scanty leisure in reading *Fortune* or one of the other special-interest magazines—and he can be reached there at a fraction of the cost.

Furthermore, if you can influence any of these elite groups, you will in time influence a much wider circle. For they are the tastemakers and opinion formers—the one per cent of the population, roughly, who are imitated by the others, who hold the leadership posts in business and government, who can articulate their views forcefully enough to command respect. To cite a minor instance, when they began to drive small foreign cars they set a fashion which eventually forced Detroit (much against its will) to change its whole scheme of design, production, and sales.

Another paradox (the industry seems to be full of them) is that the specialized publications, on the whole, are building up their readerships much faster than the mass-circulation magazines, and at far less cost. The reason is that our society, in its growing complexity, needs more and more educated people to keep it running. As our universities turn them out, they also produce, inevitably, a growing public which is dissatisfied with the bland banalities of the mass media. Nevertheless, it is improbable that the special-audience magazines will ever try to reach more than about one per cent of the population. To do so would mean a fundamental change of character; and, since this is the last thing they want, some of them already are restricting their circulation.

The central character in *The View from the Fortieth Floor* is Ridge Warren, a professional executive who has just become president of a sick publishing company. The board of directors hired him to do two things: raise a lot of new capital, and revive its two money-losing magazines. (Presumably it is only coincidence if they bear any resemblance to *Collier's* and *The Woman's Home Companion,* which bled the Crowell-Collier Publishing Company to a pale mauve in the years before their death.)

Warren's first move is to "engineer an audience"—to build

back circulation by a series of editorial gimmicks and expensive promotion stunts. He succeeds, but in the process he destroys the last remnants of the magazines' character. Because the audience he collects is nondescript and artificial, nobody (including the advertisers) has any confidence in them; because Warren never has time to figure out what he wants to say to his audience, nobody can tell what his magazines stand for.

The trouble is that Warren is a businessman, working for a board of businessmen. They think of their magazines not as a Voice but as a Property. None of them has any real interest in editorial content, or any understanding of the man who created the magazines in the first place.

That was old Ab Pepper, an editor. He never had any doubt what he wanted to say, and the most important thing in his life was to say it loud and clear. An audience gathered to listen to him, because he was saying important (though often unpopular) things—because he believed that "one man plus the truth makes a majority," because he thought he was responsible not just to his stockholders but to the country. So he made his magazines a power in American life, and incidentally made money.

When he died his publications passed into the hands of trustees, to whom making money was by no means incidental. As businessmen, they had been trained to put that first; to them, the Old Man's passion for shouting the truth as he saw it was just an embarrassing eccentricity. The Voice grew hoarse, the audience drifted away, and (though the trustees never glimpsed the connection) the money drifted with it. Because Warren, a nice honest guy, had all the right instincts except those of an editor, there really wasn't anything he could do to save the property.

This part of Mr. White's story sums up the history of many magazines, and maybe the future of some of them as well. All great publications have been created by great editors. The classic case is *The Saturday Evening Post*, a sorry starveling when George Horace Lorimer took charge in 1899. He built it into

the world's biggest weekly, by making it the authentic spokesman of America's middle class. At about the same time Norman
Hapgood was making *Collier's* the crusading leader of the reform movement which culminated in the Theodore Roosevelt
and Wilson administrations. A generation later Henry Luce,
who still thinks of himself primarily as an editor, started *Time*
on a shoestring and pyramided it into the most powerful of
today's magazine empires; and DeWitt Wallace accomplished
a similar feat with *The Reader's Digest.*

The same thing is true of the great newspapers. All of them
were the products of editorial minds—Dana, Pulitzer, Ochs,
Scripps, McCormick, Cowles, White, Daniels, and a score of
others. When the founders died and the business office took
over, many of these papers withered. William Randolph Hearst,
for instance, was an evil man, but his editorial genius was beyond
question; when it flickered out, his papers became the Property
they are today, respectable and juiceless. So too with McCormick's Chicago *Tribune* and most of the Scripps relics—while
Dana's *Sun* and Pulitzer's *World* and many another old-time
giant have simply disappeared.

Most of the great editors were also passable businessmen, but
that was not their primary role. All of them understood the
absolute necessity of keeping editorial and business matters in
water-tight compartments. Old E. W. Scripps once threw out
of his office a merchant who came to ask an editorial favor—
threw him so hard he bounced, and threw his ads out of the
paper to boot. And one of the most durable legends about
Harold Ross is that he never let an advertising man set foot on
The New Yorker's editorial floor.

Such behavior would have seemed ludicrous to the well-meaning characters in Mr. White's novel: they understand the decorum expected of a sound businessman. What they never do
understand is that they are attempting something beyond their
competence—that the creation, or salvage, of a publication is
no business for a businessman.

This, I think, is the main point Mr. White is trying to make about today's mass magazines. Those which are dominated by purely business interests may well sink into deeper trouble; while those which are guided by capable editorial minds—by men who have something to say beyond what TV can offer—will have the best chance for survival.

June, 1960

4 : A Helping Hand for a Literary Upstart

FOR THE LAST TWENTY YEARS the American Santa Claus has been almost foolishly generous to "creative" writers. (These are usually defined as the producers of fiction, plays, and poetry, although sometimes the ground rules are stretched to include criticism.) So many foundations now offer them subsidies that practically anyone with a hint of talent can pick up some kind of grant or traveling fellowship. Some two hundred medals and prizes are awarded every year to celebrate their output. Artistic game preserves such as the MacDowell Colony provide them food and lodging in pleasant surroundings so that they can cultivate their genius without distraction or anxiety. Innumerable colleges offer courses in Creative Writing, plus semisinecures for resident poets and novelists. So if the United States is not yet producing literary masterpieces by the cord, it certainly isn't for lack of financial encouragement.

Until this year, however, nobody offered such help to another kind of author at least equally important to the country's health: the nonfiction magazine writer. Because, by arbitrary definition, he is not "creative," he is ignored by the big foundations. Critics and the literary priesthood of Academia regard him as a hack unworthy of their attention. What little recognition he gets is within the small circle of his own trade. The *New York Times*, for example, regularly devotes a full page to the Pulitzer Prizes; but on those rare occasions when a magazine writer gets an award, the *Times* mentions it (if at all) in a single paragraph on page 17.

This is in the best historic tradition. Every era develops its own characteristic literary form. In Archaic Greece, it was the epic poem; in Elizabethan England, the poetic drama; in Victorian times, the romantic ballad; in the late eighteenth century and the early nineteenth, the novel. During the years of its greatest flowering, each of these forms exhibited four distinguishing marks:

1. It had a wide audience, because it was best suited to expressing the thoughts and emotions of its particular period.

2. It attracted the best writers of the time, for the same reason.

3. Its practitioners usually were well paid. Shakespeare, Byron, Dickens, and Tolstoy, to mention only a few, earned fortunes; and even Homer probably ate pretty high on the megaron hog when he recited his epics before the Ionic war lords.

4. Within their lifetimes, such writers were considered low fellows. Almost invariably the critics and academics fail to recognize their period's characteristic literary form while it is at its peak; therefore they look on its practitioners as mere commercial potboilers—"popularizer" and "best-seller" are their favorite epithets. Only after the form has begun to decline is it considered worthy of critical attention. The novel, for instance, did not become really respectable among scholars until after World War I; while Herman Melville and Henry James were living, no professor would have admitted for a moment that they might eventually become cornerstones of the dissertation industry.

Today all these things are true of nonfiction magazine writing. Every week a hundred articles will reach a bigger audience than any novel can attract in a whole year. Many of the best writers of our time—Loren Eiseley, James Baldwin, Edmund Wilson,

John Hersey, Rachel Carson, Richard Rovere, and Norman Mailer, to mention only a small sample—find the article form the most effective means of presenting what they want to say. While few of them get Big Rich, the better ones make a far more comfortable living, on the average, than the "creative" writers.

(It is also significant that the novelists who are most widely read, who earn the most, and who have the heaviest impact on public opinion are now usually the so-called "nonfiction novelists." These are writers who choose a public theme—war, the uses of power, the moral dilemmas of our society—as contrasted with the "literary" novelists who prefer to deal with purely private emotions: the miseries of drug addicts and homosexuals are two momentary favorites.* And the nonfiction novelist often develops a technique which combines the skills of the reporter with those of the classical novelist. Widely disparate examples are Camus, Theodore H. White, Knebel and Bailey in *Seven Days in May*, Burdick and Wheeler in *Fail-Safe*, and Norman Mailer in *The Naked and the Dead*. It is noteworthy, too, that Mailer's later novels have been more "creative"—i.e., less reportorial and more personal in their subject matter—and at the same time less successful. Apparently he senses this himself, since in recent years he has turned increasingly to magazine writing—which, in the view of at least one reader, is markedly superior to his later fiction. The same thing, I believe, is true of James Baldwin; it is his articles, particularly *The Fire Next Time*, which have made him a major influence on contemporary events.

---

* The division between these two schools of fiction is of course drawn most sharply in this country by the New Critics and in England by F. R. Leavis and his followers. Their hatred of the "nonfiction novelist" is exemplified by Leavis's recent attack on C. P. Snow; just as their deification of the "literary" novelist is well illustrated by Leavis's adoration of D. H. Lawrence. Personally I suspect that they are drawing too rigid a line, since many of the best novels contain elements of both schools. *War and Peace*, for example, deals pre-eminently with public themes; but it also contains profound explorations of character—while *Crime and Punishment* might be described as a novel of private emotions which has far-ranging public implications.

My bias in submitting these suggestions is obvious, since I have been involved in magazine writing and publishing most of my adult life. But I don't think I am being entirely subjective in believing that the magazine article has become the characteristic literary medium of our generation. Some reasons for this development are, it seems to me, entirely objective— observable facts rather than mere opinion.

One reason is the immediacy of the article. It can be written, printed, and distributed in a matter of weeks; while the gestation of a novel may take years. This is important in a time when events are moving with unprecedented speed—when vast changes in the structure of societies and the very map of the world, of a kind which traditionally would have taken centuries, are now being telescoped into months. Africa, for example, has changed more in the last three years than in the previous millennium; and the status of the Negro in American life probably has risen further during the past summer than in all the years since the Emancipation Proclamation.

For the reporting and analyzing of such swift-flowing social change, the magazine article is a peculiarly useful tool. It offers a way to examine and debate the issues while they are still aflame; and it provides our only truly national forum open to all voices. Newspapers can't perform this function, because they are local; they are largely staff-written; their writers have neither the time nor the space to explore a subject in much depth; and they usually don't pay enough to attract the best thinkers and writers. (An exception is the syndicated columnists, such as Walter Lippmann and Joseph Alsop, who do reach a national audience and who have enough freedom from time-pressure to do it thoughtfully. It may not be coincidence that the best columnists are also frequent contributors to magazines; and their regular columns are often, in effect, short magazine articles which happen to appear in newsprint.)

Another advantage of the article, as against both books and the daily press, is its flexibility. In length, it can range from 500 to 40,000 words. In tone, it can vary from cold reporting to burning rage; it can explain, argue, imply, exhort, or enchant. Free from the rigid conventions of newspaper journalism, it can speak either with first-person directness or third-person formality, and it can blend editorial comment into the stream of narrative. When appropriate, it can develop a character as full-fleshed as the protagonist of a novel (as many *New Yorker* profiles have demonstrated)—or it can set forth a scientific hypothesis with the impersonal precision of a micrometer. (Note that the scientist—who may turn out to be the characteristic figure of our age, just as the knight was in Medieval times or the artist during the Renaissance—customarily communicates with his fellows through articles in professional journals, and with laymen through a few serious magazines such as *Scientific American, The Saturday Review, The Atlantic Monthly,* and *Harper's.* Indeed, in many fields of scholarship the preferred mode of expression now seems to be the learned article, rather than the book—again for reasons of immediacy and flexibility.)

I am not hinting, of course, that the article will ever supplant the book, or that the quality of its writing is invariably good. On the contrary, much of our current magazine nonfiction obviously is trivial and slipshod—just as many novels are trash and most plays are nothing more than an evening's entertainment. Like any other literary form, this one can be used badly or well; and in any medium real talent is rare. All I am trying to suggest is that the magazine article, at this particular point in history, has certain unique advantages for both reader and author; that as a consequence it is increasingly attractive to many of our best writers; and that it may appear, in the eyes of future generations, to have been the means of discourse most characteristic of our time.

Furthermore, because it is still in its burgeoning (or upstart) phase, it is ignored by the literary priesthood. This may be a considerable advantage. For when the critics and professoriate get around to focusing their apparatus on any form of literature, the effect on its practitioners can be pretty chilling. Like a dog in a medical lab, when one of the lively arts is stretched on the table for dissection it is likely to lose some of its *élan.*

Within the past year, however, magazine writers have received another kind of recognition which is likely to prove very useful indeed. They are getting a first tentative boost from the helping hand that has sustained novelists and poets for so many years: foundation support.

The pioneer in this field is the Philip M. Stern Family Fund —set up by a man who is himself a magazine writer and who happened to inherit a good deal of money. One of its purposes is to make grants to writers who want to tackle an important subject, requiring extensive research or travel. In the past, many such subjects have been neglected because few, if any, magazines could pay enough to cover the travel and research costs. This has been particularly true in the fields of science, medicine, and public affairs—and it is in these areas that the Stern fund plans to try hardest to encourage more and better writers, although other subjects are not ruled out.

More recently a similar program—open only to members of the Society of Magazine Writers—has been started by the Beineke Foundation of New York; and in the last few months at least one of the major foundations has been looking into the possibility of making grants along the same lines.

The immediate results of such encouragement should be an improvement in both the quality and the range of magazine writing. (I don't know of a single magazine writer who doesn't feel, now and then, that he could do better work if he had just a little more time . . . if he could run down a few more facts, interview a couple of additional sources, see for himself the relevant experiments being conducted at Berkeley or Woods Hole. And all too often he turns away from a subject which interests him intensely, because the rent is coming due and he knows he can make a quick sale with an article on a trifling but easier subject.)

For the long run, perhaps it is not too much to hope that foundation support will encourage more gifted people to embark on magazine writing as a lifetime career. Ideally, such a career should begin with long and expensive preparation (including some graduate work, or its equivalent) in the writer's special fields of interest—whether medicine, space technology, or international affairs. Able people are not likely to undertake such training unless they can see a reasonable prospect in the years ahead of being able to do their best work on the subjects they consider most significant. By providing such a prospect, programs like those of the Stern and Beineke funds can do much to bring the talent it deserves into a branch of literature whose potential is just beginning to be fully explored.

September, 1963

5 : The Old Original Beatnik

"ALL RIGHT," Karl the Barkeep said, "so these youngsters from the West Coast are making a nice soft buck out of the beatnik business. They still look like amateurs to me.

"You see, I knew the real pros—men who had mastered the craft long before this Beat Generation was born. Why, right here at this very bar I nourished the spirit of the Old Original Beatnik—the founder of the profession, you might say. These Kerouacs and Ginsbergs you talk about aren't fit to drink out of the same gin bottle with him."

Karl turned away from the beer pump he had been polishing and lifted a shot glass from the end of the shelf along the wall.

"This was old Max's personal glass," he said. "I've never let anybody else use it since the day he was murdered in 1954. As a matter of fact, for a couple of years before that I seldom let him use it either. Max had slipped pretty far by that time, and he kept trying to cadge free drinks. I am a sentimentalist, as you well know, but not that sentimental.

"But when Maxwell Bodenheim was at his peak he had the

suckers standing in line for the honor of buying his liquor. Especially the women. He used to come in here for his breakfast about five in the afternoon, and the chicks would be waiting for him practically in serried ranks. Many's the time I've seen them screeching and pulling hair before he decided which one to take into the booth with him to steady his hand for the first slug of whisky. That booth over there."

He pointed reverently to the third booth in a row of six which stretched down the narrow room across from the bar. It looked much like any other booth in a hundred other dim Greenwich Village saloons.

"A hallowed spot," Karl explained. "The office, so to speak, where he wrote his poetry and selected his women.

"The kind of beatniks you get these days, they admit it themselves, they have to *chase* women. This Kerouac put it right down in black and white that he drove a car halfway across the country after some babe or other. Climbed a mountain for another one. A thing like that would have made Max die of shame. He had his pride. He made them come to him.

"Of course he had the advantage of operating in the good old days, when the cornfed girls were stampeding into the Village like a drove of heifers, lowing for romance, rebellion, and The Finer Things of Life. Max was equipped to supply all three. He would roll his eyes, declaim a little poetry, nuzzle them with his beard, and announce that they were at last free from the leg-irons of convention which had shackled their soaring spirits in Iowa City. Forthwith they took him to their bed and board, and washed the dishes to boot.

"Most of them didn't last long, though. Max didn't bathe much, and he tended to forget their names. Also in his later years he developed this habit of getting sick whenever he was tanked up on Sneaky Pete, which was every night that he could raise the price of a quart. Even a dedicated rebel is likely to get enough of that sort of thing sooner or later.

"In fact, some of the more sensitive girls took it pretty hard. Like that Linda Dorrance who jumped out of a third-story window. Or Virginia Drew, who made the mistake of writing some poetry herself and asking Max what he thought of it. Naturally he didn't want anyone else muscling into the poetry racket— that was an important sideline for Max, as I'll explain in a minute—and I'll admit it was tactless of her to brandish a sheaf of manuscript under his eyes when he had a hangover. But I still think it was hasty of Max to tell her it was sentimental slush. They found her body in the Hudson River the next day.

"As a rule, however, the disillusioned ones would just shove him out of the apartment, to the accompaniment of the clear, high sound of a woman wronged. Then he would come down here for a replacement. He could always count on finding a new consignment of downy, verse-starved lasses just in from the Middle West with a chunk of Papa's real estate or meat-packing fortune safety-pinned to their camisoles. In those days a virile, well-set-up artist never had to go hungry."

Karl drew himself a small beer and, after a moment's hesitation, offered me one on the house. I took it to be a reward for listening; Karl's bar is located in a highly articulate neighborhood, and when the regular customers are there he seldom gets a chance to talk himself.

"I mustn't give you the impression," Karl said, "that the Bodenheim System depended on women alone. Max had other resources.

"Didn't you tell me that this current lot of beatniks is planning to start a poetry magazine—*The Big Table*, something like that? Well, that's a mistake. A fiscal mistake, of the kind an old pro like Max never would have made, at least in his mature years. It is true that when he was an apprentice beatnik he and Ben Hecht messed around for a while with a journal they called the *Chicago Literary Times*. But he soon saw the fallacy in marketing poetry wholesale. There's more money and less work in selling it retail, by the yard.

"When he wanted a little cash, he would hang a few yards of manuscript on the railing around Washington Square, with borrowed clothespins, and then stand by to wait for a customer.

The best prospects, he always said, were rich, fat old ladies, or men wearing Homburg hats. When one of these came along, Max would start hollering.

" 'You dirty bourgeois!' he would scream. 'You soulless exploiter of the poor! It's people like you who are stifling the arts in America and stomping the flower of civilization into the bloodstained mud of Wall Street. All you think about is money-grubbing, while we men of genius starve in the gutter. How could you ever hope to appreciate poetry like this? Ah, how tragic, how ironic, that I am driven by hunger to sell my priceless manuscripts to the likes of you! Five dollars, please!'

"He nearly always got it, too. Almost any hard-working middle-class square can be conned out of a few bills, Max claimed, if you just abuse him loud and long enough. On the other hand, it is a waste of time to put the bite on another Bohemian. Max found that out when he broke the news to his disciples, admirers, and mistresses that he was dying of tuberculosis, and they would have to scratch up a fund to send him to Arizona. They were broken-hearted, but they only raised $12. Anyhow, it turned out that nothing was wrong with him but alcoholism, a normal hazard of the trade.

"The only time he ever worked a deal on his fellow avant-gardists was in 1917 during the Chicago phase of his career. Late one night he busted in on a party where a lot of painters and literary characters were sitting on the floor, drinking bathtub gin, petting the girls, and talking about Rimbaud and Freud. Bodenheim was panting and even more disheveled than usual. He told them they would have to hide him quick, because the military police were hot on his track. He had refused to register for the draft, he said, on account of being a high-minded pacifist who would never, never fight in a brutal imperialist war.

"Of course this whole crowd had pacifist and anti-imperialist convictions, which were very fashionable at the time, and they were thrilled to meet a hero who was actually defying the minions of Washington. So they hid him for about two months—smuggling him after dark from one basement apartment to another, to throw the pursuers off the scent, and plying him with all the liquor and fancy groceries he could handle.

"This happy arrangement might have gone on till World War I was over, if somebody hadn't found out that Max had served a stretch in the Army from 1910 to 1913. He had tried to re-enlist, but the Army was convinced he wasn't the soldierly type and had thrust him out into the cold civilian world. After these revelations, Chicago's advanced intellects began to take a curdled view of Max and eventually he had to migrate to New York. But you'll have to admit that it was a good dodge while it lasted. I bet there isn't a beatnik living today who could have pulled it off.

"The main trouble with these fledgling beatniks," Karl went on, "is that they don't bother to learn the basic techniques of their profession. Like for instance this boy Ginsberg, he goes around all the time *explaining* his poetry. Max never made a blunder like that in all his life; he realized that nothing is so fatal to avant-gardery as an explanation.

"So he took pains to keep his verse exalted, anguished, and incomprehensible. When people asked him what it meant, he would tell them such a question proved they were unworthy to enter into the brotherhood of the truly sensitive. A poem, he insisted, had nothing to do with meaning. It was an Act of Passion. It was a Living Protest Against the Callous Cruelty of the Business Ethos. Besides, what can you expect for fifty cents? That was about all Max was getting in the last years, when he and Ruth Fagan were peddling his poems around the saloons for drink money. Ruth was his last wife, you know, the one who got murdered along with him. He used to marry some of the girls every now and then in fits of absent-mindedness.

"In handling his line of prose, he naturally used different methods. When he wanted to, Bodenheim could run up a fairly workmanlike piece of literary carpentry—which is more than I can say for the Kerouacs. So far as I can see, they just open the spigot and let the words dribble onto the page in a sort of shapeless puddle. Max had more respect for the language; in his novels, anyhow, he used it with considerable precision and dexterity. He hammered out a lot of them, and one—*Replenishing Jessica*, I think it was—turned into a best-seller, thanks to an obscenity prosecution. Unfortunately a couple of hundred other novelists started writing fiction that was even gamier, and by the thirties Bodenheim couldn't keep up with the competition. It was getting mighty hard to shock anybody by that time, and shock was all he had to offer.

"So his last twenty years were kind of dismal. He spent most of them sleeping in subways and two-bit flophouses, and in the winters he would sit all day in the Waldorf Cafeteria, to keep warm and in hopes that somebody would offer him a cup of coffee. What hurt him most, I think, was that nobody wanted to talk to him any more.

"For the sad truth seems to be that beatniking is a young man's game. A kid can have a wonderful time at it, because some women will always be fascinated by the old reliable combination of free-flowing words, liquor, love, and juvenile despair. And some publishers will always think they detect enough promise to give him a little publicity and a contract for a couple of books. But there is nothing promising about an elderly beatnik. He's just a dirty, drunken, old bore. Even the best of them—as François Villon found out five hundred years before Max did.

"So if these West Coast youngsters are half-smart, they'll get out of the game while they are still ahead. I understand that some of them are pushing forty already."

Karl picked up the Maxwell Bodenheim Memorial Glass, gave it a pensive swipe with his bar towel, and put it back on the shelf.

August, 1959

6 : Nomination for a Nobel Prize

IT NOW SEEMS LIKELY that the chief literary event of this year will be the discovery of James Gould Cozzens.

"Discovery" may seem an odd word to use about a man who has been writing for thirty-three years with unusual success, and who has been regarded by many people for at least a decade as one of the best American novelists. But no other word will do.

For Cozzens has never been fully recognized by two groups on which a lasting literary reputation depends: (a) the mass reading public, and (b) the serious critics. Both have largely ignored him—for a set of curious but understandable reasons. They can ignore him no longer. The publication this week of *By Love Possessed* (Harcourt, Brace) makes him as hard to overlook as a giraffe in the living room.

Although it is a violation of The Cozzens Security System to say so, this is his twelfth novel. Only eight are listed in the official roster of his works. His first four—*Confusion, Michael Scarlett, Cockpit,* and *Son of Perdition*—are never mentioned these days by him or his publisher, and their very existence is supposed to be a secret. Yet they are not books of which the average novelist would be ashamed, particularly in view of the circumstances under which they were produced. The first was written while he was a nineteen-year-old Harvard sophomore. When he found a publisher for it, in 1924, Cozzens decided he was in business, dropped out of college, and plunged immediately into the grinding and precarious labor of the professional novelist. On the next three books he learned his craft. He doesn't like to have them read now—for the same reason that Yehudi Menuhin would not like to have a recording distributed of his early finger exercises—although one of them is a better-than-mine-run historical, and

132

another, about a sorely tempted priest, compares well enough with a famous Graham Greene novel on a similar theme.

(If you ever run across one of these early efforts in a second-hand bookstore, buy it. Since they are scarce, and almost sure to become collectors' items, they ought to turn out to be speculations at least as interesting as, say, General Dynamics or U.S. Borax.)

By ordinary standards, the next seven novels did well. They got respectful—sometimes enthusiastic—reviews. Three were chosen by the Book-of-the-Month Club, and all continued to sell far longer than the average novel. In fact, all but one are still in print—three in paperback editions—while the remaining one, *Men and Brethren*, will be brought back into print next year. To most novelists, whose books commonly disappear like a stone dropped in the sea about six months after publication, this looks like an enviable record.

Nevertheless, no Cozzens novel has ever become a really big seller. The last and best known—*Guard of Honor*, published in 1948—has sold about thirty thousand copies; compared with the marshmallows turned out by such wholesale confectioners as Frances Parkinson Keyes and Daphne du Maurier, its readership is tiny.

It is true that some other novelists of stature—William Faulkner, Glenway Wescott, Eudora Welty, and Thornton Wilder, for example—have seldom enjoyed enormous sales, and even Ernest Hemingway reached best-sellerdom fairly late. But they have been accorded other things which most writers value even higher: literary prizes, the honors of the American Academy of Arts and Letters, and the reverence—indeed, the adulation— of the magisterial critics whose encyclicals appear in the literary quarterlies and academic journals. Aside from a Pulitzer Prize in 1949, no such laurels have lighted on Cozzens' head, and the fashionable critics have passed him by in contemptuous silence.

This time it may be different. Certain evanescent signs, which publishers think they can recognize, seem to indicate that *By Love Possessed* will sell far better than any previous Cozzens novel. The prepublication sale is high; booksellers, a notoriously glum lot, are betraying gleams of eagerness; it is a selection of both the Book-of-the-Month Club and Reader's Digest Condensed Books; review copies have been in heavy demand; *Time* is planning a cover story on the author; and—best omen of all —stenographers in the publishers' office have been snitching advance copies to read during their lunch hour. When that happens, you can be sure that something uncommon is astir.

It would be no surprise, to this reader at least, if the new novel also collects a few prizes. At this writing, no very formidable contenders for the Pulitzer Prize and National Book Award can be spotted on the fall lists. (Although that may not mean much; in recent years each of these literary lollipops has been handed occasionally to a pretty feeble and precious specimen.)

And eventually even the most lordly of the academic critics may have to take judicial notice of Cozzens' existence. They won't like him; but from now on it will be hard for them to pretend that a man who occupies so much of the literary landscape simply isn't there.

They have preferred to ignore him all these years because he does not fit into any of the established literary patterns and they have, therefore, found it impossible to measure and dissect him with their standard calipers and scalpels.

Even his private life is, for a writer, unconventional. He attends no cocktail parties, sits on no committees, makes no speeches, signs no manifestoes, writes no reviews, appears on no television shows, scratches no backs, shuns women's clubs, cares nothing about personal publicity, and doesn't even tell his publisher how to run his advertising campaigns. He holds the queer notion that a novelist's job is to write novels; and he sticks to that last with single-minded intensity. To this end, he lives and works in a quiet old farmhouse near Lambertville, New Jersey, with the only wife he has ever had (and who happens to be, quite incidentally, one of the best literary agents in the country); he almost never visits New York; few people in the so-called literary world have ever set eyes on him. Consequently he has picked up the reputation of a recluse.

It is undeserved. Actually he spends a good many sociable hours around Lambertville and two neighboring towns, New Hope and Doylestown, Pennsylvania; and he is working every minute of them. He knows the Doylestown courthouse, for example, better than its janitor does, and its occupants—from judges to jailers—are his friends. It is no accident that the law, which figures largely in both this novel and an earlier one, is taken with precise accuracy from the Pennsylvania statutes; and that Brocton, the town which serves as a setting for the new novel, bears a family resemblance to the villages along the middle stretch of the Delaware River.

The graph line of Cozzens' career also looks remarkably different from that of many American novelists. As the literary historians have noted, talented writers in this country often start off with a bang, and then dwindle away to a whimper. Sinclair Lewis, for instance, ran steadily downhill after he reached his early high point with *Main Street* and *Babbitt*. Thomas Wolfe never again wrote anything quite up to his first novel, *Look Homeward, Angel*. Even Faulkner and Hemingway have followed much the same chart. Faulkner's most bedazzled admirers would hardly claim that his last two books are up to the level of his earlier work, and Hemingway's most recent novel, *Across the River and Into the Trees*, is best passed over in charitable silence. (A subsequent book, *The Old Man and the Sea*, is a long short story rather than a novel.) A list of similar examples could be continued for pages; but Cozzens would not be on it. His output has shown a steady growth in sureness, insight, and stature, so that the present monumental work comes not as a surprise but as a natural culmination.

These are relatively superficial differences. The essential difference between Cozzens and his contemporaries lies in the character of his work. Here he is the complete nonconformist: a classic mind, operating in a romantic period. This, I suspect, is the basic reason why he has missed both popular and critical appreciation. He puzzles ordinary readers whose palates have been dulled by the Gothic extravagance of most current fiction;

and he offends critics whose professional mission has been to exalt the romantic novel, which has been in high fashion for the last thirty years.

The Standard American Romantic novelist of today can be identified by four earmarks:

1. He habitually writes about exotic characters who are, in one fashion or another, in revolt against society. Witness Faulkner's Popeye and Joe Christmas, Steinbeck's lovable bums, Hemingway's defiant tough guys, Tennessee Williams' prostitutes and heels, Capote's Southerners, Saroyan's elfin drunks, and all the other dope addicts, cheats, thieves, goldbricks, and emotional cripples who are the stock in trade of Nelson Algren, Norman Mailer, Saul Bellow, Paul Bowles, James Jones, and the other inhabitants of our contemporary Pantheon.

2. He conventionally portrays such heroes in sentimental terms —as Edmund Fuller pointed out in last spring's issue of *The American Scholar*.

"It is not my hero's fault," the romantic novelist tells us, "that he is an irresponsible jerk. Society made him that way."

And he invites the reader to drop a kindly tear for these scalawags—what Fuller calls "the genial rapist, the jolly slasher, the fun-loving dope pusher"—just as the sentimental novelist of the last century asked us to weep over his forlorn maidens.

3. Usually, though not always, he places his picaresque heroes in a picaresque tale. Such a story need have no firm plot structure; it wanders haphazardly from one incident to another, linking anecdotes, sketches, short stories, and inner musings together with a loose and tenuous narrative line. Its setting is often as exotic as the characters—the Chicago underworld, a rum runner's boat, a bull ring, Yoknapatawpha County—and the story ordinarily involves a wholesale helping of lust and violence.

4. The novelist of this school customarily identifies himself with one of his characters, and uses him as a trumpet to express his own emotions, complaints, and political views. Sometimes (as in Wolfe) the hero is the spitting image of the author; sometimes (as in Hemingway, the highbrow's Walter Mitty)

he seems to be the way the author pictures himself in his more glorious daydreams; sometimes (as in Steinbeck and Algren) he is the ventriloquist's dummy on the author's knee. In any case, it is easy to tell which speeches in the book set forth the author's sermon; Faulkner leaves no doubt where he stands in the War Against the Snopeses.

There is much to be said for the romantic method. For one thing, it is the easiest way to catch the interest of the reader— typically a man or woman who leads a sedentary, respectable, uneventful life, and therefore is ready to shiver with excitement at the wild doings of the uninhibited outlaw. It is a timesaver, since the picaresque plot is no trouble to construct; some of its practitioners turn out a book a year. It is a simple and effective device for criticizing society—always a main purpose of the novelist in America. And it is a boon to the critic, since it gives him a built-in springboard from which to launch his own dissertation about the society we live in.

But the romantic novel has its drawbacks, too. Because it uses the extreme case—abnormal characters in an abnormal setting —as a weapon to attack the evils which exist in all societies, it can never give a full and balanced picture of society as a whole. A foreigner can (and often does) read a hundred such novels without getting the faintest ideas of what normal, day-to-day life in the United States is really like. Faulkner's guilt-haunted county and Algren's vice-pots may give accurate glimpses of tiny segments on the extreme fringe of American life—and it is, of course, useful to put these pathological specimens under the microscope. But they do not picture the rounded body of society, any more than L.-F. Céline's explorations of depravity reflect the whole truth about contemporary France.

Then, too, the sentimental stance of this sort of fiction—handy though it is for posing an indictment of society—makes it impossible for the writer to deal seriously with individual moral problems. *From Here to Eternity*, for example, made it plain that plenty was wrong with the prewar Army; but at the cost of evading all questions about the personal responsibilities of

Prewitt, who had to be pictured as a helpless victim of The System. In all such novels—*The Deer Park* and *The Man with the Golden Arm* are even better examples—one vital dimension of fiction necessarily is missing.

Finally, the romantic method tends to wear itself out in a few decades. Readers get jaded with lust and violence and bizarre heroes; to hold their attention, the novelist has to reach for ever greater extremes; and in the end his readers cease to believe in characters so remote from their own experience. The resulting boredom and indifference are perhaps largely responsible for the much-discussed decline of fiction. Maybe the romantic novel has, for a time, reached a dead end.

Cozzens may, indeed, signal a turning of the tide. In his salad days, he too flirted with the romantic technique, but in his mature novels he has moved steadily away from it. Instead he has been attempting something far more difficult: to write an engrossing story about ordinary people, living ordinary lives, in ordinary circumstances.

His first experiment in this direction was *The Last Adam*, published in 1933, an account of a small-town doctor and his patients. *Men and Brethren* dealt with the life of a New York clergyman, not very different from the parson you might meet next Sunday. *The Just and the Unjust* was a study of law and politics in a perfectly commonplace community. *Guard of Honor* examined life on a Florida airbase in all its levels and complexities; anyone who served in World War II would feel at home there, but he would encounter none of the grotesque characters who man the armies of Jones and Mailer. (It may be significant that many professional military men consider it the best of the war novels; one Air Force colonel told me it was the *only* one that showed any awareness of the actual problems of Army life.)

By Love Possessed carries this series of experiments-in-the-normal a long and brilliant step forward. On all four of the counts listed above, it is the exact antithesis of the romantic novel.

THE WRITER'S TRADE : 139

Its central characters are a group of lawyers and businessmen —middle-class, middle-aged, and respectable—in an American town no better and no worse than a dozen any of us could name. They move among people familiar to all of us: a spinster secretary, a justice of the peace, a waitress, an overworked doctor, an assortment of immediately recognizable wives and children. Nobody is presented as a rebel against society, or as its victim; these people *are* society. When they try to rebel, it is not against The System, but against life itself, and they fall victim to the mortality that awaits us all.

Of sentimentality there is no chemical trace. You are never asked to weep for any of the characters, or to rage. You are merely invited to understand them, as the author probes deeper and deeper for the final meaning in each of their lives. What he finds is not always pretty, but neither is it monstrous. It comes close to being the truth, the whole truth, and nothing but the truth, so help me God.

This is no loose-woven picaresque tale. It is the most tightly constructed of novels, with every chapter—indeed, every paragraph—carved to interlock with every other. In the end it emerges as a work of classic symmetry—the last scene foreshadowed in the first, all parts in balance, all conflicts resolved. The style is equally craftsmanlike. Every sentence has been hammered, filed, and tested until it bears precisely the weight it was designed to carry, and does it with clarity and grace. No wonder this book took nine years to write.

Not once does the author himself walk into the story. No character is autobiographical, none is a loudspeaker for the author's sermons. When you finish you know a lot about Cozzens' concept of the good life—but only because you have watched a number of lives unfold in vigorous detail before your eyes.

The theme of the book is love. Love in all its aspects—between man and woman, parent and child, friend and friend, individual and community. It is an examination of the rewards and the burdens—sometimes crushing burdens—laid on people possessed by love. And like all really first-rate novels, it is an exploration of moral responsibility. Each person who inhabits the story is constantly confronted (though he does not always realize it) with the series of moral questions which confront all of us: How should I conduct myself? What is my duty? Can I escape this hard choice before me? What do I do next?

It is a measure of Cozzens' accomplishment that he endows such a story with a feeling of suspense and excitement far greater than you will find in the typical romantic novel loaded with violent action. The explanation, it seems to me, is that the ordinary reader can identify himself with the people of Brocton, as he never can with the characters of an Algren or a Mailer. The dilemma Arthur Winner faces, as he sits in his tidy law office, is one which any of us might encounter tomorrow. The temptation which brought Ralph Detweiler into the hands of the police and his sister to her death is commonplace in every village in America. Never for a moment can you doubt these are real people, coping with real problems in the fumbling, unromantic way that all of us try to cope with our own.

To be fair, it is necessary to note two complaints about the book:

1. Several women, of sound taste and judgment, tell me that they find the story disconcerting. They are not used to seeing love handled in such an unsentimental fashion, and they are not sure they like it. Moreover, I gather that they are a little upset by the fact that the issue on which the novel hinges does not involve a woman at all. It centers on the spiritual love of a patriarch for the people who have trusted him (perhaps too much) and on a question of professional ethics. Now, most mature women realize, in their hearts, that the chief crises in a man's life may have nothing to do with females; but they don't always like to be reminded of it. The romantic legend—older than Helen of Troy—that a woman is the central core of every man's life, the focus of his worries, and the mainspring of his actions, is more soothing to the feminine ego.

2. Other people, by no means prudes, have suggested that *By*

Love Possessed is not a suitable book for the young. They may be right. It was, after all, written for adults; and some of its passages might well be both incomprehensible and disturbing to adolescents who lack the range of experience to grasp the emotions involved.

This is not to suggest that anything in the story is either salacious or sensational. Quite the contrary. Cozzens has merely tried to tell the exact truth—about sex, money, ambition, and many other things—with clinical honesty. Some aspects of the truth inevitably are unpleasant. These he has neither softened nor exaggerated. They are set down with the raw, impersonal horror of an autopsy or a police report, because they are a part of life; so, too, are warmth and devotion and quiet heroism, and these he reports with equal fidelity.

The novel is like one of those Breughel paintings which show an entire community in bustling activity—the noble, the funny, the bestial, the labor and lust, the pain and laughter, all traced out in infinitely precise detail; and all the details fitted together to form a marvelously colorful composition. Like Breughel, Cozzens tells us more than any artist of his time about the life of his day. If your great-grandchild should ever want to find out how Americans behaved and thought and felt in the mid-years of this century, Cozzens' major novels probably would be his most revealing source.

If this does not stake out his claim to be one of the very few important novelists of our generation, I don't know what would. The committee that awards the Nobel Prize for literature is said to reach its decisions not on the basis of a single book but on mature consideration of a writer's whole body of work. Where can they find a more solid body of work than this?

September, 1957

POSTSCRIPT

The foregoing probably did Mr. Cozzens a disservice. It appeared about the same time as a similarly enthusiastic review by Brendan Gill in The New Yorker; *and these comments—together with the brisk sale of the book—apparently provoked a number of critics devoted to the romantic school of fiction to attack both the novel and its author in rather immoderate terms. The barrage continued for nearly six months, culminating with a 220 mm. cannonade by Dwight MacDonald in the pages of* Commentary.

On rereading the article six years after it was first published, I find nothing that I want to change; but I now think that I might well have included an additional comment on one noteworthy characteristic of By Love Possessed. *It is written in a style quite different from that of any of Mr. Cozzens' earlier works. As he told me later, he was experimenting with a use of language much more complex, dense, and involuted than he had attempted before, because he felt that the intricate, interlacing nature of the story called for it. This did not bother me, but it did annoy some readers, including a number of the unfriendly critics. Mr. Cozzens told me that, in retrospect, he did not regard the experiment as entirely successful, and did not expect to repeat it in his subsequent novels.*   —J. F.

7 : Why Nobody Can't Write Good

SHE HAD JUST BEEN GRADUATED from one of the more expensive women's colleges and now she was looking for a job in publishing. Her grades were good. She had majored in English, with special attention to eighteenth-century poetry; and she confessed, flapping her eyelashes modestly, that she had written a little verse of her own. Her speech was civilized, her clothes were in unobtrusive good taste, her nails were clean and her appearance was presentable—indeed, quite fetching.

But when she took the routine employment test it was at once apparent that she couldn't spell, construct a grammatical sentence, or write a paragraph of coherent prose. Moreover, she was astonished that anybody expected her to do these things. She assumed that we had some drudges in a back room who took care of such grubby details. What she wanted, she explained, was "to do something creative."

The suggestion I offered was meant to be helpful, and I'm pretty sure that I put it in a fatherly—well, anyhow an avuncular —tone without the faintest hint of a leer; but she didn't take it well. In fact, she seemed to regard me as both flippant and impertinent.

Her case is by no means unusual. On the contrary, every businessman knows that it is a rare day when he can hire either a woman or a man who is capable of writing reasonably competent English. It is easier, one executive recently told me, to find people trained to write the mathematical binary language of computers.

Such complaints are becoming frequent enough to suggest that the almost-vanished art of writing has become an expensive problem for American business. The dean of the Harvard Business School, for example, reports that "an incredible number of college graduates who apply for admission can't write a passable sentence"—and he is supposed to get the cream of the crop. Langley Carleton Keyes, the head of a Boston advertising agency, has deplored the "enormous wastefulness" which results from "the great amount of dull, difficult, obscure, hackneyed, wordy writing in business." Several of the better law schools have started intensive programs in writing because—as Thomas M. Cooley, dean of the University of Pittsburgh law school, put it— "the graduates of our colleges, including the best ones, cannot write the English language," much less draft a cogent brief. The State Department has just launched a course in elementary composition for its officers, who frequently cannot comprehend one another's memoranda. And Washington University in St. Louis is starting a special project, at the cost of $135,000 a year, to translate the incomprehensible jargon of social scientists into English.

Most alarming of all is the discovery that a lot of teachers can't write either. Dr. Harold Martin, of the College Entrance

Examination Board's Commission on English, found that a third of the English teachers in secondary schools were unfit to teach their subject.

Which should surprise nobody. For we have people who make it their business to teach binary computer language, or French or Russian or Swahili. But today nobody—with a few honorable exceptions, to be noted in a moment—seems to feel that it is really his job to teach the writing of English.

Listen to Professor Paul Roberts, the author of several well-known English texts:

"Everybody who is not an English teacher," he says, "seems to think that English teachers have had special training in English composition and in how to teach it. We have not had. We have been trained in English and American literature, in Old English philology and structural linguistics. Nobody has been trained in composition . . ."

If you spend a little time around the English department of any big university, you will discover that this is an understatement. The satraps in charge of graduate work there have no interest in training people to teach children to write. What they are interested in is producing Ph.D.s—and producing them according to a formula handed down almost unchanged from the medieval universities of the Old World. They are, moreover, afflicted by feelings of inferiority, because they see most of the big money and prestige flowing to their colleagues in the science departments. Hence they try their best to imitate the scientists, in an effort to prove that their scholars are just as scholarly— indeed, just as scientific—as anybody across the road in the physics lab. Above all, they insist that every Ph.D. candidate must make some "original contribution to knowledge."

As an academic outsider you may think this an unreasonable demand. For the English scholar is not free to explore the limitless reaches of the physical universe in search of his "original contribution." He is limited to the finite body of English and American literature. This means he must write yet another dissertation on James or Melville or some other famous chestnut; or he must dig up some obscure eighteenth-century poet who hasn't already been explored to tatters. Such poets are getting mighty scarce—and when found, it is obvious that they are obscure for the best of reasons. So by the time the poor candidate has spent three years poring over his subject's hamstrung syntax and beclouded rhetoric, any natural feeling he may have had for the English language probably has been smothered for good.

If not, in most universities his preceptors will soon take care of that. They will see to it that his dissertation is not written in plain, straightforward English—that would be distressingly unscholarly—but in the peculiar argot known as Pedagese or Academic Mandarin. (For representative samples, see the bound doctoral typescripts moldering in the stacks of any university library, or any issue of *Publications of the Modern Language Association*.) In due course, then, the fledgling scholar is awarded a velvet hood to wear in academic processions and a parchment license to teach English.

His first job almost certainly will be the teaching of Freshman Composition in some college: a task for which, as Professor Roberts pointed out, he is totally unequipped. He will loathe it, for this reason and because the pay is poor and the prestige worse; he is, in fact, considered the low man on the academic totem pole. Moreover, he probably will conclude that his labors are hopeless, because his classes are far too large to teach writing in the only way it can be taught: that is, by painstakingly analyzing every sentence of an assigned paper with each student individually, pointing out his mistakes and making him do it over—and and over and over—until he gets it right. Even if he had the time and stamina, his pupils would rebel against such methods; for the one thing they learned about English in high school is that it is unimportant.

Oh, maybe an occasional fussy English teacher had carried on about it—but the high-school math and history and social-studies teachers couldn't have cared less. They seldom assigned written papers or essay-type examinations, since their classes (the old problem) were too big, and it is easier to grade true-and-false "objective" tests. In any case, they didn't bother about errors in spelling and grammar; their attitude, implicit if not openly expressed, was: "Just get down the facts and don't worry about the language." Most of them, indeed, were so insecure about their own English that they would have flinched from correcting a mistake in rhetoric, even if they had considered that part of their duties.

This was not always true. To quote Professor Roberts again: "In the last hundred years there has been a steady decline in the use of writing in the general educational process. It used to be that no one had to teach composition because everybody taught it. The student was writing all the time, not only in his literature course but also in history, in economics, even in science and mathematics. It was every teacher's responsibility, and not just the English teacher's, to keep the student up to a respectable standard and to show him how to improve his prose."

And he concludes gloomily that "very likely we can never go back to such a system, but this is no argument for having special courses in writing taught by departments of English"—because that wouldn't help either. "Students write badly. They take courses in English composition and they still write badly. And nothing has been achieved except the ruin of departments of English."

With his elders in such despair, who can blame the young instructor with his shiny new Ph.D. if he scuttles away from Freshman Composition as fast as he can manage it, and begins to teach courses in Chaucer or Milton's Use of Imagery—which is, after all, what he has been trained for?

Meanwhile, the university turns out another generation of illiterates, some of them with Ph.D.s. And the graduate schools of law and business, in desperation, launch programs in elementary composition, to give their students what they failed to acquire during the previous sixteen years—because it was nobody's business to teach them.

At this point the taxpayer may begin to wonder whether we really need all those English Ph.D.s., educated at such vast expenditure of money and talent. Wouldn't it be more sensible to train a few hundred thousand people specifically for the teaching of English composition? Maybe—O heretical thought —it isn't really necessary to make a man get a Ph.D. before permitting him to teach a writing class? Maybe a different kind of union card would be more practical?

If the taxpayer is also a businessman, plagued by illiterate employees (and his own inability to write a lucid memorandum) he may begin to suspect that our whole school system isn't worth the billions we pour into it, so long as it turns out such defective products. He is not likely, however, to devote much energy to seeing whether the school system might be improved. Usually he will just grumble in private, curse the eggheads who run the schools, and vote against the next school bond issue—as the citizens of my own community did just a few weeks ago.

Fortunately not everyone has abandoned hope. In both high schools and colleges a small band of stubborn teachers still believes that it is not only possible but essential to teach kids to write. They are convinced that American society will not permit itself to drown in the rising tide of incoherence . . . that sooner or later it will realize that no nation can survive a breakdown in communications (remember the Tower of Babel?) . . . and that it will then insist on the changes, however painful and expensive, necessary to rebuild a common skill in the use of language. After all, language is the most valuable tool *Homo sapiens* ever invented, and he is not likely to abandon it for good.*

When that day comes, they hope to be ready with a whole kit of new ideas for the teaching of English. The intellectual ferment now going on among them may well be the liveliest anywhere in the field of education. (Or so at least it seems to me, after spending a good deal of time recently with English teachers in classrooms and at their professional meetings.) The result

---

* Its value, in the crudest dollars-and-cents terms, is nicely illustrated by Frederic G. Donner, chairman of the board of General Motors, the world's biggest manufacturing firm. He is of course one of the world's best-paid executives. While at the University of Michigan he got straight A's (except for one B in history) and graduated with a Phi Beta Kappa key. One of his old professors remembers that Donner "had a great skill in writing and an excellent vocabulary. From that I assumed he could think clearly."

may be an upheaval in the teaching of English comparable to the recent revolution in the teaching of mathematics and science.

The structural linguists, for example, are developing new kinds of grammar which ought to be more logical, and therefore easier to teach, than the traditional variety. (So far, at least three different approaches have emerged, and it is not yet clear which may eventually prove the most useful.) The College Entrance Examination Board already has embarked on an ambitious program for retraining teachers, working out new curricula, and making TV films to show how outstanding teachers go about their jobs. The teachers' professional associations—there is a surprising number of them—are getting together in conferences all over the place to define what they call "the basic issues" in the teaching of English, and to figure out new ways to rejuvenate their trade.

What is likely to come of all this? Here are a few guesses, based on scores of reports, speeches, and bull sessions from which I've tried to sieve some of the ideas now boiling up among the professionals:

1. We are going to have to attract a lot more—and a lot better —people into the business of teaching English. Trained English teachers are already in short supply, and because of low pay and discouraging working conditions they are getting scarcer.

2. A cataclysmic shake-up is coming both in university English departments and in teachers' colleges. It will be resisted fiercely, because professors with a vested interest in their ancient academic habits are about the world's most deeply entrenched conservatives. But it will come. One result may be a new degree —perhaps labeled Ph.M., for Master of Philosophy—which will be awarded to people specifically trained for teaching language skills and who are not forced to waste years in the brain-numbing irrelevancies of the present English Ph.D. programs.

3. The taxpayer will have to shell out a lot more money for the teaching of English. For, done right, it is a hideously expensive undertaking. It requires higher salaries to attract enough good people. It demands smaller classes. It calls for a big investment in the colleges, in order to train the regiments of additional

teachers needed in our grade and high schools. (This may, of course, mean that the taxpayer will decide to spend less money on scholastic frills, such as driver education, home economics, vocational agriculture, and football.)

4. Teachers in other subjects—from social studies to chemistry —will have to assume once more some responsibility for making their students toe the mark in their use of language. The creeping slobbism which is endemic in many schools cannot be checked so long as a youngster is permitted to get by with sloppy writing in every classroom except one.

This too will be bitterly resisted. When Dr. Albert R. Kitzhaber of the University of Oregon recently suggested it in an influential book, *Themes, Theories, and Therapy: the Teaching of Writing in College* (McGraw-Hill), he stirred up an astonishing uproar among the pedagogues in other fields. The tone of their comments is indicated by a burlesque review of his book which appeared in the *Newsletter* of the Institute of Early American Culture and History of Williamsburg, under the title "Why Nobody Can't Write Good." Supposedly written by a history teacher, it read in part:

"It is unbelievably incredible for someone to write that other professors than in English courses should teach students, which is not their job to do. In American History, to show a specific example, the professors in actuality should stick to the subject and the facts about it, and they should not meddle in someone else's course. In fact, English hasn't got anything to do with History, which proves that his whole book is irrelevant."*

But Kitzhaber will find some allies, too, in the other departments. Already many teachers are coming to realize that sense and style can't really be separated—that a student who can't write clearly can't think clearly. For the physical act of putting words on paper is an essential part of the thought process. Until you put a thought in words—sharply and precisely—it isn't a thought at all; it is just a kind of fog rolling around inside the skull.

---

* I *think* the *Newsletter* was kidding, but quite possibly the review is genuine. I know a number of academic historians who write just like that.

Consequently, I think it likely that more and more schools will reduce their dependence on true-and-false tests, and will require an increasing amount of written work in all classes, as the better prep and high schools have been doing all along. It is conceivable that the different departments may someday get together in the planning of assignments. Then, instead of having to write both an English theme and a history paper over the weekend, Johnny will have only one task: a paper on, say, The Causes of the American Revolution—for which he will be responsible to his teachers both in history and in English. Instead of racing to slap something down any old how, he will be expected to spend twice as much time in organizing his facts, thoughts, and language. And if either teacher is dissatisfied, he can insist that Johnny do the job over again. Thus Johnny will get the idea, eventually, that anything worth putting on paper is worth the very best writing he can possibly achieve.

5. This may sound utopian, but I have hopes that the colleges will someday refuse to admit any student who cannot read and write. This would be a truly revolutionary step. For most colleges, it would immediately cut enrollments by at least half (thus solving the overcrowding problem). It would force the high schools to teach English properly—and the taxpayers to put up the money for it, if they want their little darlings to get into college. It would eliminate all those dreary courses in remedial English for undergraduates—and for students in law, business, and other postgraduate schools. It would help a lot to reduce delinquency, since an inadequate grasp of reading and writing is one of the commonest causes for school dropouts. It would cut unemployment and relief costs, since until a man has acquired the basic skill in using his native tongue he has little chance to learn the other skills necessary to earn a living.

And it would give some assurance that when a college graduate walks into an office in search of a job, he probably has at least the minimum qualifications necessary to perform it.

I should live so long.

January, 1964

PART III

POLITICIAN WATCHING

1 : Please Don't Bite the Politicians

THIS IS A PLEA for tolerance toward our most misunderstood minority: the professional politicians.

No other group in America is the butt of so much suspicion, ridicule, and contempt. All kinds of opinion-makers, from editorial writers to night-club comics—people who would never dream of insulting a Negro, Jew, Catholic, or Paiute Indian—delight in slipping their daily needle of sarcasm into the politician. They have even invented a derisive name for him: The Pol.

The hard feeling always reaches its peak at the close of a Presidential election. Countless people who ordinarily have nothing to do with politics will wake up the morning after Election Day disappointed, angry, and probably overhung. And not only the losers. Many a member of the winning party will have a sour bellyful of disillusionment about the way his Peerless Leaders (from ward chairman to Presidential candidate) handled the campaign. Bitterest of all will be the amateur politicians—the volunteers who have been working for the last four months in uneasy harness with the pros. Most of them will finger their collar galls on postelection morning and reflect that their worst suspicions are now confirmed.

A case in point is an idealistic young artist, whose cartoons probably are familiar to most of you. Recently he developed a

153

deep concern for politics. He wakes up at 3:00 A.M. to worry about Peace; he believes that all men are brothers, especially if they are brown, black, or yellow; he yearns, quite sincerely, to help the poor and oppressed everywhere. So he has been trying to Do Something About It by working with the Democratic club in his Greenwich Village election district.

A few weeks ago he showed me a series of cartoons he had just finished about "typical politicians." They emerged as wonderfully funny but sinister buffoons—both sly and stupid, corrupt, hog rich, and all callously indifferent to the Big Issues such as hunger in Asia and The Bomb.

This view distressed me because: (a) it is so similar to the conclusions reached by many earnest amateurs after their first contact with practical politicians; (b) it is wildly unfair and inaccurate; (c) it is dangerous. Unless ordinary citizens understand—and respect—the processes of political life, our society isn't going to work very well. And it is inconsistent (it seems to me) for anyone to be so passionate about democracy and yet so cynical about the instruments through which democracy has to work.

It also distressed me because I like politicians. Ever since I started work as a city-hall reporter in New Mexico some thirty years ago, I have spent a lot of time in their company—in smoke-filled rooms, jails, campaign trains, shabby courthouse offices, Senate cloakrooms, and the White House itself. Mostly I've been reporting their doings, but on occasion I have served them as speech writer, district leader, campaign choreboy, and civil servant. On the whole, they have proved better company than any other professional group I've had a chance to know well—including writers, soldiers, businessmen, doctors, and academics. Drunk or sober, they are amusing fellows. Their view of human nature is acute, unromantic, and good-humored. They are as sensitive as coloratura sopranos. Few of them have much capacity for malice, and except when making speeches they are seldom bores.

On the average, moreover, they have seemed to me at least as

honest, dedicated, and idealistic as the mine run of Americans
—including the fastidious who shrink away from the "dirtiness"
of politics.

No doubt the politicians are themselves partly to blame for
the blotchy image of their profession in the public mind. But
the rest of us, I think, are more at fault. In our lazy way, we
find it easier to accept the cartoonist's caricature than to take the
trouble to look at the politician as a breathing, complex human
being. And all too often we try (maybe unwittingly) to push
him into the mold of the caricature.

A realistic portrait of the typical politician would have to begin with his motives. Why is he in this business?

Not for money. I have never known a man who got rich
out of politics. I have known many who got poor. Nearly all of
those who are reasonably competent could have done better
financially in some other line of work. It is true that a good deal
of money passes through their hands—politics has become an
outrageously expensive business in this country—but, all legends
to the contrary, not much of it sticks.

Most wealthy politicians either inherited their bankroll (like
Kennedy and Rockefeller) or married it (like Lyndon Johnson)
or made it earlier in another trade (like Benton and Bowles).
Many have sidelines which thrive on political connections—
most commonly the law, insurance, contracting, and broadcasting. Nevertheless a political career is quite likely to drain
more dollars out of the bank account than it feeds in.

My guess is that people usually turn to politics for the same
reason actors seek the stage. They need applause.

Like the theater, politics is a great nourisher of egos. It attracts
men who are hungry for attention, for assurance that somebody
loves them, for the soul-stirring music of their own voices.
(Political speeches are not invariably made because the public
craves wisdom, but oftener just because politicians love to talk
—even when their only audience is other politicians. Note how
hard it is for the chairman to throttle down the oratory at that
lowliest of all political gatherings, a meeting of precinct leaders.)

A main ingredient in the make-up of every successful politician is a thick slice of ham.

It follows that politicians, like actors and prima donnas, are abnormally sensitive to slights. For hundreds of political infantry-men, "recognition" is their only reward. They treasure the right to sit at the speaker's table at a fund-raising dinner, to be consulted before the Governor schedules a speech in their bailiwick, to ride a few miles on the train of a whistle-stopping Presidential candidate. Above all they dote on giving advice. The late Tammany boss Ed Flynn once remarked that his most tiresome chore was listening to his henchmen report—at interminable length—on "conditions" in their districts. The strategy they suggested, he said, was almost always either obvious or silly; but he had to hear them out. For an affront to their self-esteem could make a mortal enemy.*

But vanity alone by no means explains the politician. While I have long since learned that I am not competent to disentangle anybody's mixed motives (including my own), I strongly suspect that most pros are as much moved by a sense of duty as by their thirst for status. If politics is balm for tender egos, it is equally soothing to the inflamed superego. Perhaps more than most people, politicians are prodded by conscience. Certainly the best of them sincerely feel an obligation to perform a public service. And this, I think, is true at all levels—from the housewife who spends her evenings ringing doorbells and compiling card files, up to men like the late Senator George Norris or Mayor Fiorello La Guardia. Both of these were as truly noble characters as anybody you can find in Plutarch.

A third motive is usually present too: the fun of the game. Nearly every skillful politician I have ever met enjoyed the subtleties and excitements of his craft just as a tennis player enjoys

---

* Sometimes, of course, this longing for dignity and recognition can degenerate into a simple lust for power. The extreme cases in modern times probably were Huey Long and Joe McCarthy, who seemed to get a sadistic pleasure out of kicking other people. But they represent the pathology of politics; both were products of abnormal times. When our body politic is functioning normally, it usually sloughs off such malignant types before they can do much damage.

a well-played match. Perhaps a better analogy is chess—a kind of chess played with thousands of pieces, each different and every one likely to start charging around the board on his own at any moment; demanding luck as well as art; and offering to the winners the highest of stakes, and to a loser oblivion.

If the average politician is, as I believe, a reasonably decent man, why does he have such a bad name?

This isn't a new problem. As Joyce Cary has pointed out, "almost every great statesman has been described as a crook. Metternich, Cavour, Bismarck, Gladstone, Disraeli, Lloyd George, Roosevelt: history is made up of names at which the moralist holds his nose."

Ever since Pericles, the basic indictment has been dishonesty. This can include two counts: (a) he steals money; (b) he is intellectually dishonest—a hypocrite, a trimmer, a promiser of things he can't deliver.

How far can these charges be sustained?

It certainly can't be denied that some politicians are common thieves. Almost every week the papers report some officeholder whose hand was out for a mink coat, a free vacation trip, or cold cash. I have never seen any evidence, however, that the percentage of petty chiselers is any higher in politics than in any other profession.

All of us know of salesmen who pad their expense accounts, business executives who demand kickbacks from their suppliers, doctors who will split a fee, union officers with sticky fingers, disc jockeys who welcome a little payola. The real difference is that the sharp operators in private life seldom break into the news. The politician is under closer scrutiny, and when he is caught with his hand in the till, his partisan rivals make sure that everybody hears about it. A fair verdict on this count, it seems to me, ought to read: Sometimes guilty, but probably no oftener than anybody else.

But what about the politician who takes money not for personal enrichment but to finance his political career? This is far more common—indeed almost universal. Campaigns cost plenty; so, unless we want to limit public office to rich men, somebody has to put up the cash.

At this point the moral distinctions get pretty tricky. Everybody would agree that it is wicked for a candidate to take a contribution from someone who expects a special favor in return—a gambler who wants immunity from arrest, or a contractor after that new highway job. On the other hand, if the contributor doesn't expect a specific *quid pro quo*, then most people seem to think his money is clean enough. At least so one gathers from the public reaction to Richard M. Nixon's famous Checkers speech, in which he justified accepting $18,000 from wealthy friends on grounds that none of them "ever received any consideration that he would not have received as an ordinary constituent."

All they had been promised—according to Dana Smith, who solicited the fund—was that Nixon would "continue to sell effectively . . . the economic and political systems which we all believe in." Presumably that meant lower taxes and a favorable climate for business. But suppose a candidate honestly believes in higher taxes, and a favorable climate for trade unions? Is it then all right for him to take money from union leaders? And how do you judge those Southwestern Congressmen who are largely financed by oil men desperately eager to protect their special tax privileges?

Among such cases, and many others even more shadowy, I don't see how anybody can draw a clear moral line. Ideally, of course, every campaign should be financed only by small contributions from patriotic citizens who expect nothing in return except good government. But these are about as rare as whooping cranes. It is this stinginess—of which we are nearly all guilty—that makes the candidate seek his funds from dubious sources; and it is in this way that we force him closer to conforming to that unjust caricature of The Typical Politician.

If we really wanted to mend matters, we could do two things. Individual citizens might become a lot more generous, and disinterested, in making political contributions. Or we might start financing campaigns out of the public treasury, as the late Senator Richard Neuberger suggested. At the moment, both courses sound utopian. So long, however, as we prefer to leave things as they are, it hardly becomes us to point scornful fingers at the politicians.

A fair verdict on this charge, then, might read: Guilt, if any, is usually due to circumstances beyond his control.

The amateurs in politics may grant all this, and still argue that the professional is an intellectual fraud. What makes their peeve worse is the suspicion (often well founded) that the pro doesn't quite trust them, or wholly welcome their volunteer help.

Let's see how this painful situation looks from the viewpoint of a small-time professional: for example, a ward leader.

For the last four years (and for several quadrenniums before that) he has drudged away at the dull, necessary chores—seeing that newcomers to the ward get registered, hunting likely candidates for the town council, directing widows to the Social Security office, raising money to pay the clubhouse rent. Few amateurs have ever volunteered to help. But now that a Presidential campaign has rolled around, they pour in, eager for the fun and busting their seams with enthusiasm. Can you blame him for feeling that they want to eat the icing off the cake he has been baking for so long?

But he stifles this resentment and sets them to work running the mimeograph or answering the telephone. A few (usually women) do well; some get bored after a few days and disappear. Still others feel insulted; they didn't come for this sort of scullery work. What they want is to make speeches, counsel candidates, devise strategy—in short, to take over the old pro's job.

With what tact he can dredge up, he dissuades them—and not merely to protect his selfish clutch on the levers of power. How to explain that he can't trust them with such assignments? They simply don't know the delicate network of personal relationships which holds the ward together. Being ignorant of the faces that have to be saved, the egos that require an extra oil massage, the ancient local enmities that must be respected, they might tear apart overnight the organization he has been knitting for decades.

Besides, these amateurs are mostly idealists, each dedicated to a Cause. To some, racial justice is the most important issue in the world. Others feel just as strongly about penal reform or Zionism, housing or the United Nations. Each expects the ward leader to share this burning devotion, to the exclusion of practically everything else.

God knows he tries. He hates racial discrimination as much as anybody, and besides he has twenty-three Negro families in the north end of the ward. But on the East Side he also has a bunch of Poles who don't like either Negroes or Jews; they seem to spend most of their time loathing Russia, and incidentally the United Nations, which tolerates Soviet membership. None of them gives a damn about penal reform, except old Mrs. Kruszwica, who has two sons in the state penitentiary. Both Poles and Negroes like low-rent housing, though; maybe they can be pulled together on that, if the other issues are soft-pedaled enough. . . . The real-estate men won't like it, of course, and neither will a couple of good contributors who worry a lot about high taxes. . . .

So his thoughts run, through a hundred other remembrances of his constituents' desires, antipathies, and conflicts. After all, his first job is to carry the ward in November. And that he can never do if he comes out with a ringing, clear-cut declaration on every cause which his amateur helpers hold so dear. Indeed, he has to muffle *their* enthusiasm when it gets to strident. Heavenly as their motives may be, he just can't afford to let these angels rush in where any experienced fool would fear to tread.

As a consequence, a lot of volunteers will conclude before Election Day (as my artist friend did) that the old pro is a man of no convictions. He has been lukewarm about their pet issues. He has evaded uncompromising pledges wherever he could. Sometimes his speeches sounded weaselly, as if he hoped two opposing groups might interpret them in different ways. And how about those rumors that he accepted a campaign contribution from a big realtor? Isn't it plain enough that he is guilty of the grossest kind of intellectual dishonesty?

Not to me, it isn't. For my money he looks like a good man, doing a job which is indispensable in any democracy and doing it just as honestly as he knows how. I think he deserves a lot more respect than he usually gets.

If you happen to be the other kind of amateur in politics—one of those who have developed some appreciation of the professionals—and if you in turn would like to gain their affection and trust, here is a simple recipe.

Go down to your local party headquarters on the morning after the election. It will reek of stale tobacco smoke, mimeograph ink, and cold coffee dregs. Chances are nobody will be there except the ward leader. He will be as tired as a man can get, but he will be making a limp effort to clean up the joint. Help him sweep up the crumpled Dixie cups, the trampled cigarette butts, and discarded campaign leaflets. Pick up about a million scraps of paper covered with penciled figures; nearly all the people who jammed the room last night were jotting down returns as they came in over a battery of telephones, and doing hasty sums in an effort to convince themselves that we might win yet, if the boys in the third precinct roll up a bigger majority than expected. (They didn't.) Fold up the rented chairs that have to be returned to an undertaking parlor. Call the phone company and tell them to take out the extra phones, and that, yes, the overdue bill will be paid in a day or two.

When the worst of the mess is scraped away, offer the old pro five dollars to help cover the campaign deficit. (There's always a deficit.) If he doesn't drop dead from astonishment, he will be your friend for life. For, in all probability, you will be the first volunteer who has ever given him any help *after* an election. And it could be that you have just taken the first step toward becoming a pro yourself.

November, 1960

2 : Unwritten Rules of American Politics

THE SAFEST BET anybody could make on the 1948 election is that the Progressive party will begin to come unraveled before the last votes are counted. The Communists, of course, have practically guaranteed that. The slick assurance with which they took over the management of the new party already has scared away a good many of the innocent idealists who ran a-whooping to join Gideon's army at the beginning of the campaign. By Christmas nearly all the rest (perhaps including Henry Wallace himself) can be expected to drop out of the ranks, nursing purple bruises of disillusionment. The remaining core of incurable fellow travelers most likely will dwindle, eventually, into a kind of Soviet counterpart of the late German-American Bund.

Even if Mr. Wallace weren't toting the red albatross around his neck, however, his enterprise almost certainly would fail to develop into a major party. For it violates the unwritten but enduring rules of American politics—and no group which ignored these rules has ever been able to grow out of the nursery stage.

Earlier efforts to form a third party—about one a generation —have fallen into much the same pattern. In particular, the basic argument for a third party always remains the same. It is a persuasive argument, especially for well-meaning people who have not had much firsthand experience in politics. It runs something like this:

"Both of the traditional American parties are outrageous frauds. Neither the Republicans nor the Democrats have any fundamental principles or ideology. They do not even have a program. In every campaign the platforms of both parties are simply collections of noble generalities, muffled in the vaguest possible language; and in each case the two platforms are very nearly identical.

"Obviously, then, both parties are merely machines for grabbing power and distributing favors. In their lust for office they are
quite willing to make a deal with anybody who can deliver a
sizable block of votes. As a result, each party has become an out-
landish cluster of local machines and special-interest groups
which have nothing in common except a lecherous craving for
the public trough.

"This kind of political system"—so the argument runs—"is
clearly meaningless. A man of high principles can never hope
to accomplish anything through the old parties, because they are
not interested in principle. Moreover, the whole arrangement
is so illogical that it affronts every intelligent citizen. Consequently, it is the duty of every liberal to work for a tidier and
more sensible political system.

"We ought to separate the sheep from the goats—to herd all
the progressives on one side of the fence and all the conservatives
on the other. Then politics really will have some meaning; we
will know who the enemy is and where he stands; every campaign
can be fought over clearly defined issues. The Europeans, who
are more sophisticated politically than we simple Americans,
discovered this long ago, and in each of their countries they
have arranged a neat political spectrum running from left to
right.

"As a first step toward such a logical scheme of politics, we
need to organize a progressive party with a precise ideology and
a clearly formulated program. Such a party will rally together
the labor movement, the farmers, and the white-collar liberals—
and then it should have little trouble in defeating the reactionary
businessmen who have long held such strategic positions in our
old-fashioned political system."

That, I believe, is a reasonably fair statement of the position
taken by most of the supporters of Mr. Wallace. It is much the
same as that once taken by the followers of Theodore Roosevelt
and old Bob La Follette, and a similar case has been argued in
season and out by most of the splinter groups of the American
left.

It sounds so plausible—at least on the surface—that it is

hard to see why it has never made much headway. Indeed, many veteran third-party enthusiasts have been able to account for their failure only by assuming a perverse and rockheaded stupidity among the American electorate. This, in turn, sometimes leads to a secret conviction that the dopes don't know what is good for them—and that what this country needs is a Strong Leader or a small tough party of the enlightened, which can herd the ignorant masses up the road to utopia whether they like it or not.

There is, however, one other possible explanation for the chronic failure of the third-party argument: maybe there is something wrong with the idea itself. Maybe it never gets to first base not because the American voter is a hopeless dullard but simply because he rejects instinctively a notion which doesn't make sense in terms of his own experience.

It can be argued, indeed, that a third-party movement usually is an attempt to transplant a European concept of politics into an American setting—and that it fails because our own political tradition is more vigorous, more deeply rooted, and far better suited to our own peculiar needs. Such attempts often serve a useful purpose, as we shall see; but it is not the purpose which the evangels of the new party have in mind. Their whole endeavor, in fact, springs out of a profound misunderstanding of the way in which the American political system works.

Moreover, it seems to me that a careful look will show that our native scheme of politics is a more complex and subtle conception than the crude blacks and whites of the European ideological parties. And finally there is considerable evidence that our own system—in spite of certain dangerous weaknesses—has on the whole worked out more successfully than the European.

II

Perhaps it is the very subtlety of the American political tradition which is responsible for the almost universal misunderstanding of it abroad. Every practicing American politician grasps its principles by instinct; if he does not, he soon retires into some less demanding profession. Moreover, the overwhelming majority of citizens have a sound working knowledge of the system, which they apply every day of their lives—though many of them might have a hard time putting that knowledge into words. There are almost no foreigners, however (except perhaps D. W. Brogan), who really understand the underlying theory. Even the editors of the London *Economist*—probably the most brilliant and well-informed group of journalists practicing anywhere today—display their bewilderment week after week. To them, and to virtually all other European observers, our whole political scene looks arbitrary, irrational, and dangerous.

Another reason for this misunderstanding lies in the fact that surprisingly little has been written about the rules of American politics during our generation. The newspapers, textbooks, and learned journals are running over with discussions of tactics and mechanics—but no one, so far as I know, has bothered to trace out the basic tradition for a good many years.

In fact, the most useful discussion of this tradition which I have come across is the work of John C. Calhoun, published nearly a century ago. Today of course he is an almost forgotten figure, and many people take it for granted that his views were discredited for good by the Civil War. I know of only one writer —Peter F. Drucker—who has paid much attention to him in recent years. It was he who described Calhoun's ideas as a "major if not the only key to the understanding of what is specifically and uniquely American in our political system"; and I am indebted to Dr. Drucker for much of the case set forth here.

Calhoun summed up his political thought in what he called the Doctrine of the Concurrent Majority. He saw the United States as a nation of tremendous and frightening diversity—a collection of many different climates, races, cultures, religions, and economic patterns. He saw the constant tension among all these special interests, and he realized that the central problem of American politics was to find some way of holding these conflicting groups together.

It could not be done by force; no one group was strong enough to impose its will on all the others. The goal could be achieved only by compromise—and no real compromise could be possible if any threat of coercion lurked behind the door. Therefore, Calhoun reasoned, every vital decision in American life would have to be adopted by a "concurrent majority"—by which he meant, in effect, a unanimous agreement of all interested parties. No decision which affected the interests of the slaveholders, he argued, should be taken without their consent; and by implication he would have given a similar veto to every other special interest, whether it be labor, management, the Catholic Church, old-age pensioners, the silver miners, or the corn-growers of the Middle West.

Under the goad of the slavery issue, Calhoun was driven to state his doctrine in an extreme and unworkable form. If every sectional interest had been given the explicit, legal veto power which he called for, the government obviously would have been paralyzed. It is the very essence of the idea of "concurrent majority" that it cannot be made legal and official. It can operate effectively only as an informal, highly elastic, and generally accepted understanding. Perhaps the best example is the Quaker church meeting, where decisions are not reached by formal vote at all, but rather by a give-and-take discussion which continues until "the sense of the meeting" jells and is accepted by everybody present.

Moreover, government by concurrent majority can exist only when no one power is strong enough to dominate completely, *and then only when all of the contending interest groups recognize and abide by certain rules of the game.*

These rules are the fundamental bond of unity in American political life. They can be summed up as a habit of extraordinary toleration, plus "equality" in the peculiar American meaning of that term which cannot be translated into any other language, even into the English of Great Britain. Under these rules every group tacitly binds itself to tolerate the interests and opinions of every other group. It must not try to impose its views on others, nor can it press its own special interests to the point where they seriously endanger the interests of other groups or of the nation as a whole.

Furthermore, each group must exercise its implied veto with responsibility and discrimination; and in times of great emergency it must forsake its veto right altogether. It dare not be intransigent or doctrinaire. It must make every conceivable effort to compromise, relying on its veto only as a last resort. For if any player wields this weapon recklessly, the game will break up —or all the other players will turn on him in anger, suspend the rules for the time being, and maul those very interests he is trying so desperately to protect. That was what happened in 1860, when the followers of Calhoun carried his doctrine to an unbearable extreme. Much the same thing, on a less violent scale, happened to American business interests in 1933 and to the labor unions in 1947.

This is the somewhat elusive sense, it seems to me, in which Calhoun's theory has been adopted by the American people. But elusive and subtle as it may be, it remains the basic rule of the game of politics in this country—and in this country alone. Nothing comparable exists in any other nation, although the British, in a different way, have applied their own rules of responsibility and self-restraint.

It is a rule which operates unofficially and entirely outside the Constitution—but it has given us a method by which all the official and Constitutional organs of government can be made to work. It also provides a means of selecting leaders on all levels of our political life, for hammering out policies, and for organizing and managing the conquest of political power.

III

The way in which this tradition works in practice can be observed most easily in Congress. Anyone who has ever tried to push through a piece of legislation quickly discovers that the basic units of organization on Capitol Hill are not the parties but the so-called blocs, which are familiar to everyone who reads a newspaper. There are dozens of them—the farm bloc, the silver bloc, the friends of labor, the business group, the Midwestern isolationists, the public power bloc—and they all cut across party lines.

They are loosely organized and pretty blurred at the edges, so that every Congressman belongs at different times to several different blocs. Each of them represents a special-interest group. Each of them ordinarily works hand-in-hand with that group's Washington lobby. In passing, it might be noted that these lobbies are by no means the cancerous growth which is sometimes pictured in civics textbooks. They have become an indispensable part of the political machine—the accepted channel through which American citizens make their wishes known and play their day-to-day role in the process of government. Nor is their influence measured solely by the size of the bankrolls and propaganda apparatus which they have at their disposal. Some of the smallest and poorest lobbies often are more effective than their well-heeled rivals. For example, Russell Smith, the one-man lobby of the Farmers Union, was largely responsible for conceiving and nursing through Congress the Employment Act of 1946, one of the most far-reaching measures adopted since the war.

Now it is an unwritten but firm rule of Congress that no important bloc shall ever be voted down—under normal circumstances—on any matter which touches its own rival interests. Each bloc, in other words, has a tacit right of veto on legislation in which it is primarily concerned. The ultimate expression of this right is the institution—uniquely American— of the filibuster in the Senate. Recently it has acquired a bad name among liberals because the Southern conservatives have used it ruthlessly to fight off civil rights legislation and protect white supremacy. Not so long ago, however, the filibuster was the stoutest weapon of such men as Norris and the La Follettes in defending many a progressive cause—and under some future Republican regime, the surviving handful of liberal Senators may well have occasion to use it again.

Naturally no bloc wants to exercise its veto power except when it is absolutely forced to—for this is a negative power, and one which is always subject to retaliation. Positive power to influence legislation, on the other hand, can be gained only by conciliation, compromise, and endless horse-trading.

The farm bloc, for instance, normally needs no outside aid to halt the passage of a hostile bill. As a last resort, three or four strong-lunged statesmen from the corn belt can always filibuster it to death in the Senate. If the bloc wants to put through a measure to support agricultural prices, however, it can succeed only by enlisting the help of other powerful special-interest groups. Consequently, it must always be careful not to antagonize any potential ally by a reckless use of the veto; and it must be willing to pay for such help by throwing its support from time to time behind legislation sought by the labor bloc, the National Association of Manufacturers, or the schoolteachers' lobby.

The classic alliance of this sort was formed in the early days of the New Deal, when most of the Roosevelt legislation was shoved onto the statute books by a temporary coalition of the farm bloc and urban labor, occasionally reinforced by such minor allies as the public-power group and spokesmen for the northern Negroes. Mr. Roosevelt's political genius rested largely on his ability to put together a program which would offer something to each of these groups without fatally antagonizing any of them, and then to time the presentation of each bill so that he would always retain enough bargaining power to line up a Congressional majority. It also was necessary for him to avoid the veto of the business group, which viewed much of this legislation as a barbarous assault upon its privileges; and for this purpose he employed another traditional technique, which we shall examine a little later.

This process of trading blocs of votes is generally known as logrolling, and frequently it is deplored by the more innocent type of reformer. Such pious disapproval has no effect whatever on any practicing politician. He knows that logrolling is a sensible and reasonably fair device, and that without it Congress could scarcely operate at all.

In fact, Congress gradually has developed a formal apparatus —the committee system—which is designed to make the logrolling process as smooth and efficient as possible. There is no parallel system anywhere; the committees of Parliament and of the Continental legislative bodies work in an entirely different way.

Obviously the main business of Congress—the hammering out of a series of compromises between many special-interest groups—cannot be conducted satisfactorily on the floor of the House or Senate. The meetings there are too large and far too public for such delicate negotiations. Moreover, every speech delivered on the floor must be aimed primarily at the voters back home, and not at the other members in the chamber. Therefore, Congress—especially the House—does nearly all its work in the closed sessions of its various committees, simply because the committee room is the only place where it is possible to arrange a compromise acceptable to all major interests affected.

For this reason, it is a matter of considerable importance to get a bill before the proper committee. Each committee serves as a forum for a particular cluster of special interests, and the assignment of a bill to a specific committee often decides which interest groups shall be recognized officially as affected by the measure and therefore entitled to a hand in its drafting. "Who is to have standing before the committee" is the technical term, and it is this decision that frequently decides the fate of the legislation.

IV

Calhoun's principles of the concurrent majority and of sectional compromise operate just as powerfully, though sometimes less obviously, in every other American political institution. Our cabinet, for example, is the only one in the world where the members are charged by law with the representation of special interests—labor, agriculture, commerce, and so on. In other countries, each agency of government is at least presumed to act for the nation as a whole; here most agencies are expected to behave as servants for one interest or another. The Veterans Administration, to cite the most familiar case, is frankly intended to look out for Our Boys; the Maritime Commission is the spokesman for the shipping industry; the National Labor Relations Board, as originally established under the Wagner Act, was explicitly intended to build up the bargaining power of the unions.

Even within a single department, separate agencies are sometimes set up to represent conflicting interests. Thus in the Department of Agriculture under the New Deal the old Triple-A became primarily an instrument of the large-scale commercial farmers, as represented by their lobby, the Farm Bureau Federation; while the Farm Security Administration went to bat for the tenants, the farm laborers, and the little subsistence farmers, as represented by the Farmers Union.

This is one reason why federal agencies often struggle so bitterly against each other, and why the position of the administration as a whole on any question can be determined only after a long period of interbureau squabbling and compromise. Anyone who was in Washington during the war will remember how these goings-on always confused and alarmed our British allies.

Calhoun's laws also govern the selection of virtually every candidate for public office. The mystery of "eligibility" which has eluded most foreign observers simply means that a candidate must not be unacceptable to any important special-interest group—a negative rather than a positive qualification. A notorious case of this process at work was the selection of Mr. Truman as the Democrats' Vice Presidential candidate in 1944. As Edward J. Flynn, the Boss of the Bronx, has pointed out in his memoirs, Truman was the one man "who would hurt . . . least" as Roosevelt's running mate. Many stronger men were disqualified, Flynn explained, by the tacit veto of one sectional interest or another. Wallace was unacceptable to the businessmen and to many local party machines. Byrnes was distasteful to the Catholics, the Negroes, and organized labor. Rayburn came from the wrong part of the country. Truman, however, came from a border state, his labor record was good, he had not antagonized the conservatives, and—as Flynn put it—"he had never made any 'racial' remarks. He just dropped into the slot."

The same kind of considerations govern the selection of candidates right down to the county, city, and precinct levels. Flynn, one of the most successful political operators of our time, explained in some detail the complicated job of making up a ticket in his own domain. Each of the main population groups in the Bronx—Italians, Jews, and Irish Catholics—must be properly represented on the list of nominees, and so must each of the main geographical divisions.

Comparable traditions govern the internal political life of the American Legion, the Federation of Women's Clubs, university student bodies, labor unions, Rotary Clubs, and the thousands of other quasi-political institutions which are so characteristic of our society and which give us such a rich fabric of spontaneous local government.

The stronghold of Calhoun's doctrine, however, is the American party—the wonder and despair of foreigners who cannot fit it into any of their concepts of political life.

The purpose of European parties is, of course, to divide men of different ideologies into coherent and disciplined organizations. The historic role of the American party, on the other hand, is not to divide but to unite. That task was imposed by simple necessity. If a division into ideological parties had been attempted, in addition to all the other centrifugal forces in this country, it very probably would have proved impossible to hold the nation together. The Founding Fathers understood this thoroughly; hence Washington's warning against "factions."

Indeed, on the one occasion when we did develop two ideological parties, squarely opposing each other on an issue of principle, the result was civil war. Fortunately, that was our last large-scale experiment with a third party formed on an ideological basis—for in its early days that is just what the Republican party was.

Its radical wing, led by such men as Thaddeus Stevens, Seward, and Chase, made a determined and skillful effort to substitute principles for interests as the foundations of American political life. Even within their own party, however, they were opposed by such practical politicians as Lincoln and Johnson—men who distrusted fanaticism in any form—and by the end of the Reconstruction period the experiment had been abandoned. American politics then swung back into its normal path and has never veered far away from it since. Although Calhoun's cause was defeated, his political theory came through the Civil War stronger than ever.

The result is that the American party has no permanent program and no fixed aim, except to win elections. Its one constant purpose is to unite the largest possible number of divergent interest groups in the pursuit of power. Its unity is one of compromise, not of dogma. It must—if it hopes to succeed—appeal to considerable numbers on both the left and the right, to rich and poor, Protestant and Catholic, farmer and industrial worker, native and foreign born.

It must be ready to bid for the support of any group that can deliver a sizable chunk of votes, accepting that group's program with whatever modifications may be necessary to reconcile the other members of the party. If sun worship, or Existentialism, or the nationalization of industry should ever attract any significant following in this country, you can be sure that both parties would soon whip up a plank designed to win it over.

This does not mean, of course, that there are no differences between the major parties. For the last fifty years the Republican party obviously has been, in general, the more conservative; the Democratic party the more liberal. The Republicans usually have spoken for the business community, the farmers of the Northeast and Middle West, certain professional men (especially physicians), and many residents of the smaller towns. The Democrats, on the other hand, normally can count on the support of most labor unions, and a majority of the Negroes and other ethnic groups. While it draws the votes of some Southern and Western farm organizations, the core of its strength has long been in the big cities. (There are of course

many exceptions to these rough generalizations. A few labor
unions, for example, usually endorse Republican candidates, and
a number of eminent businessmen—including for many years
the head of the J. P. Morgan banking firm—are staunch Democrats.)

What it does mean is simply that neither party operates with
an immutable ideology, or the fixed support of any class or
group. It took only a decade for the Republicans to accept the
Social Security program, which they once opposed so bitterly;
and only a generation for the mass of Negro voters to shift
from the Republican to the Democratic camp.

The ability to absorb new ideas (along with the enthusiasts
behind them) and to mold them into a shape acceptable to the
party's standpatters is, perhaps, the chief measure of vitality in
the party's leadership. Such ideas almost never germinate within
the party itself. They are stolen—very often from third parties.

Indeed, the historic function of third parties has been to
sprout new issues, nurse them along until they have gathered a
body of supporters worth stealing, and then to turn them over
(often reluctantly) to the major parties. A glance at the old
platforms of the Populists, the Bull Moosers, and the Socialists
will show what an astonishingly high percentage of their once-
radical notions have been purloined by both Republicans and
Democrats—and enacted into law. Thus the income tax, child-
labor laws, minimum wages, regulation of railroads and utilities,
and old-age pensions have all become part of the American Way
of Life. In similar fashion, Mr. Wallace has forced both the old
parties to pay a good deal more attention to such matters as
civil rights than they ever would have done on their own initia-
tive. He has compelled them to bid—and to bid high—for a
handsome block of Negro votes.

While each major party must always stand alert to grab a
promising new issue, it also must be careful never to scare off
any of the big, established interest groups. For as soon as it
alienates any one of them, it finds itself in a state of crisis.

For sixteen years the Republicans lost much of their standing as a truly national party because they had made themselves unacceptable to labor. Similarly, the Democrats, during the middle stage of the New Deal, incurred the wrath of the business interests. Ever since Mr. Truman was plumped into the White House, the Democratic leadership has struggled desperately—though rather ineptly—to regain the confidence of businessmen without at the same time driving organized labor out of the ranks. It probably would be safe to predict that if the Republican party is to regain a long period of health, it must make an equally vigorous effort to win back the confidence of at least a substantial segment of labor. For the permanent veto of any major element in American society means political death—as the ghosts of the Federalists and Whigs can testify.

V

The weaknesses of the American political system are obvious—much more obvious, in fact, than its virtues. These weaknesses have been so sharply criticized for the past hundred years, by a procession of able analysts ranging from Walter Bagehot to Thomas K. Finletter and Joseph Clark, that it is hardly necessary to mention them here. It is enough to note that most of the criticism has been aimed at two major flaws.

First, it is apparent that the doctrine of the concurrent majority is a negative one—a principle of inaction. A strong government, capable of rapid and decisive action, is difficult to achieve under a system which forbids it to do anything until virtually everybody acquiesces. In times of crisis, a dangerously long period of debate and compromise usually is necessary before any administration can carry out the drastic measures needed. The depression of the early thirties, the crisis in foreign policy which ended only with Pearl Harbor, the long struggle over civil rights for Negroes all illustrate this recurring problem.

This same characteristic of our system gives undue weight to the small but well-organized pressure group—especially when it is fighting *against* something. Hence a few power companies were able to block for twenty years the sensible use of the Muscle Shoals dam, which eventually became the nucleus of TVA; and an alliance of the railroads, rail unions, and Eastern port interests held up for many years the development of the St. Lawrence seaway.

The negative character of our political rules also makes it uncommonly difficult for us to choose a President. Many of our outstanding political operatives—notably those who serve in the Senate—are virtually barred from a Presidential nomination because they are forced to get on record on too many issues. Inevitably they offend some important interest group, and therefore become "unavailable." Moreover, the very qualities of caution and inoffensiveness which make a good candidate—Harding and Coolidge come most readily to mind—are likely to make a bad President.

An even more serious flaw in our scheme of politics is the difficulty in finding anybody to speak for the country as a whole. Calhoun would have argued that the national interest is merely the sum of all the various special interests, and therefore needs no spokesmen of its own—but in this case he clearly was wrong.

In practice, we tend to settle sectional and class conflicts at the expense of the nation as a whole—with results painful to all of us. The labor troubles in the spring of 1946, for instance, could be settled only on a basis acceptable to *both* labor and management: that is, on the basis of higher wages *plus* higher prices. The upshot was an inflationary spiral which is damaging everybody—and at this writing there is a good deal of mournful evidence that the process is about to be repeated. Countless other instances, from soil erosion to the rash of billboards along our highways, bear witness to the American tendency to neglect matters which are "only" of national interest, and therefore are left without a recognized sponsor.

Over the generations we have developed a series of practices and institutions which partly remedy these weaknesses, although we are still far from a complete cure. One such development has been the gradual strengthening of the Presidency as against Congress. As the only man elected by all the people, the President inevitably has had to take over many of the policy-making and leadership functions which the Founding Fathers originally assigned to the legislators. This meant, of course, that he could no longer behave merely as an obedient executor of the will of Congress, but was forced into increasingly frequent conflicts with Capitol Hill.

Today we have come to recognize that this conflict is one of the most important obligations of the Presidency. No really strong executive tries to avoid it—he accepts it as an essential part of his job. If he simply tries to placate the pressure groups which speak through Congress, history writes him down as a failure. For it is his duty to enlist the support of many minorities for measures rooted in the national interest, reaching beyond their own immediate concern—and, if necessary, to stand up against the ravening minorities for the interest of the whole.

In recent times this particular part of the President's job has been made easier by the growth of the Theory of Temporary Emergencies. All of us—or nearly all—have come around to admitting that in time of emergency special-interest groups must forgo their right of veto. As a result, the President often is tempted to scare up an emergency to secure legislation which could not be passed under any other pretext. Thus, most of the New Deal bills were introduced as "temporary emergency measures," although they were clearly intended to be permanent from the very first; for in no other way could Mr. Roosevelt avoid the veto of the business interests. Again, in 1939 the threat of war enabled the President to push through much legislation which would have been impossible under normal circumstances.

VI

Because we have been so preoccupied with trying to patch up the flaws in our system, we have often overlooked its unique elements of strength. The chief of these is its ability to minimize conflict—not by suppressing the conflicting forces but by absorbing and utilizing them. The result is a society which is both free and reasonably stable—a government which is as strong and effective as most dictatorships, but which can still adapt itself to social change.

The way in which the American political organism tames down the extremists of both the left and right is always fascinating to watch. Either party normally is willing to embrace any group or movement which can deliver votes—but in return it requires these groups to adjust their programs to fit the traditions, beliefs, and prejudices of the majority of the people. The fanatics, the implacable radicals cannot hope to get to first base in American politics until they abandon their fanaticism and learn the habits of conciliation. As a consequence, it is almost impossible for political movements here to become entirely irresponsible and to draw strength from the kind of demagogic obstruction which has nurtured both communist and fascist movements abroad.

The same process which gentles down the extremists also prods along the political laggards. As long as it is in a state of health, each American party has a conservative and a liberal wing. Sometimes one is dominant, sometimes the other—but even when the conservative element is most powerful, it must reckon with the left-wingers in its own family. At the moment the Republican party certainly is in one of its more conservative phases; yet it contains such men as Senators Morse, Aiken, Flanders, Tobey, and Baldwin, who are at least as progressive as most of the old New Dealers. They, and their counterparts in the Democratic party, exert a steady tug to the left which prevents either party from lapsing into complete reaction.

The strength of this tug is indicated by the fact that the major New Deal reforms have now been almost universally accepted. A mere ten years ago, the leading Republicans, plus many conservative Democrats, were hell-bent on wiping out Social Security, TVA, SEC, minimum-wage laws, rural electrification, and all the other dread innovations of the New Deal.

Today no Presidential aspirant would dare suggest the repeal of a single one of them. In this country there simply is no place for a hard core of irreconcilable reactionaries, comparable to those political groups in France which have never yet accepted the reforms of the French Revolution.

This American tendency to push extremists of both the left and right toward a middle position has enabled us, so far, to escape class warfare. This is no small achievement for any political system; for class warfare cannot be tolerated by a modern industrial society. If it seriously threatens, it is bound to be suppressed by some form of totalitarianism, as it has been in the not-very-distant past in Germany, Spain, Italy, Russia, and most of Eastern Europe.

In fact, suppression might be termed the normal method of settling conflicts in continental Europe, where parties traditionally have been drawn up along ideological battle lines. Every political campaign becomes a religious crusade; each party is fanatically convinced that it and it alone has truth by the tail; each party is certain that its opponents not only are wrong, but wicked. If the sacred ideology is to be established beyond challenge, no heresy can be tolerated. Therefore it becomes a duty not only to defeat the enemy at the polls, but to wipe him out. Any suggestion of compromise must be rejected as treason and betrayal of the true faith. The party must be disciplined like an army, and if it cannot win by other means it must be ready to take up arms in deadly fact.

Politics thus becomes merely a prelude to civil war—and all too often the prelude is short. In Italy the Partisan brigades are drilling today on the same parade grounds where Mussolini's Blackshirts once trained for their march on Rome. And in France both Communists and de Gaullists are reported to be squirreling away Bren guns against the day when each expects to "save the Republic" from the other.

Under this kind of political system the best that can be hoped for is a prolonged deadlock between parties which are too numerous and weak to exterminate one another. The classic example is prewar France, where six revolutions or near-revolutions broke out within a century, where cabinets fell every weekend, and no government could ever become strong enough to govern effectively. The more usual outcome is a complete victory for one ideology or another, after a brief period of electioneering, turmoil, and fighting in the streets; then comes the liquidation of the defeated.

Because this sort of ideological politics is so foreign to our native tradition, neither Socialists, Communists, nor Fascists have ever been accepted as normal parties. So long as that tradition retains its very considerable vitality, it seems to me unlikely that any third party founded on an ideological basis can take root. The notion of a ruthless and unlimited class struggle, the concept of a master race, a fascist elite, or a proletariat which is entitled to impose its will on all others—these are ideas which are incompatible with the main current of American political life. The uncompromising ideologist, of whatever faith, appears in our eyes peculiarly "un-American," simply because he cannot recognize the rule of the concurrent majority, nor can he accept the rules of mutual toleration which are necessary to make it work. Unless he forsakes his ideology, he cannot even understand that basic principle of American politics which was perhaps best expressed by Judge Learned Hand: "The spirit of liberty is the spirit which is not too sure that it is right."

November, 1948

POSTSCRIPT

Fifteen years later, the thesis set forth in this article still seems to me basically valid. Apparently a considerable number of political scientists think so too, because it has been more widely reprinted than anything I have written; it is included in more than a dozen textbooks and volumes of readings on American politics. As late as 1963 the United States Information Agency published a simplified version of it in Ameryka, its magazine circulated in Russia and Poland; the Communist party of the latter country took it seriously enough to print a spirited rejoinder in the local press.

In recent months, however, I have come to believe that the article may present too optimistic a picture of the American political system. During the last decade that system has developed serious flaws—mostly growing out of the overrepresentation of rural voters in both state and national legislatures—which are not touched on here. I suspect that these faults may become so dangerous in the years just ahead that they will eventually force some basic changes both in the political system and in our constitutional structure. For until such changes come, many of our problems—for example, the governing of our new supercities, such as the megalopolis stretching from Bangor, Maine, to Norfolk, Virginia, and others spreading out from the Chicago and Los Angeles areas—are likely to prove insoluble. The ancient political pattern of states and counties simply doesn't fit the kind of new society we are developing; and until some kind of sensible adjustment is worked out, our greatest danger may be not Creeping Socialism but Creeping Anarchy. —*J. F.*

3 : Why Is the Conservative Voice So Hoarse?

WHEN *National Review,* a magazine which described itself as "frankly, conservative," brought out its first issue, a good many people bought it with sympathetic curiosity, feeling that a conservative journal of opinion would be a remarkably useful addition to the American scene.

It is true that the overwhelming majority of our newspapers and magazines are basically conservative, and have been for decades. Yet in all these years they have failed to perform one function which is essential, both to the conservative interest and to the health of society. They have never developed a lucid, coherent body of conservative doctrine.

By and large, their conservatism has expressed itself merely in lopsided news coverage, invective, and in the kind of blind, automatic opposition which provokes accusations about "the one-party press." As a consequence, a reader has no difficulty in discovering what our conservatives are against; but he has great trouble in finding out what they are for. Their journalistic spokesmen—from David Lawrence to Robert Welch, from the Chicago *Tribune* to the Dallas *News*, from *Time* to *Facts Forum* —rarely give any hint of a positive program; they apparently conceive their role as almost solely critical.

Often, too, they seem to think of conservatism in purely economic terms. Money and property are of course matters of concern—and proper concern—to every genuine conservative; but they are not the only questions, or even the most important. The great conservative leaders of history have never believed that they could express all their ideals by shouting: "Lower taxes!" Instead they have focused primarily on the underlying problems of the human community—the questions of leadership; of equality (how much of it is possible, and how much a good thing?); of continuity and order; the obligations of the strong to the weak (and the other way round); the privileges necessary to encourage virtue and high achievement in culture and political life; and the safeguards needed to keep such privileges from being abused.

The contemporary application of these issues rarely gets discussed in any of our supposedly conservative publications. Nowhere in America is there any organ comparable to the London *Economist*, which argues the conservative position, week after week, with style, logic, responsibility, a wealth of documented fact, and a solid philosophic underpinning.

(In the mass-circulation field, the Cowles publications—including the Des Moines *Register and Tribune*, the Minneapolis *Star and Tribune*, and *Look* magazine—probably achieve the closest approach to a consistently intelligent conservative point of view. *Fortune* often presents impressive essays in conservative thought; but since it deliberately limits its circulation to a relatively small circle of business executives, it is generally regarded as a managerial trade journal rather than a general magazine.) This lack is especially serious because the conservative politicians of our generation also have failed to develop a systematic body of ideas. In earlier days, America spawned plenty of articulate conservative thinkers—a succession running from Hamilton and Randolph to Adams, Webster, Calhoun, Lincoln, Hanna, Lodge, and Theodore Roosevelt. They knew what they believed, and could explain it with wit and eloquence. But about 1914 the bloodline apparently played out. Since then we not only have produced no American equivalent of Winston Churchill; we haven't even come up with a Lord Percy, an L. S. Amery, or a Douglas Jerrold.

Indeed, the common trait of our recent conservatives seems to be an inability to express themselves. The archetype was Silent Cal Coolidge, who made muteness his trademark. His style was matched by Harding's sprung syntax, the mumbled apologetics of Herbert Hoover, the earnest Eisenhower platitudes. About the only exceptions to this tongue-tied tradition are Douglas MacArthur—who fairly revels in besequined prose—and the late Senator Robert A. Taft.

His talent for marshaling his ideas in a plain but forceful language promptly made Taft the dominant conservative of his time. But he, too, neglected to put together anything which could be called a philosophy of modern American conservatism. Much of his best thought went into Senate speeches; and they often dealt with the technicalities of a particular piece of legislation—for example, his brilliant defense of public housing—rather than with the large questions of human society. His one attempt to write comprehensively about fundamental issues was his little book on foreign policy; and it was far from successful, because these were the problems he had studied least. Taft's genius burned itself out in a remarkable feat of personal leadership—leaving hardly any residue of doctrine to guide and inspire his successors.

The Eisenhower Administration suffers woefully from this inherited case of intellectual laryngitis. Obviously The Team believes it is operating on some consistent political theory. Just as obviously, none of its members (including its Captain Emeritus) has ever managed to say what it is—at least not in terms that anybody can remember for five minutes. (Gabriel Hauge, the White House seer-in-residence, has perhaps made the best stab at it; but he speaks the dialect of the economist, not the political leader.) When FDR was in full bloom, nearly every man-in-the-street could tell you what the New Deal meant to him. But who ever met a taxi driver who could define Dynamic Conservatism?*

This handicap is particularly embarrassing because the conservatives (of both parties) are up against an articulate—not to say garrulous—opposition. Within the last few months books have appeared from the typewriters of Truman, Stevenson, Acheson, Bowles, and a gaggle of lesser Democrats. In fact, there is scarcely a liberal Democrat in the Senate who doesn't have at least one volume to his credit, and a dozen members of the House scribble surreptitiously at their manuscripts during every dull speech. But books by Republicans—and Democrats of the stamp of Byrd and Russell—are scarcer than Gutenberg Bibles. Similarly, every magazine editor knows that scores of leading liberals are eager to write articles at the flutter of a check—while it is all but impossible to coax a manuscript out of any conservative of standing.

If there is an explanation, it is a well-kept secret. The more uncharitable liberals sometimes suggest that conservatives aren't bright enough to write anything; but this argument—while it may be valid for such concrete stanchions of Republicanism as Joe Martin and Senator Bricker—hardly explains the silence of the party's eggheads. George Humphrey, for example, is by all

---

* John Foster Dulles' *War or Peace* (Macmillan, 1950) and Henry L. Stimson's memoirs (with McGeorge Bundy, *On Active Service in Peace and War*, Harper, 1948) are the most recent major works by conservative statesmen. A considerable number of semi-academic books on conservatism have, of course, been published in the last few years by such nonpolitical figures as Russell Kirk, Peter Viereck, Gordon Harrison, Clinton Rossiter, Daniel Bell, and Walter Lippmann; but their sale has been modest, and they do not yet appear to have had much impact either on public opinion or on working politicians.

evidence the best mind to ornament the Treasury Department in twenty-five years. In comparison with a Snyder, a Morgenthau, or a Woodin, his intellectual radiance is blinding; and in high-level conferences he expresses his views with pungency and vigor. Yet on at least one occasion, when he was invited to state these same views in either a book or a magazine article, he recoiled in horror as if he had been asked to go partners in a bawdy house.

The mystery is all the more puzzling because the Administration is composed largely of businessmen, supposedly well grounded in the value of advertising and publicity. And it is a mystery with unfortunate consequences—for the country urgently needs an explicit, continuous statement of the conservative doctrine. So long as it is lacking, our political debate is not only one-sided; it also is likely to be confused and irresponsible. For instance, McCarthy's assault on the basic conservative principles of fair play, due process, and orderly government could never have got very far if the nation's conservatives had understood their own principles clearly enough to fight for them. (Senators Watkins, Flanders, and Fulbright, to their eternal credit, did understand, and were willing to fight, with historic results.)

In these circumstances, many people welcomed *National Review* with considerable hope. Here, maybe, was the long-awaited voice. . . .

These hopes did not survive the first half-dozen issues. By that time it was plain that the new magazine was an organ not of conservatism but of radicalism.

Its radicalism is of the right, rather than the left—but the distinction is not very important. In its editorial policy, emotional attitude, and even its format, it strikingly resembles its brethren at the opposite end of the political spectrum: the *Nation*, the defunct *New Masses*, and (in Britain) the *New Statesman* and the *Tribune*, spokesmen for the Bevanite wing of the Labour party. It exhibits all the classic stigmata of extremist journalism.

1. It is dedicated to the Conspiracy Theory of politics. With

the leftists, it is an article of faith that a little clique of evil men in Wall Street runs the country; *National Review* believes that The Liberals "run just about *everything.*" ("The Liberals," according to its definition, include practically everybody from President Eisenhower to Earl Browder. The only true "conservatives" seem to be McCarthy, Jenner, Knowland, Fulton Lewis, Jr., Westbrook Pegler, and their disciples.)

2. It is dreadfully earnest. The editorial tone is one of humorless indignation, almost indistinguishable from that of *The Daily Worker.* Most of its space is devoted to sermons, rather than to factual reporting.

3. It has grave doubts about freedom. Where the extremists of the left suspect that freedom is not compatible with economic security, the writers for *National Review* hint that freedom is not compatible with political security. Just as the leftists yearn for planning, so these apostles of the far right yearn for discipline—often with heavy clerical overtones.

4. It is utopian. As the Communist theorists want to bound ahead to 1984, it would like to leap back to 1928. Neither has any patience with the inch-by-inch realities of contemporary politics.

5. It has a persecution complex. In the first issue it complained that "radical conservatives in this country" are "being suppressed or mutilated by the Liberals." An echo, clearly, of the familiar whine of "progressives" that they are being stomped under the iron heel of the capitalist bosses.

6. It is unhampered by consistency. *National Review* is violently opposed to communism; but it is equally opposed to fighting communism with the economic and propaganda weapons which are likely to be decisive, during the next ten years, in the still uncommitted areas of the world.

7. Like most of the extremist little magazines, it seems to be aimed primarily at an audience of True Believers. As Eric Hoffer noted in his classic work on this species, they are emotional people who throw themselves frantically into a cause —often to make up for some kind of frustration in their

private lives. They form the hard core of many religious, nationalist, and revolutionary movements; they have great capacity, in Hoffer's words, for "enthusiasm, fervent hope, hatred, and intolerance . . . blind faith and single-hearted allegiance." They are the precise opposite of conservatives.

Maybe all of this should have been expected. The symptoms were foreshadowed in two books by William F. Buckley, Jr., editor of the new magazine: *God and Man at Yale* and *McCarthy and His Enemies*. Moreover, some of his editorial associates have, themselves, long been True Believers. Yet it is sad to see an opportunity missed. . . .

No doubt *National Review* will serve a useful purpose in feeding the emotional hungers of a small congregation of the faithful; and it will have a certain interest for students of political splinter movements. But the far greater need for a journal to express the philosophy of modern American conservatism still remains unfilled.

March, 1956

4 : The Country Slickers Take Us Again

OUR PAMPERED TYRANT, the American farmer, is about to get his boots licked again by both political parties.

Before next November's elections, Democrats and Republicans alike will be groveling all over the barnyard as they court the country vote—but the Democratic antics will be the most embarrassing. Nearly all Democratic politicians are now convinced that the farmers offer the largest single block of detachable votes—and many seem willing to use almost any tool of demagoguery which promises to pry it loose from the Republican grasp.

So when Congress opens up for business, the Democrats will set up a pious, baritone moan about the wretched plight of American agriculture. They will pass a farm-relief bill, loaded till its axles creak with rigid price supports, loans, "conservation" payments, and other shabbily disguised subsidies. Then they will pray for the President to veto it. Quite possibly he will have the courage and honesty to do just that—and Democratic Congressmen will then be sure that they have the farm vote in a gunny sack.

This cynicism is probably justified. The record of recent elections indicates that the farmer is generally eager to sell his vote to the highest bidder, and that city people are too indifferent (or benumbed) to resent this legalized corruption, even when the bribe is lifted right out of their own pockets. But don't blame the politicians for this record. They didn't make it. We did—all of us.

Our only excuse is that for twenty years—from 1920 until 1940—the farmers *were* in pretty bad shape. During these decades, city people got in the habit of giving them handouts, and haven't yet discovered that times have changed. The farmer not only got in the habit of accepting his dole; he came to believe that it belonged to him permanently, as a matter of right. When any hog keeps his jowls in the trough long enough, he gets to thinking he owns the trough.

Just how rugged is the farmer's plight today?

You should have such a plight.

When Harrison Salisbury of the New York Times traveled through the Middle West last summer, he reported that "The ordinary Iowa farmer . . . has a minimum of two new cars and they are usually brand-new Buicks or Oldsmobiles or Cadillacs." These Iowa swine-growers and steer-fatteners are of course better off than many of their brethren in other states. Still, the average farm family, taken the country over, has assets totaling about $22,000.

It is true that the slice of the national income which goes to agriculture has shrunk in the last four years—that is what the moaning is all about—but the farm population has dwindled too. As a result, the individual farmer isn't much worse off— only about 5 per cent—than he was at the peak of his scandalous wartime prosperity.

Everybody knows that it is the taxpayer who keeps the farmers (or rather, a favored group of them) living in clover and Cadillacs; but even the taxpayer seldom realizes how much it is costing him. The Treasury spent nearly $3 billion during the last fiscal year to support farm prices—but that was just the beginning. The scheme is rigged to nick the taxpayer twice; once when he pays to take surplus crops off the market, thus propping up prices; and again when he has to pay these artificial prices at the grocery store.

If you complain, the farmer—or rather the highly skilled lobbyists who front for him in Washington—have a plausible answer:

"Why shouldn't I get a subsidy, when nearly everybody else does? Look at the airlines, the steamship companies, the manufacturers with their tariffs—all getting fat at the taxpayer's expense. That has become The American Way of Life."

But there is a catch to this argument. The other subsidized industries are producing something that we need, or at least can use. The farmers are being subsidized to produce millions of tons of things—cotton, wheat, rice, butter, and so on—which we don't need, can't possibly use, and can't even give away.

The government has "invested" $7 billion to hide these useless crops away in dead storage. Wheat, for example, almost a billion bushels of it, is now overflowing from every grain elevator in the country, stored in old Liberty ships tied up as floating warehouses, heaped in long yellow mounds on the bare ground all through the Southwest. Nobody wants it, because wheat is in mountainous surplus the world over. Yet Washington is encouraging the farmers to plant still more, and promising to take it off their hands at a guaranteed high price.

Who gets the money?

Not the needy farmers. There *are* some of them—about one

and a half million families whose acreage produces less than $1,000 a year. If the federal bounty went to them, maybe it could be justified as sheer charity. In fact, relatively little of this river of greenbacks ever trickles in their direction. The big subsidies go to the big farmers.

Such as the Delta Pine & Land Company of Scott, Mississippi. It has $1,292,472 worth of cotton "under loan" to the government. ("Loan" is part of the elaborate semantics used by the farm lobbyists to conceal the real nature of these subsidies. "Pawn" would be more accurate, since the government is going to keep the cotton and the farmer the money. Nobody even pretends that these "loans" will ever be paid off.)

The Chandler Company of Saragosa, Texas, is into the treasury for $814,000 worth of cotton. Senator Homer E. Capehart, farmer, of Indiana is on the records for a $21,742 wheat loan. Adams Brothers & Company of Odebolt, Iowa, got $179,127. The Louisiana Irrigation & Mill Company of Crowley, Lousiana, turned its surplus rice over to the taxpayers for $486,-727.

The list runs on for page after alarming page. What it shows is that the big helpings of government gravy are going to about two million farmers—many of them corporations—who grow 85 per cent of the total farm output. They operate a little more than a third of the farms. Yet they form the most powerful vested interest in the American economy. Since they dug into their positions of special privilege during Democratic administrations, Mr. Truman does not sound entirely convincing when he describes the Eisenhower regime as "a special privilege government."

In fact, Secretary of Agriculture Ezra Taft Benson has made a few gingerly efforts to bring a little sense back into our farm economy. Whereupon Democratic Congressmen—and some Republicans—promptly denounced him as a callous-hearted ogre. They pounced with even more indecent glee on one of his understrappers, Assistant Secretary Earl L. Butz, who was indiscreet enough to blurt out the truth.

"Too many people are trying to stay in agriculture," Butz said.

That is the nub of the whole story—and politicians of both parties have been avoiding it for years. At least 40 million of our 350 million acres of crop land ought to be taken out of production. At least one million out of our 5½ million farm families ought to be nudged gradually off the land, and helped to find some useful occupation.

One respected economist—Ross D. Robertson of the St. Louis Federal Reserve Bank—goes much further. He suggests that "it is not inconceivable that 5 per cent of the work force could produce all the farm products which the United States and a part of the rest of the world would take at profitable prices." If he is right, we could get along with less than half of the people we are now supporting in agriculture.

The explanation is that during the past twenty years farming has undergone a more sweeping technological revolution than anything industry has yet seen. New machinery, new fertilizers, new varieties of hybrid seed, new pest killers, new techniques have caused an astronomical rise in output, per man and per acre. Elementary common sense, then, would suggest that the unneeded people ought to be shifted into other jobs, and the unneeded acres into better uses—notably timber and grass.

Our present farm policy, of course, works in precisely the opposite direction. It tends to freeze both manpower and resources into their present obsolete and wasteful patterns. Moreover, the nostrum favored by most Democratic Congressmen —higher and even less flexible farm supports—would merely freeze these patterns higher still.

Why is it that any word of common sense about farm problems is such political dynamite? Fundamentally, because our whole political structure, on every level, is stacked in favor of the farmer. North Dakota with its 680,000 people (mostly farmers) elects just as many Senators as New York with its 12 million (mostly city folks). Many a rural Congressman represents only one-half to one-fourth as many voters as his colleagues from city districts. In like fashion, nearly every state legislature is rigged to give an outrageously oversized representation to the country districts. (The political boundaries were drawn years ago, before the cities grew up; they can be changed only by legislative action; and the cornfed statesmen don't like to vote themselves out.)

A grand-scale reshuffling of districts, both for Congress and the legislatures, seems to be the only long-range remedy. That will require something akin to an insurrection by the long-swindled city voters—followed by years of patient logrolling and political maneuver. We can make a start next November, however, by throwing eggs at every candidate who poses as The Farmer's Friend. That will help get rid of one surplus, and a lot of political hypocrisy at the same time.

By way of footnote, it might be well to add that the writer of these churlish lines is not merely an exasperated city taxpayer. He is that, all right. But he also comes from a farming family, grew up in farming communities, did a certain amount of farmwork himself, owns an interest in farm property, and benefits from farm subsidies which he has done nothing to deserve. This is worth mentioning only because it suggests that there may be other people with a financial stake in our present ridiculous farming system—perhaps more than anybody suspects—who are ready for a change in the direction of sanity.

December, 1955

5 : TV and Its Critics

IN THE HURT TONES of a misunderstood man, Robert W. Sarnoff recently complained that television is getting a raw deal. Its critics, he said, are calling it bad names—"mediocre". . . "unworthy" . . . "time-wasting."

This, he intimated, is both unfair and damaging to the industry. TV is giving the public what it wants, and the public loves it. Its critics are either misinformed, or they have a selfish interest in discrediting TV; or they are intolerant intellectuals who despise the mass taste and want to impose their own arcane standards on a reluctant America.

If this keeps up, he warned, TV will face two hideous dangers. Its audience and advertisers may drift away, because they are constantly being told that watching their favorite programs is "a shameful act." Worse yet, the government might start meddling with TV programing.

So Mr. Sarnoff urged his industry to launch "a massive communications effort" to answer its critics. It should explain that "a principal function" is to serve up light entertainment—to "meet the need of most active Americans for relaxation." (Well, all right, maybe it ought to provide something for "minority tastes" as well—but that is secondary.) And the industry ought to make clear that it finds no conflict between serving the public and serving advertisers; what is good for the sponsor is good for the United States.

Since Mr. Sarnoff is boss of NBC and since he was talking to the broadcasters' trade association, he got action. Committees were set up, money was raised, and the industry is now planning a heavy-caliber campaign to defend itself.

Mr. Sarnoff has a point. Four points, to be precise.

Much criticism of TV *has* been misinformed. Some of it has come from professional intellectuals whose main stock in trade is lament over the malodorous decay of American culture. (A classic example is Gunther Anders' essay in *Mass Culture: The Popular Arts in America,** in which he deplores TV for 4,500 words without once touching on anything so vulgar as a fact. One of his conclusions is that "because the world is brought into our homes, we do not have to explore it . . . modern man

---

* Edited by Bernard Rosenberg and David Manning White; published in 1957 by The Free Press, Glencoe, Illinois.

travels only as a last resort." To preserve his intellectual purity, Dr. Anders evidently avoids not only TV, but also highways, airports, trains, and docks.)

Perhaps it is also true—though hard to prove—that some of the newspaper and magazine criticism of TV has been snide and hostile, because TV is a strong competitor for audience and advertising.

Surely, Mr. Sarnoff is right in fearing that government domination would be a bad thing. The Federal Communications Commission has made sorry use of what power over broadcasting it now has; and foreign experience—notably in England—suggests that government-operated TV has about as many (though different) failings as the American system. Then, too, it is always dangerous to let politicians or bureaucrats get their fingers on *any* channel of communication. The temptation to use it for propaganda is too great a strain to put on any conscience.

Finally, for whatever one man's opinion is worth, it seems to me that TV is better than many of its critics are willing to admit. In a slow and spotty way, it may actually be improving. At least in the New York area, where the network programs usually originate, anybody willing to hunt a little can now find one or two worthwhile programs almost every day—ranging from history lectures to Eugene O'Neill, from first-rate jazz to Leonard Bernstein. (True enough, local stations in the hinterland often refuse to carry the best of the network offerings; they can make more money by running ancient movies.) In the household I know best, TV has caused none of the disasters predicted by the gloomier sociologists. My children haven't turned into videots, or even neglected their homework much. And if my own brain is softening, I can't honestly blame it on my watching an occasional prize fight, baseball game, or Phil Silvers comedy.

But if we grant all this, the fact remains that Mr. Sarnoff and many of his fellow broadcasters don't seem to understand what their responsible critics are really saying. These critics too have some valid points—and they cannot be answered by any "communications effort," however massive. The only possible answer would be a basic change in the organization of the industry.

The true indictment against TV is not that it is all bad, but rather that it is not nearly as good as it could be—nor as good as the public has a right to expect. The public is now paying a high price for something it has been promised, and is not getting. With the best will in the world, the industry *in its present form* evidently is powerless to deliver what it has promised—solemnly and legally—that it would deliver.

Some specifications of this charge were set forth most vigorously not by a cloistered intellectual but by one of the most respected and successful executives in broadcasting, Edward R. Murrow. He scandalized the industry by saying, right out loud, that its performance is timid, trivial, and escapist. He pointed out that in the all-important prime-time period—the hours between 8:00 and 11:00 P.M., which are the only ones when most people are free to use their sets—the air is full of froth. Normally all three networks and all local stations offer much the same fare: frivolous entertainment, consisting of Westerns, vaudeville, quiz shows, and an occasional detective story.

In practice, then, during the prime hours you and I do not have that "freedom of choice" which Mr. Sarnoff speaks of so reverently. Candy is dandy, as Ogden Nash has observed—but what if you want beefsteak for a change? You won't get it. The sponsors in their infinite wisdom have decided that most people want candy between 8:00 and 11:00 P.M.—and you will, by God, take it or go hungry.

The result is that the best brains in television, its best hours, and its best dollars are dedicated to making the American people fat, dumb, and happy. Or, as Mr. Murrow put it, to "decadence, escapism, and insulation from the world in which we live."

Is this good enough? Can we afford to use our best resources in this way, at a moment when the Soviets are straining all their resources to make *their* people lean, smart, and tough? Even if most of the customers (and sponsors) do eat it up, does it really make sense? Isn't it like feeding candy to a diabetic—without warning him that sugar may kill him? For, as Mr. Murrow pointed out, prime-hour TV makes "only fleeting and spasmodic reference to the fact that this nation is in mortal danger."*

Many people in television are aware of these questions, and uneasy about them. One is Mr. Sarnoff. Shortly after his speech about the critics, I talked to him at some length, and have no doubt that he is a conscientious and intelligent man, eager to do what he can to improve his industry. So too with the responsible executives at CBS—notably its president, Dr. Frank Stanton, a former professor who is at least as thoughtful as any of his intellectual critics.

The trouble is they can't do much.

As the industry is now organized, *nobody*—neither networks, nor local stations, nor sponsors—has much leeway to attempt anything more than marginal improvements.

Some such modest improvements already are in prospect. Mr. Sarnoff recently announced that NBC is planning seven hour-long informational programs, plus some operas and original plays, to be presented at peak viewing periods. Dr. Stanton has said that next year CBS will schedule "regular hour-long informational broadcasts once a month in prime evening time," and that later he hopes to offer such programs twice a month and eventually every week.

---

* On rare occasions the networks do venture to slip a morsel of protein into the evening menu—a documentary, a prestige show, an interview with Walter Lippmann. But ordinarily, as we all know, if you want to get your teeth into something, you have to search for it at unearthly hours—such as 6:30 A.M., midnight, or Sunday afternoon.

Even then we don't have much freedom of choice. On Sundays, for example, the sponsors assume that all right-thinking consumers are outdoors playing golf or inhaling exhaust fumes. Consequently these relatively worthless hours can be used as sops for the intellectual—and all the sops are tossed on his plate at once. On May 10, for instance, if you had wanted to listen to Senator Javits and Bergen Evans and Tom Mboya and the *New York Times* Youth Forum and a panel of scientists, you couldn't do it. All were scheduled on different channels at the same hour.

These are remarkably courageous steps. Even if the network chiefs get away with them, however, that will still mean that only about one-twenty-eighth of the prime hours will be salvaged from the froth. And to judge from past experience, many of the networks' affiliated stations will refuse to carry such programs.

The reason why such improvements are so daring and difficult is, in a word: Money. Those prime hours are enormously valuable. Their sale to advertisers brings in most of the network's income. From this profit it pays for unsponsored programs, for its costly news service, and for those cultural items which appear at dawn and on Sunday afternoon. From this same profit it must pay its dividends. If the networks give away too many of these golden hours for "informational broadcasts," the stockholders will soon want to know why. They may even want a new president. After all, TV is not a philanthropic enterprise.

Each local station is under similar pressure. When it carries an unsponsored network public-service program it is actually out of pocket; but if it rejects that program and sells the time to half a dozen local sponsors, it makes a tempting profit. What would you do if you were the station manager?

Why, then, don't some of the big corporations sponsor an occasional program dealing with "ideas and information," as Mr. Murrow suggested? Again, because they feel they can't afford to. It costs a sizable fortune to put an evening program on a national network. The sponsor will get his money back only if he draws the largest possible audience. If horse opera sells more autos than Ed Murrow—as it does—then the advertiser has to go for horse opera. The fact that he, personally, may prefer Murrow makes no difference. If he should yield to such a whim, his harder-headed competitors will soon run him out of the market.

Actually the sponsor doesn't even have the freedom to take that chance. Once in a long while some advertiser may be rich enough—or stubborn enough—to put on a program which strikes his fancy, even though it does not fetch a whopping audience.

One such was Firestone. Until recently it presented a program of semiserious music—not great art, but certainly a high cut above the quality of most evening shows. Although its audience was relatively small, Firestone was content.

The ABC network was not. It was afraid to carry a low-rating show at 9:00 P.M., because millions of viewers might switch to a competing channel—and stay there for the rest of the evening. So ABC told Firestone that it would have to shift to a less strategic hour or get off the air.

Everybody feels awfully sorry about this—and everybody is helpless. Them, as Jimmy Durante used to say, is the conditions which prevail.

Our system of broadcasting was not meant to work that way. When it got started, a generation ago, everybody recognized that radio (and later TV) could serve as an immensely powerful instrument of public education and enlightenment. In theory, every station is supposed to put that purpose first. It is licensed to broadcast, under the Federal Communications Act, in order to serve "the public convenience and necessity."

Such a license is a gold mine. It gives the lucky applicant a monopoly on the use of a particular piece of public property —a radio wave length or TV channel. It costs him nothing, though it may earn him a fortune. Some licenses have been sold, shortly after they were granted by the FCC, for as much as $8 million.

In return for this magnificent gift of public property, the station owner is supposed to devote a considerable part of his air time to public-service programs. Naturally the competition is keen for every one of the available channels, and each of the competing applicants makes impressive promises about the public service he will provide. (Sometimes, as the Harris Committee discovered, he also tries to bribe an FCC commissioner.)

These promises are seldom, if ever, kept. The Federal Communications Commission has made no serious effort to enforce them. No station's license has ever been revoked, or refused renewal, because the operator broke his pledge. In practice, therefore, most stations simply ignore this obligation, and sell every hour they can for as much money as they can get. Much of their programing consists of showing old movies in fifteen-minute slices—with as many as six consecutive commercials sandwiched in between all the segments. (Watching one of these mutilated dramas is enough to make a man wonder about Mr. Sarnoff's conviction that "broadcasting's responsibility to the public is harmonious with its responsibility to advertisers.")

If some undesirable time remains unsold, then the station may use it as a cheap gesture toward the public service—often by running a sermon by some local minister.

The upshot is that we are all paying dearly for something we don't get. We are letting the broadcasters use valuable public property, for free—and they are not delivering in return the public service which they promised.

Can anything be done to stop this scandal?

Well, of course the FCC might try to enforce its own rules —but that seems most unlikely with the caliber of men now on the commission and the political atmosphere in which it operates.

There is, however, another possible solution. It would, I think, meet most of the points raised by the responsible critics of broadcasting. It would give the public real freedom of choice in programs. It would avoid the dangers of government control. Finally, it would remove the economic pressures which now bear down so painfully on people like Sarnoff, Stanton, Murrow, and others who would like to improve TV and radio, but can do so only with great difficulty and risk.

In bare outline, it might work something like this:

1. Instead of giving away its air channels, from now on the government would rent them. Each local TV and radio station would pay a modest percentage of its annual earnings—say 10 or 15 per cent. This would be no great hardship, since most broadcasters are now making very comfortable profits. For ex-

ample, CBS earned $7 million in the first quarter of the year, a gain of nearly 8 per cent over the same period in 1958. Radio Corporation of America, the parent company of NBC, reported first-quarter earnings of nearly $13 million, for a 44 per cent gain; but some of this came from the sale of TV sets and other equipment, rather than from broadcasting.

The earnings of all the hundreds of local stations are hard to discover, so I have no idea how much money such rentals might bring in. Certainly it would be substantial. For the sake of illustration, let's assume that they might total $50 million a year.

2. This money would be turned over to a National Broadcasting Authority—a public body chartered by Congress but carefully insulated from politics. Its directors would be five men who already hold responsible positions in the fields of education, culture, and information. They must not be governmental appointees; they must be free from economic and political pressures; they must not represent any competing media; they should represent a broad spectrum of the public interest; and they must command respect.

Such a board might include the president of Harvard, the heads of the Carnegie and Rockefeller foundations, the director of the Metropolitan Museum, and the chief of the National Radio and Television Center. (Again, this list is merely illustrative; no doubt it could be improved upon.) The essential point is that the men who hold such jobs at any given moment would ex officio become directors of the National Broadcasting Authority. They should be well paid for their part-time services. I can think of no better method to select a board of assured competence, and above suspicion of any interest except the public welfare.

3. The board would hire a Program Manager, and would give him general policy directives—much as a corporation board of directors deals with the company's president. This manager would, of course, be an experienced broadcasting executive. Mr. Murrow, for example.

4. The main job of the Authority and its manager would

be to produce public-service programs—news-in-depth, top-quality music and theater, documentaries dealing with science, the arts, and public affairs, plus any kind of experimental features they might want to try. In the beginning, they might attempt three hour-long programs each week for TV and an equal number for radio.

5. Each program would have to be carried by one of the major networks and all of its affiliated stations, in prime evening time. Monday's program, for example, might be assigned to NBC, Wednesday's to CBS, and Friday's to ABC. This hour would be an additional rental-in-kind, demanded of the broadcasters in part payment for the privilege of using the public's airwaves. (Unaffiliated stations might be required to devote an equal amount of time to showing the Authority's kinescopes.)

Thus the viewer would have genuine freedom of choice. If he is not interested in the Authority's report on the Berlin crisis, scheduled for 9:00 P.M. Monday on NBC, then he can turn to a Western on CBS or a song-and-dance act on ABC. And vice versa. (He would even get a chance to see an occasional program uninterrupted by commercials, since the Authority would have no need for advertising.) Such an arrangement would, moreover, expose the Authority's program producers to the bracing effects of competition for their audience.

6. This system would cost the broadcasters far less than you might think. For the networks and the few conscientious local stations would be relieved of the painful and expensive duty of producing public-service programs. And those stations which now evade this duty would be forced to bear their fair share of the Authority's cost.

All broadcasters could then go merrily about their primary business of selling advertising—undistracted by the present conflict between their duty to their stockholders and their duty to the public service. Nagging consciences would be stilled, snarling critics would be silenced—or, at least, largely diverted to watching the Authority's programs—and ulcers might no longer be the TV man's occupational disease.

7. The Authority would open up a stimulating new opportunity for broadcasting talent. I personally know a dozen top-flight producers, writers, and actors who would jump at the chance to work for such an outfit, even if it meant a cut in salary—simply because they are tired, as one of them put it, of "producing garbage."

8. The plan would not cost the taxpayer a penny; it could be put into effect with a simple piece of legislation; and it would require no governmental machinery to operate it.

July, 1959

6 : Recovery from the Plague

IT SEEMS LIKELY that future historians will note the summer of 1954 as the point at which America began to recover its political health. The country now shows signs of passing the crisis stage in one of its periodical bouts of Congressional government—a peculiar disease which afflicts our body politic in regular cycles, like malaria or undulant fever. Its ravages are always damaging, but never fatal; and we usually recuperate fast, once convalescence sets in.

Normally the attack starts just at the end of a war. It is foreshadowed by the administration of a strong President—a Lincoln, Wilson, or Roosevelt—who has concentrated an abnormal amount of governmental authority in the White House. The first symptom is a public weariness—a sort of moral lassitude—which follows quite naturally after the strain of the emergency. Instinctively the voters turn to a candidate who promises them a vacation from the strenuous life, a "return to normalcy." So we get a Grant, a Harding, or an Eisenhower—well-meaning men, who honestly believe that their job is to serve as choreboy for Congress, rather than to lead the country.

(As Bruce Catton, the Pulitzer Prize historian, has pointed out, this is a common failing of the soldier-turned-politician. Since he is trained in "the traditional army officer's view that Congress is the boss," he usually makes a disappointing President, "not because the man will use too much authority in that position, but because he will try to use too little.")

Meanwhile, Congress goes on a rampage. Resentful because they were forced to play second fiddle during the war, the men on The Hill now try to take over the whole orchestra. Their investigating committees run wild. They bully the civil service, try to conduct diplomacy from a Capitol hearing room, and snatch all the executive power they can from the peaceable and bewildered man in the White House.

The result, of course, is a horrifying mess. By its very nature, this bellowing herd of prima donnas is incapable of administering anything. (A fact that the Founding Fathers underlined repeatedly when they drew up the Constitution.) Their attempt leads promptly to a near-paralysis of the machinery of government. Our foreign policy falls into confusion and impotence. Under cover of the uproar, somebody usually manages to raid the national domain; witness the post-Civil War scandals, the Teapot Dome affair, and the current Congressional schemes to give away the public grazing lands, timber, and water power.

The classic case of this malady was the Reconstruction Era. Then a little group of Congressional radicals—blood brothers to Knowland, Jenner, McCarran, and McCarthy—managed to wreck the South, impeach one President, disgrace another, and reduce the noble profession of politics to its lowest level in our history.

Our most recent plague of Congressional usurpation, however, looks very nearly as bad. No doubt it was aggravated by the long preceding period of executive dominance—unhealthily stretched out by the Depression, World War II, and Korea. In that twenty-year span, Republican Congressmen forgot the habit of responsibility. Not a single one of the present crop had ever before served under a Republican President; so it is hardly surprising that they had come to think of themselves as a per-

204 : THE STUPIDITY PROBLEM

petual opposition, and to look on the White House as a permanent enemy.

At any rate, they have been displaying all the textbook symptoms—the attempt to rob the President of his Congressional responsibility for foreign affairs, by such means as the Bricker amendment and constant harassment of the Secretary of State; the planting of stooges and spies in executive agencies; the use of threats and smears to force civil servants to report to Congress rather than the White House; the pilfering of executive documents; the pretense of a few Senators that they are the only patriotic Americans, that they alone speak for the country, and that all their critics are traitors.

McCarthyism is merely one aspect of this disease—precisely like the Bloody Shirt phase of the Reconstruction. Alarmed foreigners often mistake Our Joe for a budding Hitler; if they were less ignorant of American history, they would have realized long ago that he is merely another Thaddeus Stevens. In his day, this spiteful little man was even more of a terror than McCarthy; he actually managed to deprive President Johnson of his command of the Army, and of his power to fire federal employees. But who remembers him now? Like annoying pimples, the Thaddeus Stevenses and Joe McCarthys are forgotten as soon as the underlying disorder clears up.

Which won't be long now. Sooner or later the voters always get fed up with these Congressional forays, and herd the legislators back onto their reservation. This time the tide of opinion apparently began to turn in mid-spring—thanks, in part, to the vaudeville team of Cohn, Schine & McCarthy. Their tantrums, their phony documents, their childish insults to honorable men—all projected on millions of television screens—helped awaken an incredulous public to what has been going on in Washington. And there are some degrees of national indignity which even the most lethargic citizen cannot stomach.

To President Eisenhower, this wave of revulsion may offer a last opportunity. Millions of Americans still hope that he may finally grasp the nature of his job—that he will stop cringing before the Senatorial wild men, defend the integrity of the executive branch, and restore the balance of constitutional power. In recent weeks he has shown signs of bracing himself for the fight. If he does, he may yet escape the historians' piteous list of weak Presidents. If he does not, he will be remembered— in Gerald Johnson's phrase—"as merely another Grant, minus the whisky and the whiskers."

The root of this national sickness is, of course, the temporary indifference of the average citizen. The guilt rests on each of us, more than on Congress or the President; for we always get the kind of government we deserve.

But for a year or more this postwar fatigue, this shirking of individual political responsibility, quite evidently has been fading. The earliest sign of the change is hard to note, because it is undramatic, purely local, and seldom reported by the wire services or national press. It is a gradual influx of new blood into the precinct and county organizations of both parties. A lot of ordinary citizens—with no personal political ambitions— begin to drop into headquarters in the evening, to lick envelopes, sit in on committee meetings, and ask embarrassing questions. Gradually they demand a say in local party affairs; sometimes they reach for control.

The upshot, in rare instances, may be the overturn of an entire state political machine, like the ousting of the Republican Old Guard in Indiana last May. More frequently it is a quiet shift of power—a village primary fight, a change in a few ward leaders, the nomination of a maverick such as Clifford Case in New Jersey or Dick Neuberger in Oregon. Lately this has been happening in scores of scattered areas throughout the country; nobody has yet attempted to add up the many little rebellions and assay their total significance—but it may turn out to be considerable.

Meanwhile, the professional politician watches this invasion of the amateurs with uneasiness.

July, 1954

7 : By Any Other Name It Would Smell Sweeter

WHAT THIS COUNTRY NEEDS is a good five-cent word to describe itself. We have invented a new social system—perhaps the most interesting social contraption since Mumtaz Mahal invented the brassiere in 1608—but we haven't yet thought up a name for it. So we keep on trying to describe it with a set of labels which were devised long ago to fit something entirely different.

This confuses everybody. We are in much the same fix as an airline which would insist on referring to its jets as Covered Wagons. This would preserve the fine old pioneering tradition, all right. But a certain number of elderly passengers inevitably would complain that they couldn't find the reins. The Minute Women of America would keep trying to hitch the plane to a span of oxen. And foreigners—who often take our sentimental language literally—would scoff at our Oregon Trail mentality, and try to sell us their more up-to-date conveyances, such as the hansom cab.

The new society which we have invented obviously is quite different from anything the world has ever seen. It doesn't resemble the "capitalism" of Adam Smith any more than a transport plane resembles a prairie schooner. It certainly isn't "free enterprise" as Andrew Carnegie used that phrase—or as some of his mental contemporaries, such as Senator Homer E. Capehart, still use it. The New Tycoons don't look a bit like the traditional stereotype of The Capitalist—that paunchy character with the top hat, the big cigar, the cutaway coat, and the dollar signs on his vest—and the economy they run looks just as unlike any of its predecessors.

Yet because we are so fond of the ancient, hallowed words, we conceal the fact (even, sometimes, from ourselves) that we have invented something pretty wonderful. This unaccustomed modesty does a good deal of harm. For the labels which sound so cozy to us sound perfectly horrid in the ears of millions of people overseas.

To many Europeans, for example, "capitalism" is an evil word. The only sort of capitalism they know—their own—worked very badly indeed during its heyday before World War II. On the whole it was inefficient, cruel, corrupt, irresponsible, and riddled with nepotism. It differed just as sharply from the American system as it does from, say, communism. But there is no way for *them* to know that. So long as we keep on describing America as a "capitalist" society, we can hardly blame the French and Yugoslavs for thinking that we are talking about the same kind of society which failed them so miserably for about five generations.

Such confusion over semantics often works in the other direction, too. "Planning," for instance, is a highly popular word abroad. To the European and Asian, it carries echoes of order, of economic justice, of faster progress than their ramshackle variety of "free enterprise" can ever offer. But in the American language, "planning" means a nasty habit, like selling dirty postcards or eating snails. Such things must be expected of those deplorable foreigners—but for any clean-cut American boy they would be unthinkable.

Nevertheless, it is a cold fact—reluctant as we may be to admit it—that we can plan circles around the Socialists who profess to be good at this sort of thing. Indeed, we do it every day. In his Council of Economic Advisers, the Interdepartmental Board on Growth and Stability, the National Security Council, and half a dozen related agencies, the President has an apparatus for planning which probably is more elaborate—and more effective—than any Socialist government ever set up. Through other machinery—ranging from the Interstate Commerce Commission to the tax laws and crop-control programs—he has ample power to direct the course of our whole economy. Nobody can plant an acre of cotton, start a radio station, change a railway fare, locate a new factory, issue a share of stock, write an advertisement, drill an oil well, or sail a ship without feeling the guiding hand of the federal government. The results are pretty good—as Republican orators gladly admit, at least when a Republican administration is in power. Though of course they never use a four-letter word like "plan."

Or compare the planning that went into the Grand Coulee project with that of the British Socialists' notorious African ground-nut scheme. Both undertakings aimed to make fertile vast tracts of desert land; both involved starting new towns; laying out roads, schools, and water supplies; meshing together the work of many agencies; settling thousands of families in a strange environment. The Socialist project was a spectacular fiasco, because of bad planning. Grand Coulee is a triumph of foresight and careful organization. Who was primarily responsible for it? Milton Eisenhower, at that time Coordinator of Land Use Planning for the Department of Agriculture. (This disclosure will not, we hope, blast the career of a first-rate Republican public servant.)

Similar examples can be found almost everywhere. No British Socialist government has ever dared to enact such a radical measure as our capital-gains tax. Or to demand the intimate statistical information—indispensable for sound planning— which American businessmen regularly send in to Washington without a whimper. Or to interfere with the "private enterprise" of the deeply entrenched British cartels and price rings, in the way our Anti-Trust Division and Federal Trade Commission have been doing for years.

Moreover, every major American industry now has to plan its own investments and operations for years in advance. Such private planning obviously can work only when it is keyed in with the government's overall planning for the economy; the regional scheme for watershed development; the states' plan for traffic and schools and housing; the projected supply of electric power, public and private; prospective shifts in population; the construction program of the local sanitary district; and maybe a dozen other sets of similar blueprints.

This is rugged individualism?

A few weeks ago a Senate committee heard about a woman who went to work for Sears Roebuck at the age of fifteen for $6 a week. Now 54, she earns $80 a week; and through the Sears pension fund and bonus plan she has acquired $104,000 worth of the company's stock, plus $17,000 in other assets. With her fellow employees, she owns the controlling interest in the firm. What should we call this woman? Is she a laborer or a capitalist—or something new? Which side of their class struggle do the Marxists think she belongs on?

It would be equally puzzling to try to explain who owns United States Steel. The one thing sure is that nobody "owns" it, in the sense that Andrew Carnegie owned his steel mills. The corporation now has more stockholders than it has employees; no one of them holds more than a tiny share of the total stock; potential control rests with a small group of semipublic trustees, who don't exercise it; and actual control could easily be purchased by the steel workers' union, any time it might care to invest its considerable war chest in that way. (A similar possibility is open to many unions. So far, however, none of them has taken over control of its employing company—perhaps because it would be confusing for the same man to sit on both sides of the bargaining table.)

Our peasants don't fit into the foreigner's picture of "capitalism" either. They have banded together into revolutionary organizations, such as the Ohio Farm Bureau Federation—an outfit that operates office buildings, huge marketing facilities, and a network of insurance companies which makes it one of the biggest investors in the Midwest. Similar kulaks' associations run everything from oil refineries to quick-freeze plants—and a number of their officers pull down more pay than the Premier of France.

This sort of thing was what the late Frederick Lewis Allen had in mind when he suggested that "the United States is not evolving *toward* Socialism, but *past* Socialism."

It is a sad and curious fact that no European reporter or economist has ever taken a hard look at this new society. If one did, his first startled conclusion might well be like that of the

Tennessee farmer when he saw his first giraffe: "There ain't no such animal." Meanwhile, we can't blame them for their indifference. After all, we have never told them that we are producing a new kind of animal over here. We keep insisting that all we've got is the same sort of motheaten dog that they have been kicking around their own house for years.

May, 1955

8 : Khrushchev As a Host

IN THE SPRING of 1946 I had a chance to get acquainted with Nikita Khrushchev under somewhat unusual circumstances— including one evening when he got staggering, glassy-eyed drunk.

His behavior on such relaxed occasions may throw a gleam of light on one facet of a personality which has become important to all of us. Since he now has the power to kill a good many Americans at any hour he might choose, even the smallest scrap of data about his habits and character may be worth noting. Moreover, the impression of that character which I picked up does not altogether tally with the newspaper speculations which have been appearing since he overthrew Malenkov.

I had not used my notes about him before because I had been, in a way, his guest. He was still a long way from the top of the Soviet hierarchy; and any suggestion that he had behaved indiscreetly in the presence of foreigners might have caused him embarrassment. Now, however, he clearly is above any such concerns.

For a couple of months that spring I was working in the Ukraine as a member of a small official mission sent out to check on the use made of some $125 million worth of United Nations Relief and Rehabilitation Administration supplies. Khrushchev was political boss of the Ukraine and a junior member of the

Politburo. Because our mission had authority to cut off shipments if our work was impeded, he and his subordinates treated us always with at least surface cordiality. With some of the lesser bureaucrats, this developed into a fairly easy, informal working relationship.

Such contacts provide a scant basis for judging the character of any man—let alone one as complicated as Khrushchev. Other members of the mission (including Marshall MacDuffie, its chief) have interpreted them somewhat differently. These comments, therefore, are far from dogmatic. Yet I got no impression that Nikita Khrushchev was either "an amiable chatterbox"—as one recent news story described him—or a Second Stalin. For what it may be worth, this is the way he looked to one observer:

1. In appearance he is remarkably like another empire-builder who came up fast: Robert R. Young, the collector of railroads. He has much the same stature—about five feet, four inches—the same restless energy, the same impatient self-confidence of manner, and even a certain resemblance in facial expression. Like Mr. Young when talking to a Senate committee, he knows how to assume an air of earnest, wide-eyed sincerity which is most persuasive. He is equally dapper about his clothes. (When he reviewed a May Day parade in Kiev, Khrushchev turned up in the cloth cap which is *de rigueur* for such occasions—a fashion set by Lenin, and symbolic of the Working Man. But his was specially tailored of cream-colored linen, with a suit to match.)

2. He frankly enjoys the luxuries that go with power. His office—located high up in the eleven-story, heavily guarded Palace of Ministers of the Ukraine—was furnished with the heavy Victorian lavishness which seems to characterize upper-class Soviet taste. At that time he maintained four houses—residences in Kiev and Moscow, a country *dacha*, and a Black Sea vacation place—which one of his subordinates described as "true palaces."

The dinner party at which he drank so freely was ostentatious even by Soviet standards. Each guest was attended by an indi-

212 : THE STUPIDITY PROBLEM

vidual waiter, liveried in the style of Louis XIV; and the procession of courses—which marched on from 8:00 P.M. until nearly 2:00 A.M.—ranged from sturgeon and caviar (four varieties) through a dazzling array of elaborate desserts. Up to the point where he had to be led out of the room by two worried aides, Khrushchev tackled all of them with obvious gusto. (Curiously, however, he passed up the vodka and the wines, drinking all nine of the formal toasts in French cognac.)

Such tastes are hardly surprising in a man who had spent his younger years as a coal miner, sheepherder, mill hand, and pipe fitter. But the frankness with which he displayed them was, perhaps, a little unexpected in a Soviet politician—especially at a moment when the backwash of war had left his people in extreme privation. Maybe it is related to his strange streak of recklessness, noted below.

3. Like Billis in *South Pacific*, he loves projects. He seemed to get his main fun in life out of conceiving and pushing through a variety of grandiose schemes. When I knew him, his chief project was the rebuilding of the devastated Ukrainian cities. The conference table in his office was littered with blueprints, samples of plywood and ceramic tile, and models of buildings— all of which he explained with boundless enthusiasm. Later he plunged into big schemes for prefabricated concrete construction; for settling millions of acres of virgin land on the sub-Arctic frontier: for transforming whole provinces to corn-hog farming, modeled on the Iowa pattern; and for replacing the traditional Russian villages with supercollective farms, each centering on a big "agricultural city."

Some of these projects evidently were tackled with more enthusiasm than forethought. The supercollectives, for example, never worked very well; and his diversion of thousands of tractors from the old farming areas to the undeveloped frontier helped bring on the present crisis in Soviet food production. (He has managed, however—at least for the moment—to blame these failures on Malenkov.) The same headlong trait reportedly characterized some of his tactics during World War II, when he was in charge of guerrilla operations in the Ukraine. And his drinking habits have never been exactly circumspect.

So far as I know, there are no symptoms of alcoholism. But he does seem to have some inner tension which periodically demands alcoholic relief. His prowess with the bottle was mentioned, half jocularly, by several Ukrainians who had known him a long time. During the war, for example, he sometimes would enlist partisan leaders in drinking bouts, where he liked to down a water tumbler full of vodka in one long gulp.

4. He is dangerously ignorant of the outside world. Except for one recent trip to China, there is no record that he has ever traveled outside of the Soviet domain.* His questions about America suggested that his views about it conform strictly to the Marxist legend. My guess is that he really believes that sooner or later the United States "inevitably" must attack the Soviet Union. On the night he drank too much, his one verbal indiscretion—if it can be called that—came near the end of a rambling, somewhat incoherent speech about Stalin and his glorious leadership during The Great Patriotic War. Bracing his fists on the table, Khrushchev looked fixedly at the Americans present and said (according to the translator at my elbow): "We don't ever want to fight again. But I want you to remember that if anyone attacks us—anyone—we will fight to the last drop of blood."

5. He has certain human qualities that Stalin never displayed. It goes without saying that he is ruthless, passionately ambitious, and skilled in intrigue. Without these qualifications, no Soviet bureaucrat rises very far. Yet where Stalin was withdrawn, cold, and reptilian, Khrushchev is outgoing, gregarious, and quite capable of turning on a high voltage of politician's charm. While by no means a "chatterbox"—his conversation always was to the point—he undoubtedly does like to talk. (His Russian, according to my translator, is crude and rather slipshod.)

He gets around more than most inmates of the Kremlin;

---

* This was of course written before his memorable shoe-pounding visit to the UN, and his subsequent travels through Western Europe.

during harvest season he used to visit a collective farm almost every day, shaking hands and kissing babies like an Alabama Congressman. His mind is by no means closed to new ideas; and he might be capable of diluting Communist ideology with a little sensible pragmatism. In comparison with Stalin, he seems to be a little more the politician, a little less the conspirator. He is never likely to yield an inch of the Soviet conquests—but it is just possible that he might prove a trifle more reasonable in international negotiations.

The oddest thing about Khrushchev's seizure of power was the fact that Malenkov was demoted, not executed. Possibly Malenkov's survival means that politics—in the Western sense —is beginning to seep into the Soviet system.

If politics can be defined as the art of governing without murder, then it is fair to say that this art has been virtually unknown to the Russians throughout their history. Indeed, the very concept of government by consent, rather than coercion, seems to be hard for the Russian mind to grasp. I have no idea whether Khrushchev is, in fact, attempting a first tentative experiment with this kind of politics. (If so, it may turn out to be his most reckless venture yet.) But he does show indications of some talent for it—and even the frailest and most temporary sprouting of a less violent political life in Russia would be a hopeful sign for the rest of the world.

April, 1955

9 : Gone, Wind and All

A COUPLE OF WEEKS ago one of our editors stepped into the Senate press gallery to watch the new Senate knuckle down to its work. He realized at once that something about the place was strange, but for a moment he couldn't figure out what it was. The ritual snuffboxes were in their niches, the pageboys scampered around with their usual adolescent, blue-serged awkwardness, Alben Barkley was still telling that story about the Kentucky moonshiner which he had found so serviceable in 1936. Then dawned the horrid truth: there was nobody on the floor who looked like a Senator.

Politically there is no great difference between this batch of lawmakers and the one before it—but the difference in style is enormous. Indeed, it is probably more significant than any mere passing shift in the balance of parties; for what we have here is the first big change in political fashion in more than a century.

Ever since Webster and Calhoun, the style in Senators has been as rigid, classic, and widely recognized as the Washington Monument. Everybody knew what a proper Senator was supposed to look like; the mane of white hair sweeping down over his collar, the dignified paunch, the black string tie knotted like a Mississippi gambler's, the frock coat, the broad-brimmed Stetson, the mottled jowls, the countenance of a slightly apprehensive Roman emperor. He had been born in a log cabin; his voice sounded like a church organ with the *vox humana* stop pulled out; he walked as if he were leading a parade.

Not every Senator could live up to the pattern, of course, any more than all women can look like Gina Lollobrigida; but most of them tried. Always, until this year, there was at least one perfect specimen to set the standard and keep the tradition pure—Blanton, Watson, Borah, Ashurst, and that flamboyant gem of the collection, Texas' Tom Connally.

But last summer when death got Pat McCarran, the Senate lost its one remaining archetype of Gates-Ajar Gothic. Like the late examples of any great style, he was a trifle decadent and overblown; he lacked the courtliness of a Hoey, the Vandenberg gift for four-color oratory, the awesome righteousness of the elder La Follette. But he was authentic, if a little seedy, and he will be remembered as the relic of a once-mighty species, like the last whooping crane.

Extinction was, no doubt, inevitable. Only one incumbent—Kerr of Oklahoma—claims to have been born in a log cabin, and it is unlikely that any Senator can ever make the claim again. (Though there is some talk in Washington of building a Log Cabin Maternity Home, within easy taxi distance of the Mayflower bar, for the benefit of those parents who might have political ambitions for their offspring.) Not even Kerr fits the classic recipe in any other respect, and at least one newcomer—Kennedy of Massachusetts—flouts tradition to the shocking extreme of a semicrew haircut.

It can't honestly be said that the current crop have set a new style. They just don't have any style at all. Where you could once spot a Senator as far as you could see him, you would now find it hard to sift one out of a convention of master plumbers, stockbrokers, or YMCA secretaries. The most typical figures in the upper house—Nixon, Johnson, Case, Humphrey, and Knowland, to cite only a few—look like somewhat disillusioned versions of the all-American boy. They are real clean-cut. They obviously know the Boy Scout oath, and—whatever their political differences—they come equipped with similar models of the neon smile, the Junior Executive suit, the sincere handclasp, the engine-turned personality, and the litmuslike sensitivity to public feeling.

Unquestionably they are better public servants than the old boys; they work harder, demagog less, and are on the whole more honest. But it would have been fun if we could have kept one pristine Claghorn-type—perhaps preserved in alcohol, a congenial medium—just for the hell of it, and for the instruction of posterity. They were crusty, bombastical, opinionated, and eye-filling; and they were never dull.

February, 1954

PART IV

LEGENDS

1 : The Embarrassing Truth About
Davy Crockett

ADMITTEDLY the Chinese are pretty good at retail brain-washing. Given enough time, they apparently can chivvy a few dozen forlorn prisoners into believing almost anything. When it comes to a wholesale operation, however, they still have plenty to learn from the United States.

A bare six months ago, for example, practically all American boys from five to eight were loyal Space Cadets, wholly devoted to blasting each other out of galactic apple trees with their atomic disintegrators. (A few backward types were still in the Hopalong, or chrysalis, stage; but they were merely waiting for their space helmets to arrive from the breakfast-food company.)

Then, almost overnight, two million clean, patriotic youngsters were seduced into switching allegiance. Forgetting all about their sworn duty to defend the planet against swarming Martians, they turned—within the course of a single television program —into Davy Crocketts. Crowned with coonskin, they now infest the trash-can forests and parking-lot prairies from coast to coast, brandishing their Old Betsys in an endless war for the kingship of The Wild Frontier.

Moreover, these infant brain-washees have been bedazzled

into worshiping a Crockett who never was—a myth as phony as the Russian legend about Kind Papa Stalin. The historic truth is that Davy Crockett was a juvenile delinquent who ran away from home at the age of thirteen, to dodge a well-deserved licking by his father, a country saloonkeeper. For three years he bummed around Baltimore, scratching a living in various ways he never cared to talk about. At eighteen he went to school for six months, while making a pass at a girl who preferred a boy friend who could read, but he gave it up as soon as he found that even the ABCs wouldn't get him to first base. (Later he married a less intellectual woman, whom he deserted after she had produced a small herd of children.) He proved himself— according to accepted historical authority—"a poor farmer, indolent and shiftless." He also was an unenthusiastic soldier; during the Creek War he weaseled his way out of the army by hiring a substitute to fill out his term of service.

Since work was distasteful to Davy, he became, in turn, a backwoods justice of the peace who boasted about his ignorance of law; an unsuccessful politician; a hack writer, heavily dependent on some unidentified ghost; and—hear this, Junior— a violinist. Whenever a steady job threatened, he took to the woods. He never was king of anything, except maybe the Tennessee Tall Tales and Bourbon Samplers' Association. When he claimed that he had shot 105 bear in nine months, his fellow tipplers refused to believe a word of it, on the sensible grounds that Davy couldn't count that high.

If our youngsters spurn these unheroic facts in favor of a Simonized, Disneyfied version of history, they can at least plead an adult example. As everybody knows, Crockett managed to get himself killed in the Alamo. This is the blood-splashed ruin which every Texan—little or big—venerates as his national shrine. Every year it is drenched with geysers of high-decibel oratory—steamy, impassioned, and gloriously inaccurate. Indeed, such inaccuracy has now become a matter of self-defense; for on this subject—and a few others—the Texans have brainwashed themselves so thoroughly that any speaker who told the whole truth would invite a lynching.

So no orator ever hints that the Alamo was, in fact, the worst military blooper in American history, short of Pearl Harbor. The bungling started when a little band of hotheads occupied an indefensible and strategically dubious outpost, in open defiance of orders from their commander-in-chief.* Because they couldn't agree on a leader, they broke the cardinal military rule by dividing authority between two co-commanders, William Travis and James Bowie. Neither of them had much confidence in the other—Travis described Bowie as a drunk—and neither could maintain discipline.

They established no line of supply, nor did they bother to lay in an adequate store of ammunition—or even food, although plenty was available close at hand. (They did make sure, however, that they had enough liquor; some of the volunteers traded their rifles for whisky.) Although the troops—less than two hundred—were too few to man the outlying walls, they were too lazy to build a shorter line of fortifications or even to cut loopholes. They neglected to send out patrols, or to collect intelligence about the approaching enemy; when friendly Mexicans volunteered information, it was mostly ignored. Only a lucky rainstorm, which bogged down Santa Anna's cavalry, kept the Texans from being taken entirely by surprise.

When it finally dawned on them that a vastly superior force was breathing down their necks, they refused to rejoin the main Texas army, which needed them urgently. (Except for Louis Rose, a French mercenary, who had the Gallic good sense—or something—to slip out of the trap while the getting was good.) The rest were determined to become heroes if it killed them; which of course it did.

They died well. From a military standpoint, that is about all that can be said for them; and it is the only solid fact about

---

* Sam Houston's instructions, January 17, 1836, were to "remove all the canon [*sic*] . . . blow up the Alamo and abandon the place."

the Alamo which most Americans ever hear. (Hardly anyone bothers to note that their Mexican opponents died pretty well, too; the Toluca Battalion alone lost 670 out of its 800 men.) But maybe the plain historic truth is something we can no longer afford. It would be bad for business—the Davy Crockett Industry, for example.

July, 1955

2 : Geronimo's Blanket

THIS DEPARTMENT had a grandfather who became a close friend of Geronimo, the eminent Apache philosopher and war chief, after the old gentleman had taken up enforced residence in his declining years at Fort Sill, Oklahoma. During his livelier days, Geronimo had painfully assembled a blanket—or piece-quilt— of white women's scalps. It was warm and fashionable—the envy of every chief from the Gila River to the Arapaho country —but it was a nuisance to keep well groomed on the march, because of a tendency to collect fleas and sandburrs. Moreover, as the Southwest became infested with General Nelson Miles's cavalry, the owner realized that it was becoming increasingly hard to replace (or even to patch up) if he wore it out.

So eventually he reserved it for purely thaumaturgic purposes, with splendid results. When spread over a wounded brave, it would heal him up faster than rattlesnake oil or any other available medication. At night it would make the wearer invisible, so he could steal horses from the best guarded remuda.

Worn in battle, it would bounce off the slugs from a Winchester carbine, as Geronimo himself demonstrated on many occasions. He never would have surrendered, if his women and children hadn't been starving. He never could resist a squaw's tears.

All this Geronimo related as he sat on a bench in the winter sunshine outside his stone cell, cuddling on his knee the five-year-old daughter of a Fort Sill artillery instructor. She was fond of him; and he loved to stroke her blonde curls.

March, 1955

3 : The Sure 'nuff Truth About the Civil War

As EVERY SOUTHERNER KNOWS, there is a sharp distinction between the truth and the sure 'nuff truth. One is concerned with facts, the other with essence.

The only inheritance I got from my two grandfathers—one a Confederate, the other a Union man—was the sure 'nuff truth about the Civil War. It sounded a lot different from the truth put out by the historians. For this reason I had always considered it a purely private treasure, of no value to anybody except the family.

Recently, however, I have begun to suspect that it might be a vital asset to the national economy. For a major industry, the writing of Civil War books, is now sputtering to a dead stop because it has run out of raw material. The official records and generals' memoirs were used up long ago; prospectors armed with Geiger counters have rummaged through every attic in the country in search of letters and diaries; and by late 1960 the last surviving scraps of paper, from every sutler, cook, and camp follower who could write, had been run through the mills.*

* Notably Catton's Nostalgia Foundry and the Miers Distillery, bottler of 90-proof blood.

Today, with a recession already threatening, thousands of writers, printers, and booksellers are facing unemployment—even though the demand for Civil War books apparently remains as insatiable as ever. Under the circumstances I don't feel that in good conscience I can keep my little hoard of raw material cached away any longer.

The first bit of sure 'nuff truth I picked up—at about the age of six—was that the Civil War was fun. This seems to have escaped the historians and all of the stuffier generals, such as Sherman. (Not Lee. He believed it might be fortunate that war is a bloody business, lest men learn to like it too much. And until the Battle of Yellow Tavern Jeb Stuart evidently regarded the whole thing as a wonderful lark.)

Anyhow, as my grandfathers told it the war was a four-year picnic, with fireworks. A partial explanation, no doubt, is that familiar trick of old men's memories, which filter out the unpleasant. (My Confederate data trickled through a double filter. Because my Grandfather Caperton died before I was born, his story reached me secondhand, mostly from three uncles.) Certainly both youngsters, like any other soldiers, were often cold, hungry, scared, and in pain. But I am pretty sure that on the whole they had an uproarious good time.

For one thing, neither of them had to walk. The Caperton family (none of whose members has ever cared for walking) managed to spare one of its plow horses so that George could enlist in the Fourth Alabama Cavalry. Grandfather Fischer was born beside the Ohio, on a farm near Marietta, and from the time he was old enough to lift a hoe he had looked with envy at the sailors lounging on the decks of the paddle-wheelers that steamed past. So at the age of twelve he signed up as a cabin boy on one of Commodore Foote's gunboats.

"One of the saddest days of my life," he told me later, "was when they paid me off at the end of the war and sent me back to that damned farm."

They ate better than most. The cavalry had endless chances to steal chickens, hogs, and roasting ears (plus an occasional jug of whisky), and it is one of America's oldest military traditions that the Navy always gets better food, and more of it, than the Army.

Their bloodshed was modest. That old infantry jibe—"Who ever saw a dead cavalryman?"—wasn't quite fair, but it wasn't altogether baseless either. And among the river sailors, squatting behind their armor of boiler plate and railroad rails, the casualty rate was lower still.

Finally, my grandfathers found time between battles for some memorable parties. The Fourth Alabama was commanded by disciplinarians—Nathan Bedford Forrest and later Joe Wheeler—who never encouraged the sort of carousing which was legendary among Stuart's troopers; but they couldn't prevent a campfire brawl now and then. One of these ended up in a bowie-knife argument, in which George Caperton got his most serious, if not exactly glorious, wound. (Later he broke an arm when a horse was shot out from under him at Shiloh. Since the surgeons weren't bothering with trifles at the time, he never got it properly set and carried a lump of ill-knit bone for the rest of his life.)

Cabin boy John Fischer got his only wound, his biggest party, and his worst disgrace in the Vicksburg campaign.

He had volunteered for service on one of the transports which Admiral David Porter had chosen for the supposedly desperate race down the Mississippi under the muzzles of the Vicksburg batteries on the night of April 16, 1863. Some sixty years later he told me about it, during the course of a long, hot afternoon of post-hole-digging, in words about like this:

"Everybody except Grant and Porter thought the scheme was crazy. While I was cleaning up the officers' mess table I heard them say that even Sherman was against it, and that all of our unarmored transports were bound to be sunk before we could steam a hundred yards beyond Big Bend. All that afternoon I helped stack cotton bales and barrels of hardtack along the rail, to give the deck hands a little cover. They made a mighty flimsy-looking breastwork, and I figured that I'd never live to see morning.

"What really happened was a sort of anticlimax. The night was real dark, and of course there wasn't a single candle or seegar alight in our whole string of ships. Besides, we stuck close to the west bank, so that the Reb gunners couldn't see us too well even after they set afire some barns and houses to light up the river.

"But they sure tried. For nearly two hours they blazed away with every cannon they could bring to bear, and I guess maybe ten thousand riflemen kept popping at us as fast as they could load. I watched the whole thing through a crack between two cotton bales, jumping like a rabbit every time a shell slammed into our boat. One transport ran aground and sank, and all the others got splintered up pretty bad—but we didn't lose a man.

"Seemed like I was always hungry those days, like a teen-age boy generally is, and as soon as the shooting was over I slipped along the deck till I found a smashed cracker barrel. I started eating hardtack as fast as I could stuff it in my mouth, aiming to get my fill before an officer caught me. In the dark I couldn't see that a Minié ball had stuck in one of those crackers, and I broke a tooth. It wasn't what you could call a combat wound, I guess, but it *was* caused by an enemy weapon."

Toward the end of the campaign some of the transports were ordered to Natchez for repair. In those days it was two towns— a dignified cluster of porticoed mansions on the bluff, and below it a rowdy port, Natchez-under-the-Hill.

"The minute we tied up," my grandfather said, "every man aboard lit out for the saloons, which were loud and plentiful. But the Captain told me and Henry that the cabin boys would have to stay and look after the ship. He also ordered us to have plenty of hot coffee ready by daybreak, on the theory that he and the other officers would need it when they got back.

"Neither of us knew much about cooking, but we filled a ten-gallon wash boiler full of water and ten pounds of coffee and set it on the galley stove. By midnight it was boiling good, but an awful lot of coffee grounds seemed to be floating on the top.

"Now somewhere I had heard that eggshells would settle coffee grounds. Henry argued that didn't stand to reason. What the situation called for was something with more body to it, like whole eggs. So we broke a dozen eggs into the boiler and stirred for a while. That helped some, but not much. So we added another dozen, and threw in the shells after them.

"Naturally we were pretty sore about missing the fun in Natchez-under-the-Hill, and when Henry found a bottle of vanilla extract in the pantry we decided to have a party of our own. Come daylight, we were smelling like a pair of angel-food cakes. At about that point it occurred to us that the coffee better be real good when the Captain got home. We broke in all the rest of the eggs in the galley, including those which weren't too fresh, and we were stirring hard when the officers wobbled up the gangplank.

"In spite of all the pains we had taken, the Captain wasn't happy about that coffee. In fact, he was downright irritable. Said we tried to poison him. Said we probably were Rebel spies. Said that anyhow we were no-good brats, and we would sure God spend the rest of the war in the brig.

"Maybe we would have, too, if the officers hadn't got tired of waiting on their own table. We never were officially pardoned, exactly, but the First Officer let us out in time to see the surrender of Vicksburg in July."

For officers in general my grandfather had scant respect. Sherman, for example, he described as "a nervous ol' fuss-budget" who nearly lost the Army of the Tennessee at Shiloh out of sheer carelessness, and who was saved only by the last-minute arrival of the river flotilla with firepower and reinforcements. But Grant, he admitted, "probably knew what he was up to." Sometimes he added that "Grant wasn't as flighty as most of them generals"—a rare compliment from the old man, who regarded flightiness (or any other display of emotion) with chill contempt.

This judgment apparently was based less on Grant's record of victories than on a cabin boy's observation of his behavior under fire. Grandpa's best chance for a close-up appraisal came at the siege of Fort Donelson. For hours there the gunboats tossed shells into the Confederate entrenchments, while Grant watched from the riverbank a few yards away. The weather was near freezing and an icy rain fell at intervals all through the day.

"He scootched up in his saddle like a wet chicken," Grandpa remembered, "while the water dripped down his coat collar and the Reb cannon balls splashed mud all over his boots."

For his juvenile listener this was exciting stuff—an eyeball witness's account of History in the Making. I nagged for details. What I wanted, I suppose, though I didn't know how to ask for it, was an insight into the character of a hero, some explanation of what it is that makes a great man great. What did he do to win that battle?

"He didn't do anything so far as I could see," Grandpa said. "He just sat there like a hickory stump."

Well, then, how did he *really* look?

"He looked cold."

That was as close to the sure 'nuff truth about Grant as I ever got. At the time it seemed unsatisfactory, but years later I began to suspect that it summed up the essential facts pretty well: a cold man, unbudgeable as a hickory stump.

Every one of the Southern children I knew in my knee-pants days would confess, when pressed, that:

1. Before "The War" his family had owned a thousand slaves. (Never 973 or 1,012; always an even thousand.)

2. It lived in a mansion with white columns in front.

3. Not only was it aristocratic—that went without saying—but wealthy until the Yankees ruined everything.

For a long while I assumed that the Southern half of my family had enjoyed this vanished grandeur, like everybody else. Then, over the years, I gradually picked up from my innumerable kinfolk the disillusioning sure 'nuff truth:

1. The Capertons had owned three slaves. Each of these

had a large family, but nobody seemed sure whether the wives and children were slaves or not. While the Caperton men were off at war, the Negroes worked the farm, hid the livestock from Yankee raiders, and in general took good care of the little community. When they were "liberated" by a Union column which marched across the farm on its way to Chickamauga, a few miles to the east, they thanked the soldiers kindly, cheered the Stars and Stripes, and went right back to work. After the war they stayed on, living the same as always; and when the family moved to Texas in 1891, an ex-slave—Wellesley Caperton—went along. (He found the Panhandle too windy and lonesome, and finally moved back to De Kalb County, Alabama.)

2. The "mansion" had no columns. Like most of the other old farmhouses on Sand Mountain, it was a dogtrot log cabin with an ell at the back. The same practical pattern is still being used by builders throughout the South, but the dogtrot is now called a breezeway and the construction isn't as solid. The walls of that cabin were made of squared-off walnut logs, some of which must have been four feet thick. When I saw it a few years back, they looked good for at least another century. (They had another and bigger house, for winter use, down in the valley, but it didn't have any columns either.)

3. The Yankees didn't ruin the place. Aside from stealing a few fence rails for their campfires, they apparently behaved with decorum. The family was poor because the soil on Sand Mountain never was much good, the Tennessee River habitually flooded the better fields in the bottoms, and malaria was endemic. Contrary to legend, it wasn't The War that forced such families to the West; they just hoped to make a better living on free homestead land. For the Capertons, TVA came a century too late.

Another favorite legend of my boyhood was that the war divided many families in the Tennessee River country, with the result that kinfolks met on the battlefield, usually at bayonet point. I now know that my two grandfathers must have been on opposite sides in at least two battles—Shiloh and Donelson—and probably at Fort Henry. But it is most unlikely that they ever got within shooting distance, and they never did meet on the battlefield or elsewhere.

Moral: The sure 'nuff truth may be stranger than fiction, but it doesn't make as satisfying a story.

April, 1961

4 : How to Cure Bird Watchers

ONE OF OUR READERS—a young woman living in Sacramento—has written to ask whether there is any known cure for bird-watching. Her father, she says, keeps gawking around the neighborhood with field glasses, often at unseemly hours. This causes embarrassment to her and her friends. Only last week a couple parked in a quiet lane was startled by the old gentleman at an unfortunate moment, and matters weren't helped much by his explanation that he was only looking for a spiny-toed nightingale.

The lady has come to the right place. This is a service magazine, in a soulful kind of way. We aim to help with the spiritual problems of our readers, just as *McCall's* takes care of the grosser human needs by printing all those articles about forty-three new ways to cook hamburger. Besides I have been plagued by birds for years, and while I can't say that I've learned to cope with them I at least know how to give them a good fight.

It is true that I have never suffered myself from bird-watching. Since childhood, when I was forced to take care of a herd of malevolent chickens, I have regarded all varieties of *Aves neognathae* as smelly, noisy, feather-brained, hysterical little beasts, from which any sensitive man naturally averts his eyes. Nevertheless at a tender age I stumbled by accident on a sure-fire remedy for the affliction. The only difficulty is that the young woman will have to persuade her father to do his bird-watching, at least once, barefooted and along the banks of some Southern stream. The Suwannee River would serve. Or Dead Man's Bayou.

My own discovery was made on Sweetwater Creek in northern Texas. I was after catfish, using a No. 6 hook baited with boiled potato. (This method is neither as sporting nor as efficient as dynamite, but my parents—who had never heard of Dr. Spock and permissive child-raising—discouraged me from playing with explosives.) So I was ambling along barefoot, brooding over parental tyranny and looking hard for one of those muddy backwaters where catfish hold their committee meetings.

All of a sudden my left foot came down on something unpleasant. I had never stepped on a water moccasin before, but somehow I knew right off what to do. The moccasin is a fat and sluggish snake, and before he knew what was squushing him I was ten feet in the air; and by the time he got his fangs cleared for action, I had hit the ground about five yards off in a high lope.

Ever since I have been a compulsive snake watcher. Anyone, I believe, who has felt the coils of a water moccasin under his toes will thereafter keep his eyes firmly on the ground. Never again is he likely to be bothered with the sight of birds, aside from sandpipers and those little squinch owls that live in prairie-dog holes.

Even a reformed bird watcher, however, is by no means out of the woods. With any decent animal—a grizzly, for instance —you can be reasonably sure that if you don't bother him, he won't bother you. But not birds; they seek out their victims with the vindictive persistence of the Kremlin's secret police. If you go to earth, so to speak, on the twenty-fourth floor of a Manhattan apartment, a posse of pigeons is sure to turn up at six the next morning to hoot and sneer at you from the windowsill. Starlings will build a nest in the intake of your air conditioner.

Or you will find, as one inoffensive New Yorker did recently, that something of the order *Columbiformes* has flown right inside and laid an egg on your bedspread.

Take the case of George and Helen Papashvily, sculptor and writer, who sought tranquillity in the upper fastnesses of Bucks County. They had hardly got the plumbing into their old stone farmhouse when they were beset by a retarded cardinal.

Like so many of his genus, he was belligerent as well as stupid. For weeks he carried on a running battle with his own reflection in the dining-room window—swooping into the pane like a *kamikaze* pilot, beating it with his wings, and pecking at it till his beak dripped blood. The round ended when he had knocked himself out or collapsed on the grass in exhaustion.

At this point the Papashvilys—who are kindly to the verge of simple-mindedness and constantly imposed upon by man and beast—would rise wearily from their dining table and rescue the dope. After they had trickled brandy down his throat with an eye dropper, plied him with smelling salts, and pressed cold towels to his forehead, he usually revived enough for another assault.

This might have kept up indefinitely, or anyhow until the brandy ran out, if a she-cardinal hadn't come along one day and diverted him to other interests. They are now, presumably, populating the thickets of northern Pennsylvania with generation after generation of half-witted *Richmondena*.

Smart birds are even worse. Everything that wears feathers is a criminal at heart—as Dr. A. C. Bent demonstrated in his classic fourteen-volume *Life Histories of North American Birds* —but the elite of this overworld obviously are the crows. They are as well organized as the Mafia, and more cunning. Nobody has ever rounded up a gang of crows in an Apalachin farmhouse.

The reason is that—unlike Barbara, Genovese & Company— crows do their conspiring in an open field, with guards posted to cover every approach. These sentries apparently carry binoculars, and are trained not only to spot a gun at five hundred yards but to tell whether it is a rifle or shotgun; and they have learned the range of each. Consequently, as every hunter knows, they are about the most elusive game on this continent.

I once tried to beat their system by sneaking up on a crow convention in a station wagon. They know that autos are harmless, and ordinarily pay them no attention. So I pulled up, in an offhand way, beside a pasture where maybe twenty-five of them were plotting their next job.

Sure enough, after one contemptuous glance they went right on with their scheming. I rolled down a window. Still no alarm. Then I reached for the carbine I had hidden under a gunny sack, and started to poke it—slowly and cautiously—over the sill. Not more than an inch of the muzzle was sticking out when the nearest sentry saw it, recognized instantly what it was, and blew the whistle. The whole gang took off, jeering vulgarly, before I could get in a shot.

The only practical way to outwit a crow is with dynamite, the sportsman's best friend on water or land. Here is a tested recipe, bearing the Harper's Seal of Approval:

First you find a thicket of shinnery oaks where crows gather to roost. These scrubby little trees grow in dense clumps all over the Texas Panhandle; they make an ideal lair for crows, as they once did for horse thieves and train robbers. As many as five thousand birds may infest a single clump.

At daybreak they leave in small bands, scattering over miles of countryside on their criminal pursuits—stealing pheasant eggs, devastating grain fields, pecking the eyes out of newborn calves. As soon as you are sure they are all gone, you slip into the shinnery and start stringing up your dynamite. Half-sticks will do, tied to branches at about head height and spaced roughly five yards apart all through the thicket. Their detonators all have to be connected to a single wire, which runs to a hiding place a safe distance away—usually a neighboring patch of brush. There you wait, beside your storage battery and switch, until the enemy comes home at sundown.

This is the crucial moment. You have to lie well ambushed and absolutely still; for if an advance patrol spots you, it will warn the whole flock—which at once will line out for another roost miles away. If you escape detection, however, you simply bide your time until the whole colony is assembled; then close the switch. The results are gratifying. A rain of black feathers, shinnery leaves, and crows' feet will cover the landscape for acres around.

In our struggle with the birds, the most dangerous chink in man's armor is sentimentality. They are alert for any sign of this weakness; and, as we have seen in The Papashvily Case, they know how to take instant advantage of it.

My aunt Annie was, I guess, the softest-hearted woman in Comanche County, Oklahoma. For many years she lived on a homestead there, keeping house for her widower father. One Christmas a neighbor gave her a jar of brandied cherries and—though Annie disapproved of liquor even in semisolid form—the guests at dinner that night managed to put away the whole quart.

In her thrifty way, Annie saved the pits and fed them next morning to her flock of hens. This was meant in the kindliest spirit—Annie felt that even Plymouth Rocks deserved a Christmas treat—but it turned out to be a mistake. When Annie went out at noon to collect the eggs, she found every one of the chickens lying stone cold dead with its claws sticking up stiff in the air.

Crushed by grief as she was, she didn't mean to let those chickens go to waste. Annie couldn't bring herself to chop off their heads—that was man's work anyhow, and could wait till her father came in from plowing the northeast forty—but she could at least begin to get them ready for the cold-storage locker. With tears sliding down her nose, and muttering prayers against the evil of drink, she plucked them all—carefully saving the feathers for pillow-stuffing. Then she laid the corpses in a row along the shady side of the barn to await the ax.

Trouble was, they didn't stay dead. When her father brought in the team at suppertime, he encountered a spectacle which, he said, beat anything he had seen since the night a Kiowa war party scalped the whole village of Chillicothe. Twenty-three hens were staggering around the barnyard—overhung, shivering, and naked as September Morn.

The sight so scandalized the mules—a high-strung pair at best—that it took him twenty minutes to get off the harness.

Annie worked all night, cutting up old burlap bags and sewing them into hen chemises, while her outraged flock huddled squawking behind the stove. By morning they were the best-dressed chickens in Oklahoma; but they didn't seem to appreciate it. For the next six weeks, while they were growing a new crop of feathers, they wore their smocks with a look both sheepish and hangdog—which for chickens is quite a trick. I am willing to grant (grudgingly) that they, anyhow, must have been birds worth watching.

HOWL: A Beatnik-type Ode to Our Little Feathered Friends

Canto I

Hark, the robin
And his uncle and his cousins and his aunts
Plus some grackles or something
And a lot of asthmatic thrushes
Are starting up their harebrained noises
Again just outside my window.
Which means it is
Four A.M. (Eastern Daylight Saving Time)
And there will be no more
Sleep around here this night.

Canto II

Ah, why can't God's blithe spirits
Keep their throbbing little throats
Shut until seven o'clock

Like cats and horses
And other reasonable animals?

Canto III
Anybody want to join
The Little Daisy Air Rifle
Bird-watching Association?

April, 1961

5 : Here Today and Gone Today, Too

FOR HIS SEVENTIETH BIRTHDAY, I took a fifth of bourbon to
Joe L. Williams, who had been in his time about the best cow-
hand in the Texas Panhandle. Later, as an oilman and wheat
farmer, he had made and lost three fortunes. When I was a
teen-ager I had worked for him now and then, driving a tractor
and painting cattle sheds; we had remained close friends. As we
sampled the whisky, which he took straight, he told me the
following cautionary tale:

It was 1892, when I was foreman of the RO ranch, that Henry
Quiller, one of my cowhands, told me how he got rich and
learned never to worry about money.

Henry came from a big family, and a poor one, in the
Concho River country. On his eighteenth birthday his father
told Henry it was time for him to get moving.

"You'll never have much chance here," he said. "On this
land and with this drought it's all I can do to feed your mother
and the young ones. The best I can do for you is to give you
part of the sheepherd; they'll starve anyway if we keep them
here. I've heard there is plenty of fresh grass up north, where

the country hasn't been settled much yet. So you take two hundred head and line out that way. When you come to a likely piece of land with nobody on it, file your claim."

Henry kissed his mother good-by, tied a sack of beans behind his saddle, and started chaperoning those sheep. He grazed them along easy, a few miles a day. It was early in the year, the weather wasn't too hot, and he sort of enjoyed himself until his beans-and-mutton diet began to get monotonous.

About that time, though, he came across a Mexican family living in a sod shack way off by itself in the middle of the prairie. They were trying to make a go of farming, and first off they had planted a little garden patch with chiles and tomatoes and such truck, as Mexicans usually do. The sight made Henry's mouth water. He offered to work a few days, setting fence posts and stringing wire, in return for all the vegetables he could eat. The Monteros were glad to have him—they needed help and company, too—and he got along with them fine. When the time came for him to move on, the old man said he wanted to give Henry a present.

A couple of years earlier the Mexican kids had found a stray lamb. They had named him Santa Anna and raised him as a pet. In the beginning he had been mighty cute, but now he had grown into a full-sized ram, and a mean one. He would hide around the corner of the shack until Doña Montero came out the door with an armload of laundry or something, and then he would butt her clear across the lot. He butted all the rest, too, whenever he could catch them with their backs turned. Old Man Montero wanted to butcher him, but the kids wouldn't hear of it. So would Henry please take Santa Anna along with his herd?

Henry would. He had a few rams already—good gentle ones —but he thought his ewes might be grateful for some more rambunctious companionship. At his age he thought he could handle anything, and he headed north again without a care in the world.

Next evening when he was picking up buffalo chips to make

a cookfire, that ram got him. For a minute Henry thought he
had been hit by a locomotive, and he couldn't sit his saddle
with any comfort for two days.

From then on he tried to keep an eye on Santa Anna, but the
ram was just as smart and treacherous as his namesake. He
got in a couple more good licks in Henry's absent-minded
moments, and a certain coolness began to grow up between
them.

By this time Henry had been traveling for nearly three months,
and he had reached a country different from anything he had
ever seen. It was flat and empty and the bunchgrass grew almost
as high as his saddle girth. He was beginning to look for a
spring or year-round creek where he could build a homestead,
when he came to a canyon a mile wide and half that deep. It
was the Palo Duro, on the Prairie Dog Town Fork of the Red
River, but of course Henry didn't know that at the time. All he
knew was that he had found a sight like he never dreamed of—
miles and miles of red cliffs, with cedar growing on the slopes
below and a pretty stream winding along the bottom.

He sat down in the shade of a mesquite tree right on the rim-
rock, and tried to figure some way to get his sheep down into
that canyon without breaking their necks, and his. Once he
reached the bottom, he would have everything—water, grass,
wood, shelter from the wind—to make the prettiest ranch you
ever saw. (Later on Colonel Charles Goodnight and John Adair
had the same idea, and the Adair family are running their JA
brand there to this day.)

The shade and the scenery were mighty comfortable, and
pretty soon Henry remembered another present the Monteros
had given him—a bundle of old newspapers. He had stuffed
them in his saddlebag and forgotten about them—Henry never
was much of a reader—but now they came to mind he thought
he might as well find out what had happened in the world
since he left home.

At first he couldn't find anything in the papers of much
interest—some wars going on in Europe, a big fire in Chicago,

a steamboat collision on the Mississippi. Then he found a page of livestock price quotations, and he began to get excited. Cattle and sheep had both been going up—fast—on the Kansas City market. Henry fished out a stub of pencil and began to do some arithmetic on the edge of the paper. He calculated the present value of his herd. Then he figured what the natural increase might be each year, especially if he could shelter his sheep in that deep canyon and keep the coyotes away from the lambs. Gradually it dawned on him that he was a poor boy no longer. Already he was well off—and if the livestock market kept rising for a few more years, he could count himself a wealthy man.

He looked at his woolies, grazing peacefully in that tall grass, with a new affection. And then he saw Santa Anna at the edge of the herd, pawing the ground with his head down and getting bunched up for a charge.

"Let him come," Henry said to himself. "A rich man like me doesn't have to put up with that damned old outlaw any longer."

He stood there, with his back to the canyon, and held out his newspaper at arm's length, like a bullfighter's cape, to give the ram a good target. Santa Anna aimed right at it, with a full head of steam.

What Henry hadn't figured was that the rest of the sheep had got in the habit of following Santa Anna. When the ram lunged past that newspaper and took off over the cliff, the whole herd was strung out behind him, running hell-for-leather.

"There wasn't much I could do," Henry said when he told me about it years later, "except to start grabbing with both hands. One minute I was practically a rich man. The next minute I didn't have a thing in the world but nine pounds of wool and seven sheep tails.

"Right then I realized that wealth was a snare and an illusion, and from that day on I've never even tried to make a lot of money. I knew I never could hold on to it if I got it."

May, 1957

6 : Social Status in the Underworld

THE CRIME INVESTIGATIONS now under way in Washington and elsewhere have given the impression that the underworld is managed like a feudal barony by a few overlords, such as Luciano, Genovese, Costello, and the late Mr. Anastasia. This theory was reinforced by the publicity given the ill-arranged mobsters' convention at Apalachin, New York, and by the subsequent newspaper accounts of what is usually assumed to be gangland's Supreme Command—variously labeled as The Syndicate, The Mafia, or Cosa Nostra.

This notion is wrong. The Organization (actually a loose confederation of several separate and occasionally hostile mobs) undoubtedly does command a lot of money, guns, and sometimes political influence. Evidently it does administer and discipline a certain sharply defined field of criminal activity.

But it does not rule the entire underworld, and its members are by no means the upper crust of that society. They are, in fact, viewed with contempt and suspicion by the real criminal elite. The social hierarchy of the underworld—a structure just as complex as that of the so-called normal community—ranks the racketeers well below the middle rung. Their status, regardless of the size of their bankrolls, remains about the equivalent of a shoe salesman's; for money alone counts for a lot less here than in more respectable circles.

What follows is a report on some of the social values of the criminal—the ways in which he measures the prestige and respect due to each class of his fellow professionals. It is based in large part on the testimony of a man who enjoyed for many years a secure niche in the underworld's topmost social group: The Heavies.

240

The worst mistake I ever made, editorially speaking, was to help Henry get out of jail.

He had the ideal setup for a writer: a quiet cell with a type-writer, plenty of paper, and no telephone; an unlimited supply of source material close at hand; no worries about where the next meal was coming from, and no women to take his mind off his work; the ministrations, for free, of a psychiatrist who would have cost an ordinary writer $25 an hour; experts on every branch of his subject matter available for instant consultation; a staff of alert guards to protect him from the delivery boys, insurance salesmen, Jehovah's Witnesses, subscription peddlers, and other interrupters who make it so difficult for most authors to get their work done.

So his literary career blossomed fast. He sold several magazine articles—including a classic how-to-do-it piece in *Harper's* on the theory and practice of armed robbery. He held a publisher's contract for a book on crime which might well have become a best-seller. And he was making splendid progress with his masterwork, *A Dictionary of Modern American Slang, Cant, and Underworld Argot, on Interpretive Principles*. H. L. Mencken himself had given Henry advice and encouragement, in the belief that the book might someday make a place for itself on the permanent reference shelf, alongside Mencken's own monumental work, *The American Language*. Henry had written 646 pages and was nearly finished with the O's, when his pardon came through.

He has hardly written a line since. Understandably enough, he has been too busy getting caught up with all the living he missed during his seventeen years in prisons. The last I heard of him he was happily married, earning a comfortable salary as a consultant on crime films for a Hollywood studio, and hadn't looted a single bank, payroll truck, or even a filling station since the day he walked out of the Big Gate.

As a friend I am of course delighted that Henry is doing so well on the outside; but as an editor I can't help mourning the contributions he might have made to literature and sociology.

One of the manuscripts we bought from him, to help finance his debut into what he called "the legit life," was an unfinished treatise on the social nuances of his former society. From it I have gleaned some of the following notes; others came from many conversations with Henry and equally knowledgeable people.*

The moral standards, traditions, and folkways of the underworld are very ancient indeed; some of them run back to the beginnings of recorded history. They were developed to guide the behavior of a group in perpetual rebellion—thus enabling it to survive the pressures of an overwhelmingly powerful enemy. Naturally they are very different from the standards of conventional society; in some ways they resemble the ethical code of underground fighters in wartime.

For example, the underworld accords its greatest honor and admiration—logically enough—to those who are the most fanatically rebellious. By the same token it disdains and distrusts those who are willing to compromise or deal with the enemy. Socially, therefore, it divides itself into two main classes, each

---

* Since my first assignment as a police reporter in 1930, my work has from time to time thrown me into the company of nonpious characters—ranging from such big-time operators as Machine Gun Kelly, Frank Nash, and Pretty Boy Floyd to the most feckless sort of bootleggers, marijuana pushers, and alley creeps. Most of them did not have endearing personalities, but a few I liked and trusted as much as any of my more conventional friends.

For example, Matt Kimes, an amiable gunman whom I first met when he was a kitchen trusty in the Oklahoma State Penitentiary at McAlester. He used to fry up big steaks for me on those nights when I had to go there to witness an electrocution. They equaled anything you can get at the Waldorf, since the warden made it a rule to be attentive to reporters, but I could never manage more than a few bites; some reporters claim that they get used to covering executions, but I never did.

One evening while I was loafing around the kitchen, waiting for midnight— the customary hour for executions, since the condemned man is entitled to all of his final day—I muttered some routine complaint about the unreasonable demands of my city editor.

"If that bum gives you any trouble," Matt said, "just let me know and I'll tell one of my sidekicks in Oklahoma City to take care of him."

I hurriedly explained that drastic remedies weren't really necessary. Jack Bell was a hard man but one of the best bosses I ever worked for; he is now an ornament of the Associated Press staff in Washington. And, like Matt, he was always ready to do anything for a friend.

with a number of subdivisions. The smallest, and most respected, group consists of The Heavies. The other is made up of Grifters.

The heavy is a specialist in armed robbery. He takes what he wants by violence, or threat of violence. He scorns the use of guile or chicanery, and above all he refuses to employ the fix: that is, the bribery of police officers, by giving them either money or information about other criminals.

His name originated in England about two hundred years ago, when a bounty of forty pounds was offered for any criminal accused of a capital offense. Highwaymen, burglars, and others whose professional activities made them eligible for hanging were known, therefore, as "heavy-men" because of their extra forty pounds of "weight." (Later the term, in its contracted form, also was applied to stage villains.)

The distinguishing mark of the heavy is his eagerness to combat the forces of respectable society on an all-out basis, no quarter asked or given. His motive is pure hostility. Money is not important, except as a measure of his "score" and therefore of the successfulness of his aggression. When he has it, he flings it about with contemptuous carelessness (which often leads to his arrest). Money is, after all, one of the idols of the society he is defying, so he refuses to worship it; in fact the argot he commonly uses equates cash with filth.

Also significant are the heavy's terms for his professional operations. They always imply aggression: he will "clout" a payroll or "knock off" a bank. So too the language in which he speaks of sex connotes aggression, never tenderness. Henry's dictionary is full of illuminating, though rude, examples.

Henry became a heavy before he knew what the word meant. He had been raised in a genteel, prosperous upstate New York family with deep religious convictions. So deep, indeed, that his father demanded an impossibly high level of conduct, and beat him mercilessly for any lapse—usually two or three times a day. By the time he was adolescent, Henry was convinced that he was a worthless and irredeemable sinner, who could never placate Authority. Eventually he defied it, by running away.

At this stage, defiance seemed to be almost his only emotion. When he saw a "No Spitting" sign on a streetcar, he would spit; the mere sight of a policeman would drive him into a red-eyed rage. Pretty soon he attempted a petty robbery—on impulse, without proper planning, and therefore bungled from the start. He ended up in the penitentiary at the age of nineteen.

There he got in trouble with the guards the first day. Throughout that term and several later ones (all for armed robbery) he remained implacably uncooperative, in spite of all punishment. This earned him the respect and friendship of the other heavies in stir, and before long he found himself a member of the clique that dominated the social life of the prison. Its members were few, but they had no trouble imposing their will by simple violence and intractability—or, as Henry put it, "by their force of character." Eventually he reached the apex of personal leadership by heading a prison riot. Soon afterward a psychiatrist was assigned to the penitentiary. The warden, who didn't hold with newfangled notions, ordered him to keep his hands off the "good" prisoners and to concentrate his efforts on Henry: nothing could make *that* one any worse. Consequently Henry got about $50,000 worth of psychoanalysis during the next couple of years; it enabled him, finally, to understand the reasons for his pathological aggressiveness and to turn his energies in another direction: i.e., writing. Later the doctor was largely responsible for getting him pardoned, by certifying that he would no longer be a menace.

Like his fellow heavies, however, Henry remained forever disdainful of the grifters. In this class are included all thieves who try to outwit the sucker, rather than overpower him. They operate with fraud, not weapons. Therefore, in the eyes of the heavy they are "short of belly"—that is, lacking in courage. Moreover, they are primarily out for money, and thus accept one part of the enemy's value system.

What is even more scandalous, they are willing to connive with the police. Whenever possible, they prefer to operate under their gutlessness and crummy, chiseling natures, they are held in low esteem.

Clear outside of the underworld—outcasts, who have no social standing whatever—are the nonprofessionals. These are the ordinary suckers, or John Citizens, who get entangled with the law more or less by happenstance: the clerk who passes a bad check, the woman who sticks a bread knife into her husband in a fit of pique, the bank cashier who got to playing the horses and dipped his hand into the till to make good his loss. Most despised of all are the sex offenders, who (in Henry's phrase) "have about as much social prestige in prisons as a garbage collector in Westchester."

The racketeers, now the most prosperous group in the underworld, form a special class of grifters. They are businessmen who deal in forbidden commodities and services—notably narcotics, organized gambling, and the labor rackets. Like the hustlers, they are not wholehearted rebels; many, in fact, operate legitimate businesses as a cover for their illegal enterprises, and some of them show yearnings for respectability—if not for themselves, at least for their children.

Like the grifters, they work with a fix whenever they can. They dislike unnecessary violence, since it is likely to attract unfavorable public attention. When force is necessary, however —to discipline members of their organization, to intimidate a victim of extortion, to eliminate obstreperous members of a captive labor union, or to protect their territory against the encroachment of another mob—they don't hesitate to use it. In such cases, they often will hire a heavy to do the actual killing.

Unlike most other criminals, they operate through elaborate and relatively permanent organizations—sometimes with lawyers, accountants, and other such technicians on the payroll. (Heavies and most grifters either work alone or in small groups—seldom larger than six—which form and split up as readily as an amoeb frequently such a mob will last only for a single job. Usually, t each member is considered co-equal with every other, and proceeds are split evenly.)

the protection of a fix. Consequently decent criminals can neve
be sure that a grifter will not turn stool pigeon, in order to bu
himself temporary immunity from the law. This moral ur
reliability is the chief reason for the grifters' low standing on th
underworld's social scale.

Among the grifters there are about twenty-five subclasse
Each has its own procedures and code of ethics, although a fe
doctrines hold good throughout all reaches of criminal societ
For instance, all thieves share an attitude of derision towar
working stiffs, and a conviction that it is wicked to educate
mark: that is, to warn an intended victim.

At one time the cannon-mobs—i.e., pickpocket teams—wer
regarded as an elite among grifters, because their profession r
quired training, skill, and steady nerves in a high degree. (The
name derived from the Yiddish *gonif*; it has nothing to do wit
firearms, which a pickpocket shuns.) They are a dwindling trib
however, because the young talent is now turning to easier, mor
lucrative capers.

Other main categories of the grifters are con men; boosters, c
shoplifters—many of them women; crooked gamblers; heelmer
or the kind of sneak thieves who pick up unwatched luggage i
railway stations and overcoats in restaurants; car snatchers; an
prowls, or house burglars.

At the very bottom of the social hierarchy are the hustlers. Th
term covers a whole group of occupations that entail little risl
minor penalties, and no great skill, intelligence, or courage. On
example is the pitchmen, who hawk fake jewelry and the magi
spot remover which also, in a matter of hours, removes the clotl
Others are the pushers, who change counterfeit currency; tout
pimps, and prostitutes; pool sharks; retail dope peddlers; steerer
who guide suckers to gambling gaffs, clip joints, and night clut
for a percentage of the take; and anyone else who is hungry t
turn a safe and dishonest dollar. The hustlers—by far the mos
populous group in the underworld—are not really dedicate
rebels; when forced to it by penury, they have no scruples agains
loving temporarily into upperworld jobs. For this, as well a

According to my informants—and contrary to popular mythology—there is no overall national organization of the rackets, and no single master mind. The major outfits or syndicates have, however, divided up the country into clearly defined territories; and in some cases of jurisdictional disputes they have apparently called in the top man of the Mafia to serve as referee. It has an enviable reputation for skillful management, founded on four hundred years of experience in Sicily; for *omertà*, or adamant refusal to talk to the law; and trustworthiness. A Mafia man's word—to another criminal—is supposed to be as good as a government bond. (Incidentally, it is generally believed that Anastasia was executed because he refused to accept a Mafia ruling which awarded the gambling business in Cuba to a rival mobster.)

The attitude of the heavy toward the racketeers is a compound of dislike, mistrust, resentment, and envy. He dislikes their acceptance of business-world mores, and suspects the worst of their close tie-ups with politicians and the police. For, to quote an underworld maxim, "Sleep with the dogs, and you're bound to catch fleas." At the same time he envies their prosperity, and resents their relative immunity to punishment. (The heavy is far more likely to end up in jail than either the grifter or the racketeer; he is more reckless, he has less political and legal protection, and crimes of violence have always provoked the most vigorous retaliation by the upperworld.)

Relations between the two groups also are curiously ambivalent. The heavy will work for a racket mob, on occasion, but he is also likely to prey upon it. For example, the Syndicate's horse parlors in Chicago have repeatedly been raided by independent holdup men, and gang bosses live in constant fear of kidnaping. Naturally they try to punish such outrages in their own way. As a result, a heavy will not be surprised to find himself hunted simultaneously by the police and the Syndicate's shotgun specialists—although, to quote Henry again, "he never ceases to express horror and indignation that such things can be." If the police locate him first, they may not bother to arrest him; a simpler and more permanent solution, they may decide, is to finger him—i.e., point him out to the mob's enforcers.

This necessarily oversimplified account of a complicated situation might well be rounded off with one of Henry's tales, which nicely illustrates the complexities of a criminal's life.

Willie the Beef-lugger was a respected holdup artist. (He also was conspicuously overweight; hence his moniker.) One night, with a Smith and Wesson .38 in his hand, he walked into a hotel apartment where a dozen racket big shots were relaxing at a private crap game, and helped himself to a half-bushel of coarse bills lying on the table. For a man of his build, disguise was out of the question, so he didn't even bother to wrap a scarf around his face.

As he backed out the door, he bade a cheery good night to one and all, and added: "I know you as well as you know me."

Willie depended on this implied threat to save him from the attentions of the mob's enforcers. His readiness to argue an issue at gun point was well known, and besides he had friends who might resent it if Willie encountered an accident, such as a stick of dynamite wired to the starter of his car.

What concerned him more was the city detective squad which, at that time, worked in cordial and lucrative symbiosis with the rackets. He knew that there would be no formal complaint about the robbery, and that there was no other charge outstanding for which he could be arraigned. But he was not eager to be held "for questioning," since the squad's method of inquiry was notoriously strenuous. To this matter he had given much thought.

As a consequence he had made arrangements in advance with one of the city's leading trial lawyers. His office was alerted to expect a telephone call from Willie every hour on the hour for two weeks after the heist. If a call ever failed to come through on schedule, the lawyer was immediately supposed to scour the police stations until he found Willie, and then get him released on a writ of habeas corpus.

A pair of detectives did indeed pick Willie up within twenty-four hours. They took him to a back room in an outlying precinct station and worked him over at intervals for nearly two days—to such effect that he eventually had to spend a good part of his loot on personal repairs. If he hadn't been so well upholstered, Willie believes, he might well have been maimed for life.

The lawyer never did show up. What particularly incensed Willie was that he had foreseen everything—or everything except the fact that his lawyer had for years been taking a surreptitious retainer from the mob. He regards such conduct as lousy and unethical, and swears he never again will trust either lawyers or racketeers.

October, 1958

7 : Legend Aloft

NEXT TO THE COVERED WAGON and the Model T Ford, the DC-3 probably is embedded deeper in American history and legend than any machine we have ever made. It is the plane in which most of us made our first flight. It also is a work of art—clean, functional, and (like a good piece of sculpture) superbly balanced from any angle of vision. It is designed in what John Kouwenhoven has christened the American Vernacular, the great tradition ranging from the Mississippi steamboat to the San Francisco Bay Bridge, the Johnson Wax Company Building, the New Jersey Turnpike, and the Hoover Dam. (Every culture, of course, develops its own distinctive idiom and media. The materials of our major artists are steel, aluminum, glass, and concrete, rather than canvas, paint, and marble; and they are intended for the delight and use of millions, rather than for the private pleasures of an elite. Because European intellectuals find this hard to understand—because they can hardly conceive of any culture so different from their own—many of them still cling to the illusion that America simply doesn't have any.)

Then, too, the DC-3 has become legendary because it figures in the sharpest memories of so many Americans. Hundreds of thousands of us have had some experience with the plane which we are never likely to forget—a magic-carpet arrival in a strange land, a journey to a sick child, a glimpse of Manhattan's towers at night, an air drop into battle, or an encounter with fear.

For example, on a hot August morning in 1944, three strangers climbed aboard a DC-3 cargo plane at Dum-dum airfield. (This ancient military post, near Calcutta, is memorable only because the dum-dum bullet—which mushrooms on impact—was invented there about a hundred years ago; and because the outlawry of this unpleasant weapon is almost the only international Rule of War which is still universally respected.) None of the three had any proper military authorization to get on that plane; they were merely hitchhikers, thumbing a ride to Delhi.

Like most cargo planes at that time and place, this one was overloaded. It took off heavily, under a five-hundred-foot ceiling, and slid up into the monsoon cloudbank—some 16,000 feet thick —which covered most of India and Burma. You couldn't see the wingtips; everybody felt claustrophobic and uneasy.

Forty minutes out of Dum-dum the starboard engine quit. The pilot revved up the remaining engine, and swung into a slow turn back toward the field. Then the second engine began to splutter.

At this moment the navigator opened the door from the pilot's compartment, and grinned at his three passengers.

"Looks like we may have to get out," he said. "We got a couple of extra parachutes—you guys divide up."

He tossed the two khaki packs on the floor, between the rows of bucket seats, and closed the door.

For perhaps thirty seconds, the three strangers stared at each other, each one grappling in silent panic with the same moral problem: Do I let the others have the chutes—or do I fight like a tiger to get one for myself?

Before anybody could make up his mind, the port engine stopped spluttering and a few seconds later the starboard motor roared back to life. The passengers fumbled for cigarettes with sweaty fingers and talked about something else. The two parachutes were still lying untouched on the floor when the plane rolled down the landing strip.

At least one of the passengers still bothers about the incident now and then. He wonders: (a) What should he have done, if the engines hadn't caught on?—Toss a coin? Try to guess whose life was most important to the war effort?—and (b) What would he actually have done? These unanswered questions—and the awareness that one of them now cannot ever be answered for sure—leave an annoying kind of gap, a hole in his psychic sock. He remembers it uncomfortably every time he sees a DC-3 parked at an airport.

August, 1954

8 : How They Saved New York

ALTHOUGH IT STARTED about twenty years too late, the New York Chamber of Anti-Commerce swung into its job with the energy and imagination which always have characterized the metropolis. The first pamphlet—"It's a Lousy Place to Visit and You Wouldn't Want to Live Here"—appeared in June, 1968, just three weeks after the organization was founded.

In that same month the Chamber gave the full treatment to the American Legion, which insisted on holding its annual convention in New York City in spite of repeated warnings. A battalion of goons, recruited from the Pistol Local of the International Longshoremen's Association, welcomed the Legionnaires with their own traditional weapons—squirt guns, electrified canes, and water-filled paper bags dropped from hotel windows. The barkeepers cooperated by inventing a new drink, the Forty-and-Eight Mickey Finn Special, and the police called the wagon for every conventioneer who dared to complain over a clip-joint check. One prisoner from every state was forwarded to the back room at the Twenty-sixth Precinct; there they were methodically marked up by the strong-arm squad (though seldom with anything worse than a broken nose) as an example to folks back home.

Later that summer the Chamber of Anti-Commerce brought into action its Official Greeters Corps—a collection of Broadway types selected for their two-tone personalities, obtrusive muscle, and Damon Runyon accents. They met tourists at all terminals with a brief message: Get out of town before dark.

Regrettably, these activities led to some misunderstanding in the hinterland. The President of the Chamber—Robert Moses, who was also at that time State and City Coordinator in Charge of Everything—tried to clear the matter up with his famous Waldorf-Astoria address to the National Association of Manufacturers. Speaking on the subject "Go West, Old Man," he outlined the New York program for discouraging new industry. He also announced a handsome bounty for any enterprise already established in the city which would move to Kansas, or anywhere more than five hundred miles away.

"For New York has become overgrown," Mr. Moses explained, "to the verge of municipal suicide. Like a circus fat lady, it is paralyzed by its own bulk.

"We have built superhighways, tunnels, and bridges, that are engineering marvels; but our traffic arteries are still clogged with chronic thrombosis. We have latched onto every trickle of fresh water within two hundred miles, but our air conditioners still run dry. In spite of the highest tax rates in the country, we still have the most overcrowded schools, the sorriest police force, and the filthiest streets. A civic machinery grown insanely complex harasses all of us with its constant breakdowns—ranging from a tugboat strike to a stuck elevator, a broken water main, or a subway short circuit. In a normal city, these things would be inconveniences; here they are often disasters.

"We have realized, at last," he went on, "that nature imposes an upper limit on the size of every organism, whether it is a brontosaurus or a city. Beyond that limit, every additional 10 per cent of growth doubles the expense and trebles the inconvenience. New York passed the limit long ago. It is no longer practical: indeed, it is hardly tolerable. Our goal therefore is to siphon off a million population within the next five years. . . ."

With his customary tact, Mr. Moses added that anyone who disagreed with him was a utopian dreamer, a lily-fingered theorist, and a tool of the vested interests. As he sat down, amid stormy applause, the city's leading real-estate operator grabbed the microphone. In a voice choked with emotion, he proclaimed his conversion to The Cause—and offered to tear down four new skyscrapers immediately, plant the site in trees, and christen it the William Zeckendorf Memorial Gardens.

Next morning four manufacturers of ladies' girdles, twelve stockbrokers, and a publisher advertised for out-of-town locations, and the great exodus really got under way. . . .

June, 1954

9 : The City That Hid Itself:
An Archaeological Mystery Story

SAMOTHRACE

TO GET TO THIS ISLAND, you first have to find the *Holy Virgin of Samothrace*. She usually turns up about twice a week along the waterfront of Alexandroupolis, a dusty little fishing port in the far corner of Greece, close to the Turkish border. She is a kind of seagoing omnibus, and if you can squeeze yourself onto the deck among the wool bales, sacks of charcoal, melons, chickens, children, and barefoot women, she will carry you to Samothrace in about four hours. When a herd of goats is aboard the best seat is upwind on the coil of mooring rope in the bow.

The *Holy Virgin* will stop, on request, at almost any spot along the island's shore. If you want to land at Palaeopolis, as I did, a couple of crewmen will row you to the rocky beach. There, if you have the favor of the Nikolaides clan, a charming young man named Ulysses will be waiting to carry your bags through the surf. He is the member of the family who speaks English, and he will lead you up the trail to their guesthouse, which is Samothrace's only approximation to a hotel.

It isn't really in Palaeopolis, but on the opposite side of a gulch which once guarded the western wall of the Old City. In fact, nobody lives in Palaeopolis now, and visitors are rare. Few tourists come to this remote stretch of the Mediterranean, and few of those ever heard of the Old City or the curious story of its disappearance.

But for a thousand years it was one of the great tourist centers of the world. Maybe it was the first. Some ancient historians thought that the people who "sprang from the soil" of this island were the earliest in Greece. The Great Gods of Samothrace probably were being worshiped here long before anybody ever heard of Zeus or Apollo, and certainly were still venerated after those Olympian upstarts had been forsaken.

Their shrine drew the pious in multitudes, as Jerusalem and Lourdes do today. Pilgrims came from as far as Syria, Egypt, and Rome, and their trade and their offerings made the city rich. (Among them was the Emperor Hadrian, himself worshiped as a god, and St. Paul, who was spreading the word of a new, subversive deity.) You can get some idea of the old splendor of Samothrace from the Winged Victory in the Louvre; it was one of many statues which adorned the sanctuary of the Great Gods.

This sanctuary was almost a little town itself—a cluster of

shrines, monuments, treasure houses, souvenir shops, and priestly halls, mostly of imported marble. It lay outside the ramparts of Palaeopolis, in a wooded valley between the west gate of the city and the ridge where the Nikolaides house now stands. Such a holy spot, its founders thought, needed no protection except that of the Gods.

The city proper, nourished by its tourist trade, grew powerful as well as rich. In its heyday, some six hundred years before Christ, perhaps 75,000 people lived on the craggy headland which rises above the sanctuary and juts northward to the sea. They were sheltered behind a wall twenty feet thick, in which some stones weigh many tons—a wall so strong that miles of it still stand in spite of unnumbered sieges and earthquakes. Their navy dominated the strategic sea lanes to the Dardanelles. Their palaces could offer entertainment suitable for the wealthiest of kings; it was here, for example, that Philip of Macedonia met and wooed the princess—also a visitor to the holy sanctuary—who became the mother of Alexander the Great.

It is not unusual for such a city to vanish. Many cities in this part of the world, once just as proud and strong, are only mounds of rubble today. What is peculiar is the manner of its disappearance. For Palaeopolis was not razed by conquerors, like Pella and Corinth, nor wiped out by disease, like Paestum. It simply went into hiding. In the end its people got so frightened and discouraged that they ran away—abandoning their homes and shops and churches—and took refuge in a secret valley about four miles into the hills.

Their descendants—some three thousand of them—are hiding there yet. Until a couple of years ago, they refused even to build a road to their village. When they finally decided that a road would not necessarily be a dangerous invitation to invading strangers, they did not aim it toward the Old City, but to another spot on the coast where the *Holy Virgin* can tie up at a dock. Many of them still seem to have misgivings about this innovation, and the beat-up truck (the only car on the island) which it accommodates. When they venture out of their valley, they usually go on foot or muleback, by way of obscure and break-neck paths.

Not that they have much of anywhere to go. Their village, which they call Chora, is the one surviving remnant of a great and graceful civilization. A few scattered farms and hamlets are the only other habitations on Samothrace.

Exactly what happened to Palaeopolis is still something of a mystery. But the main clues are now beginning to emerge—thanks to a handful of archaeologist-detectives, most of them Americans. The story they are uncovering may have a certain melancholy interest for people who live in confident cities elsewhere.

It began more than three thousand years ago, when the pre-historic men who then lived there discovered an outcropping of colored porphyry beside a little stream on the north side of the island. They decided that these rocks were sacred—probably because their red, blue, green, and gray mottling was different from anything they had ever seen, and prettier. Besides, chunks of magnetic iron ore were scattered around the neighborhood; and they obviously contained some sort of magic. Reasonably enough, these primitive people figured that an earthy deity—the Mother of the Rocks—lurked somewhere about, and was showing her power through these odd manifestations. It was only prudent to offer her sacrifices; and so the porphyry boulders became a group of altars.

Apparently it wasn't long before some bright young man decided to set himself up in the priest business—a profession more dignified and less strenuous than hunting and fishing. Probably he simply announced that the Goddess had informed him in a vision that he enjoyed her special confidence, and that from now on he should supervise the sacrifices on her sacred rocks.

The next logical step was to build a crude stone enclosure around the holy spot, so that nobody could approach it without making a payment—or votive offering—to the priest. (Its lower courses are still in place.) In time, as the fame of the sanctuary spread and as it acquired more priests and worshipers, they built shrines above first one of the sacred boulders and then another. Eventually, after the Greeks had arrived and adopted the local cult—in addition to their own gods—the whole glade was filled with splendid buildings.

And as the years rolled past, the ritual naturally became more elaborate. The Goddess acquired a spouse—Kadmilos, a fertility god whose demeanor would now be considered rude—plus a couple of attendant young demons known as Kabeiroi. She also seems to have had a pair of senior underworld assistants, Axioker-sos and Axiokersa. Together these divinities were called the Great Gods, and their rites were conducted in an ancient language, probably Thracian in origin. It persisted for centuries after the original inhabitants had been absorbed by the Greeks—in much the same way that Latin has survived in church services today.

By the time the religion had reached its full flower, it was giving the pilgrims who swarmed here good value for their money. They were initiated into the Mystery Cult of the Great Gods by means of an awesome ceremonial—complete with torchlight processions, a ritual drama, libations, sacrifices, oracles, oaths of secrecy, and perhaps a baptism with blood. It was a uniquely democratic order, open to everybody—a wealthy Roman and his slaves were once accepted in the same rite—but it had two degrees. The higher apparently was open only to people of sterling moral character, and even they had to confess their sins before admission.* Initiates of both degrees, however, were awarded valuable talismans—a sacred purple sash, to be worn around the waist as a protection against shipwreck, and a finger ring of magnetic iron to bring good fortune.

When these produced the expected results, the communicant showed a proper gratitude. If they failed, this was plain evidence that he had not been living right, or perhaps had been too stingy with his offerings. In either case, the renown and riches of the gods increased.

---

* The cult foreshadowed Christianity in several other curious ways. For example, its shrines—unlike the Greek temples—were used for congregational worship, and contained no graven images. One of them even had a rudimentary apse, the only thing of its kind I ever heard of in a pre-Christian building.

The Nike Fountain, for instance, probably was the thank offering of a naval commander whom the Great Gods had helped in battle. Its square, stone-lined niche is cut into the hillside above the sanctuary. The floor was a basin of rippled marble, fed with water by a terra-cotta pipe which still leads from a now-vanished spring on the slope above. Out of this little pool rose the marble prow of a warship, and on it—as if she had just alighted—stood the Winged Victory, looking over the shining colonnades of the temples toward the sea. The prevailing north wind molded her clothes against her body—as it will now, for any girl in summer dress who cares to step onto the foundation stones which once held the marble ship.

But the scene below has changed. In the holy valley the ruins of the sanctuary still gleam with a haunted grandeur; but on the far slope, where their guardian city once stood, there is nothing but the long wall, a single tower, and acres of scrub thorn.

This ruin apparently was brought about by five agents—Christians, goats, pirates, earthquakes, and lime burners—in that order.

So long as the Greeks (and the Romans who followed them) held Samothrace, they not only tolerated its cult but encouraged it. Although they had perfectly good deities of their own, it did no harm, in their view, to take out reinsurance with the Great Gods. Their embellishments, in fact, brought the sanctuary to its peak of magnificence.

Christians, however, had no patience with competitors. As soon as they came to power in the eastern Mediterranean, during the fourth century, they closed down the sanctuary for good. With its stream of pilgrims cut off, Palaeopolis was left stranded—much as Miami Beach would be, if its tourist traffic were abandoned overnight.

Meanwhile the goats had been at work. Like most Greek islands, Samothrace is a mountain peak thrust above the sea. Its stony ridges never carried much topsoil, and that little was held in precarious place only by its mantle of vegetation. On such a landscape, the goat is (for a time) the most efficient animal; he grows fat where cows or sheep would starve. The reason is that he can eat almost anything, including brush and saplings—

and grass he pulls up by the roots. When a flock of these four-legged bulldozers grazes over a mountainside, they leave it naked, so that the next storm scours the soil off into the sea. As a result the high pastures of Samothrace gradually washed away, and the scanty fields below were covered with flood-borne gravel.

At the same time, the harbor of Palaeopolis was silting up, so that its merchant ships could no longer bring in grain nor its triremes fight off pirates. The first great raid came in 84 B.C. Later, when Rome grew too weak to police these waters, looting parties swept in at increasingly frequent intervals. The dwindling and hungry population could no longer man the walls—and in the end it hardly seemed worthwhile to try.

The amazing thing is that they held on for so long. Not until the fifteenth century did the last of the Samothracians give up their city and flee inland. Then they chose for their new settlement of Chora a spot that had two advantages: it could not be seen from a masthead, and if pirates did find out about it, they could reach it only by a wearisome and dangerous march. (I tried it, and can't recommend the route to a raiding party or anyone else. The path winds through a dozen narrow passes and oleander-choked gullies, each a natural ambush. Underfoot the rocks are so sharp that the local mules cannot wear ordinary horseshoes, but have to be shod with oval plates.)

It's a sad irony that some of the noblest buildings men have yet achieved were built in earthquake country. Like so many Greek monuments—in Olympia, for example, and Delphi—the shrines of Samothrace were repeatedly shaken. So long as heathenism thrived, they were promptly rebuilt; but after the coming of Christianity nobody bothered when a pagan altar toppled. Good riddance.

An earthquake, however, saved the Winged Victory. She fell into the basin of her fountain, where dirt from the eroding slope above soon covered most of her shattered fragments. (One of her hands washed into the channel which drained the fountain, and there it was found in 1950—with results to be noted in a moment.) Providentially, the lime burners never found her, except perhaps the head and a few other missing parts.

They found nearly all the other statues, columns, and cornices that had been the glory of the city. Since they were hardheaded businessmen, they set up a kiln in the heart of the sanctuary, and others at convenient intervals throughout the streets of Palaeopolis. Then for centuries they burned the marble, which lay about in such profusion, to make lime for mortar and whitewash. It was a profitable trade, because Samothrace has little native marble or limestone; the material for Palaeopolis and its shrine was mostly shipped in from Thasos, an island fifty miles to the west. So until as recently as 1938 the lime burners were earning a nice drachma from this windfall. A visitor poking through the ruins will often stumble on the kilns where masterpieces of men who may have been the peers of Phidias and Praxiteles were converted to practical use.

The kilns stopped glowing only after Dr. Karl Lehmann arrived. He is an elderly, fragile-looking scholar from New York University, with a German accent, a remarkable wife, and an even more remarkable collection of talents. A friend of mine in Chora calls him "the savior of Samothrace."

Twenty years ago, armed with a grant from an anonymous donor, he landed on the island to begin the first thorough exploration of the lost city. Earlier diggers had worked here in a desultory fashion ever since 1863—when a visiting French consul discovered fragments of the Winged Victory and a few other sculptures and whisked them off to the Louvre—but nobody had undertaken a systematic excavation. That is what Dr. Lehmann has been doing ever since (minus the interruption of the war years) and he is just now bringing in the harvest. When I dropped in on him, he and his companion archaeologists had laid aside their shovels to write a nine-volume report on their work—which will, I suspect, long stand as a model of its kind.*

A more exciting career would be hard to imagine, or a more

---

* The first three volumes have been published, in a magnificent edition, by Pantheon Books for the Bollingen Foundation, which is helping to finance Dr. Lehmann's work; others are in press. Many of the facts cited here came from these books and from Dr. Lehmann's pamphlet on Samothrace, published in 1955 by New York University Press.

demanding one. It requires the intuition of a Sherlock Holmes; a flair for raising money; a mastery of languages (Dr. Lehmann speaks German, Turkish, English, French, Italian, and Greek, and is an authority on several archaic tongues); the managerial talent to organize, train, and direct a large crew of native workmen, plus a staff of sometimes-temperamental scholars; a diplomat's tact in dealing with local governments (and lime burners); an encyclopedic knowledge of history; a grasp of architecture, anthropology, art, and geology; an explorer's constitution; the highly specialized techniques of archaeological investigation; and a superhuman patience.

This patience—self-restraint might be a better term—struck me as the hardest qualification of all. One evening Georgios Nikolaides, the expedition's foreman, innkeeper, cook, and Grand Vizier, remarked that he had come across three graves in an unexpected spot: the garden of the little guesthouse where we were all staying. My impulse was to grab a spade immediately, and to hell with supper. Only a few hours earlier in the expedition's museum I had been handling a fantastic collection of jewelry, statuettes, vases, coins, and gold wreaths which had come from similar graves.

Gently, Dr. Lehmann explained that nobody would dig in the garden today—and maybe not for years. The schedule of work he had laid out could not be changed every time a new lead turned up, no matter how enticing.

"Already we have had too many such interruptions," he said. "We built the guesthouse on this particular site because we were pretty sure that nothing of importance lay beneath. We were wrong. As soon as we started on the foundations, we found we were in an ancient graveyard, and we had to sift every handful of earth before we could pour concrete. My wife wanted to call it The Hotel Necropolis, a Tomb in Every Room. But calmer heads prevailed."

Anyhow, the Lehmanns already have found enough treasures for one lifetime. Among them is another Winged Victory, smaller than the one in the Louvre but equally sophisticated in its carving. (She looks so remarkably like an angel that one wonders whether the cult of the Great Gods really was destroyed completely, or whether some of its traditions slipped into Christianity in disguise.) Appropriately, it was discovered not by a man but by Mrs. Lehmann—who is herself strikingly statuesque and who teaches at Smith College when she is not engaged in fieldwork. Like nearly everything else turned up at Samothrace, the new Nike is displayed in a charming little museum which the expedition has put up in a grove just west of the diggings.

This is one of the things which has so endeared Dr. Lehmann to the islanders and the Greek government. Ever since Lord Elgin picked up his marbles and went home, European archaeologists have been in the habit of carting off their finds—or at best turning them over in bulk to the Greeks, who then had to find money in their anemic budget to house them. The Americans, however—here, in the Stoa of Athens, and at a few other sites —have arranged to preserve and show their discoveries near the spot where they were found. Incidentally, the building of the museum and the guesthouse was the biggest public-works project the island has had in centuries, and some optimists believe they eventually will attract a tourist traffic. (A modest one. The guesthouse has only seven bedrooms.)

One discovery which you will not find in the Samothrace display is the hand of Nike. Since the French already had the rest of her, the Greek government (with Dr. Lehmann's advice) traded it to the Louvre for three other valuable carvings which had been lifted from the sanctuary. Because the arm is still missing, the hand cannot be fitted back in place; but a ribald art historian tells me that the position of the fingers makes it plain that the Winged Victory's thumb was originally close to her nose.

The main work of the New York University party has been to clear the underbrush and silt out of the sanctuary, re-erect part of the Hieron (the initiation hall for the higher degree of the mysteries), and to collect and study every surviving fragment of the holy buildings and their contents. This is an incredibly painstaking job. Each inscription on stone or potsherd has to be translated, drawn, and photographed, even when it is only a single letter. Each building stone has been measured to a fraction of a millimeter, and its location recorded. From this data, Mrs. Lehmann and three architect-scholars—Stuart Shaw of the Metropolitan Museum, and a couple of young Englishmen—have been able to reconstruct on paper exactly what some of the main buildings originally looked like. Indeed, a considerable part of the Rotunda—the largest round building known in Greek architecture—has been restored to its original form within the shelter of the museum.

Yet two decades of such labor, in which more than a score of investigators have taken part, is only a beginning. The city itself and its main graveyards have hardly been touched, and the silted-up harbor might well contain a trove of relics washed down from the once-populous slopes above. Anyone who climbs up there, from the shore to the site of the old citadel, will find himself stepping on innumerable fragments of pottery, most of them considerably more than a thousand years old and some three times that. They are the broken wine jars, the goblets, vases, dishes, and toys of a rather untidy people, who apparently dumped their rubbish in the streets or their own back yards.

Such bits of clay sometimes yield unexpected information. One of Dr. Lehmann's favorite artifacts is a ball about two inches in diameter, made as a child's plaything—presumably in imitation of a larger ball of sewn hide which was used in some unknown sport. For seams are incised in the baked clay, indicating that the life-sized model had been sewn from skins cut in exactly the same pattern as a modern basketball.

So we can guess that the old Samothracians enjoyed games something like our own. But there is vastly more about them that we cannot yet guess. Centuries of their history are completely blank, the names of their kings unknown, the invaders who looted the sanctuary unrecorded. Such information awaits, perhaps, another generation of diggers; and with it—who knows?— maybe other finds comparable to the gold of Troy, the stunning

mosaics which have just been uncovered in Alexander's old capital of Pella, or the archaic statues which were hauled from beneath a street in Piraeus.

What better adventure can you ask for these days than to hunt
such treasures, to ferret out ancient mysteries—and to get paid
for it, even at a university's wage scale? If I were eighteen again,
I know exactly what I would do. I would start studying Greek,
memorizing the old maps of Samothrace, and sharpening my
spade.

November, 1959

10 : A Small Buried Treasure

ALEKO became a grave robber mostly out of boredom, though
hunger had something to do with it.

He is not a talkative man, so I learned about his profession only
obliquely and over a considerable period of time. (His former
profession, that is. Now he is a businessman of monumental respectability, the owner of a cherished secondhand Cadillac in
which he will drive you anywhere in Europe for quite a reasonable
fee.) The first hint came in Salonika, after we had been traveling
for days over the rutted, dusty roads of northern Greece.

We had stopped at a sidewalk café for a cup of coffee. On the
way back to the car we passed one of those little open-front shops
which seem to be the commonest form of enterprise in Macedonia. Its counter was piled with canvas shoes, old clothes, bat-
tered lamps, and similar castoffs. At one end was a tray of jewelry.
I wouldn't have given it a second glance if Aleko hadn't stopped
and begun to poke around among the earrings and bangles.
Most of them looked as if they had come originally from the
Greek equivalent of a dime store, and the one he pointed out to

me—a copper-colored bracelet—was even more tarnished than the rest.

"You might buy that," he said. "It won't cost much."

There was nothing I needed less, but I had learned to follow Aleko's suggestions, however odd. He conducted the mandatory haggling and bought it in the end for a few drachmas.

When we were on the road again I asked him why.

"It's old," he said. "Probably about eighth century B.C. I think it came, maybe, from the grave of a little girl. Because it wasn't gold, the grave robbers sold it cheap. They are ignorant fellows mostly." He was silent for a couple of miles, and then added: "I know a little about such things."

(At the time all this sounded unlikely, but weeks later I found out that Aleko was right. Museum people told me that the bracelet was bronze, not copper; its incised decorations were Early Geometric; a few similar pieces are in the Binaki collection in Athens.)

Two days later Aleko asked, diffidently, if I would mind our making a short detour. We were driving east, toward the Turkish border, along the narrow strip of coastal plain at the top of the Aegean Sea. The road originally had been built by the Roman emperors to link their two great seats of power, Constantinople and Rome, but it had deteriorated considerably since their time. A few miles to the north rose the long crest of mountains that mark the Bulgarian border. In their foothills, Aleko said, was the village of Moustheni. No, I wouldn't find it on the map— just a dozen or so stone huts.

"When I left there twenty years ago," he said, "I wore hand-cuffs. I never expected to go back—but now that we are so close, I would like to drop by and see if they remember me. It would be good for them to see me traveling in my own car and with an American friend."

As we turned onto the rocky track that led toward the foot-hills, he told me about his boyhood in Moustheni. His family, like most of the others, were tobacco farmers. Except for the few weeks each year when he helped plant, hoe, and harvest their three-acre patch, he had no work. Nor was there much else to do—no school, no movies, not even any girls; for in this part of the country, so long under Turkish rule, the women are still secluded. (Many of the older ones never appear in public without their heavy, tentlike veils; the younger ones, never without a chaperon.) So Aleko spent much time with a few other idle youngsters at a table in front of the town's only café, playing cards, nursing a thimbleful of coffee through the long hot afternoons, grumbling about their poverty and boredom.

He doesn't remember who first thought of the tumuli. These are mounds, about ten feet high, which rise like pimples all over the Macedonian plain; along some stretches of road you pass one about every quarter of a mile. Each of them covers a tomb, usually a rough stone enclosure which contains (or once did) the bones of some Bronze Age chief, and sometimes those of his family, servants, and horses. (Common people were, presumably, buried with less pretension.) A stranger finds it hard to believe that there could have been so many of them; but, as Aleko pointed out, people as bellicose as the Achaeans and Dorians could manage over a few thousand years of tribal warfare to run through quite a few chiefs.

The young men of Moustheni had heard that archaeologists from Athens recently had been digging in such a mound near the ancient ruins of Amphipolis, not far away. Nobody knew for sure what, if anything, they had found; but there were rumors of much treasure—jeweled sword hilts, necklaces, armlets, statues of solid gold. Why shouldn't the boys do a little digging on their own?

Such enterprises are of course illegal in Greece, and the penalties are severe. But policemen are scarce in the country districts; besides, the Moustheni explorers planned to work at night. As an extra precaution they organized themselves into two shifts of four men each—one to stand sentry while the other dug.

"For the next year," Aleko said, "I labored harder than I ever have in my life. We would tackle a grave just like the archaeologists do—cutting a trench about two feet wide straight through the middle of the mound. If we hit anything promising, we would then open branch trenches to the left or right. And always we would try to finish the job and fill in the trenches before daybreak. We even replaced the sod and bushes as best we could, to avoid attracting attention to our business.

"We must have opened a hundred tumuli without finding a thing except bones and bits of useless pottery. Other grave robbers, you see, had got there first, maybe hundreds of years ago. So all we got for our trouble was calloused palms and aching backs, and naturally we began to get discouraged. Then one night we found it.

"This mound looked exactly like all the others, but somehow the earlier diggers had missed it. Alongside the bones of the old warrior we found all the equipment his people had given him for his last journey—three pots that must have held food and wine, a bronze spearhead, a wreath of gold leaves, and a little statue of Hercules. It was only about six inches high, but it was gold—probably from the ancient mines near the headwaters of the Strymon River—and to us the workmanship seemed very fine. None of us had ever seen anything like it.

"But what could we do with it? If we tried to sell such a rarity anywhere in Greece, the authorities would begin to ask questions at once. And how could we find out what it was worth? After so much labor, you understand, we didn't propose to let ourselves be cheated.

"We stopped our nighttime ventures, and for days we sat around the café and talked about this problem. In the end we worked out a very clever scheme. . . ."

At this point Aleko's account was interrupted by our arrival at Moustheni. It looked even grimmer than he had led me to expect —a single cobbled street twisting up the hillside between two rows of gray hovels. But there was nothing grim about the people. As we came abreast of the first house, Aleko began to honk his horn, and the whole village—including a remarkable number of dogs and babies—poured out to follow. The appearance of any automobile here was cause for excitement enough, but when they recognized the man at the wheel the uproar really cut loose.

If St. Demetrios himself had ridden into town on his spectral white stallion, he couldn't have produced more astonishment, or noise.

Aleko inched the car along to the café, where he had plotted with his friends so many years ago, and stopped to receive homage. At this place the street widens a little, to form a sort of village square. Though it was crowded to the walls, somebody managed to drag a couple of tables out to the center, and after Aleko had introduced me to what I took to be the village elders, we sat down with them for a ceremonial round of *ouzo* and thick, bitter coffee. Aleko insisted on paying for everything. While I couldn't understand a word of the conversation, it was clear that he was enacting—with great dignity—the Prodigal's Return.

His sense of timing was flawless. In precisely twenty minutes he rose, shook hands again with everybody, and led the procession back to his car—the very image of the man of affairs who has to be off to the pressing business of the outside world. A swarm of children and dogs, in full cry, raced beside us until we passed the last house.

All the way back to the main road Aleko grinned in silent satisfaction. I had a hard time getting him to pick up the thread of his story.

"One of the men you met back there—the one who passed around the tobacco and cigarette papers—is Philip Galas," he said. "He is a farmer now, but in the old days he was one of our diggers. He had relatives in Kavala, and there he had met a jeweler and pawnbroker—a rich man but trustworthy. To get our scheme under way, Philip took the statue to him and persuaded him to make an exact copy. Naturally we had to promise him a share—a full one-ninth—of the wealth we expected to have before long.

"The jeweler then carried his copy to the local museum and tried to sell it, saying that it had been pawned in his shop over a year ago and that the owner had never reclaimed it. The curator, of course, refused. He explained that it was only a modern reproduction, though a good one, and therefore worth little more than the metal it contained. Our friend pretended great disappointment. But if it *had* been genuine, he asked, what price would it have brought? At least a million drachmas, the museum man told him. Perhaps more, for such works of art from the archaic period were very rare indeed.

"Once we had that information, we knew just what to do next. From our fathers and the jeweler we borrowed enough money to send one member of our band—you will forgive me if I don't mention his name—to Paris. He carried the little Hercules, the real one, baked inside a loaf of bread. It was a safe hiding place, since nearly all peasants carry a parcel of bread and sausage when they go traveling, and the customs guards never pay it any attention.

"In Paris our messenger had no great trouble in finding a dealer willing to pay a fair price and ask no questions."

Aleko lapsed into one of his long silences; I thought the story was finished. When he began talking again, it was about Greek history.

"The habit of betrayal has always been our great weakness," he said. "Remember Alcibiades? Remember Ephialtes, who sold the pass at Thermopylae? Such men are more typical than you might think. Every city in Greece has its legend of at least one betrayer. So has Moustheni.

"Our agent didn't come home. Instead he went to Athens with our money in his pocket, and wrote an unsigned letter to the national police, telling them all about our little venture in midnight archaeology. So a truckload of policemen pulled into the village one morning, and arrested all seven of us. They took us to the Kavala court, where the judge sentenced us to a big fine and many years in jail. If the war hadn't broken out that fall, I might have been in prison yet."

What happened, he explained, was that the royal government had opened the jail doors for every man who wanted to fight the invaders. Aleko and his friends set off for the mountains, with no equipment except a rifle and a belt of cartridges apiece, and fought for five years against Italians, Germans, and Bulgarians. When the war was over, nobody felt inclined to remember the old charges.

"But the archaeologists didn't forget our statue," he added. "With the help of the French police they eventually got their hands on the little Hercules. You can see it any day you like in the Kavala museum—the finest piece in its collection. We never got a penny for it, of course."

Did he know, I asked, what had become of the man who turned them in?

"Yes," Aleko said, "he came back to Macedonia after the war. Perhaps he too thought that old scores would be forgotten. He was mistaken."

For a long while we had met no one along the road. Now we saw ahead of us two old women on minute donkeys, riding side-saddle in the fashion of the country. Aleko pulled up beside them to ask about the turnoff for Keramoti, the fishing village where he was to leave me and where I hoped to find some sort of boat to take me on the next leg of my journey. When we were on our way again, he said:

"There is one thing about these old graves. When everybody knows that one of them has been opened—as, for example, the one where we found the treasure—it is no longer of interest. Nobody else is likely to look inside it again, maybe not for centuries. It makes an ideal place to hide a body."

July, 1960

11 : The Nonsexual Behavior of the Human Female

THOSE KINSEY PEOPLE are at it again.

Dr. Alfred C. Kinsey lies a-moldering in the grave, but his studies go marching on—apparently forever—under the banner of his Institute for Sex Research at the University of Indiana. His disciples there have just turned out another of those clinical, chart-studded books about the sexual behavior of the human female, and they hint that any number of similar volumes are in the works.

This labor of love (if that is the term) probably is a mistake. Any man of discreet years already has a working knowledge of such matters, or anyhow as much as may be good for his ego. What he really needs is a reliable guide to the nonsexual behavior of the human female—a mystery which has caused more rage and grief throughout the ages than the bubonic plague.

So far researchers haven't even scratched the surface of this subject, probably because they are afraid it might scratch back. But cowardice won't block the path of science much longer. The Haroun-al-Raschid Fund for Benevolent and Hell-Raising Purposes—the foundation which fears neither woman nor devil —is about to embark on an investigation which holds infinite promise for the happiness of the species, or at least the male half of it.

Its first project, naturally, will be to try to discover why women are deciduous. Every male inevitably spends a large part of his life picking up the *débris de femme*—Kleenex, gloves, lipsticks, handbags, and the like—which they leave in their wakes. On rare occasions this can serve a useful purpose. During World War II, for example, Mr. Horace T. Quimby, a civilian employee of the Norfolk Navy Yard, decided it was his patriotic duty to collect the bobby pins which showered down from the lovely heads of his wife and three daughters; within nine months he had saved enough steel to armor a battleship.

But ordinarily the enormous energies expended in tidying up after women produce nothing but abraded nerves. To cite one pitiful case, a janitor at the Radio City Music Hall is nearly going out of his mind because he keeps finding under the seats, about once a month, a single high-heeled slipper. What he can't figure out is: How in Heaven's name can even the most fog-

272 : THE STUPIDITY PROBLEM

bound female get out of the theater without noticing that she is walking in only one shoe?

One New York bank tries to cope with the shedding problem, at considerable expense, by providing combination locks for those women who lose an excessive number of keys to their safe deposit boxes. It has never been able to develop a theory, however, to explain why some are so much worse than others. One vice president, who reads Freud in the evenings, thinks guilt feelings may have something to do with it. The widows who are most remorseful lose one key after another, he believes, as a form of unconscious self-punishment, thus cutting themselves off (temporarily) from the enjoyment of their inheritance.

Trouble is he can't find any tactful way to measure remorse. After his first attempts resulted in three rich old biddies' withdrawing their accounts, this line of inquiry had to be abandoned. He is now working on an even more Freudian explanation which is hardly suitable for discussion in pages as chaste as these.

What the Fund hopes to discover is the hormone, or whatever it is, that makes some women shed like an elm in autumn while others are reasonably prehensile. Then—by a careful process of selective breeding, or retraining, or something—it may eventually produce a strain of nonshedding females. (In the beginning the Fund thought that pockets might be the answer, until a secretary in its office pointed out that no woman will ever use them because they cause bulges in the wrong places.)

A second research team will look into feeding habits. Already it has collected a number of case histories which seem to defy rational interpretation.

Take, for instance, the strange case of Gerda Himmelreich. She is a Chicago girl, nineteen years old, gentle, sound in wind and limb, sixteen hands high and not a blemish on her. To the casual male observer, she appears to have all the essential parts, arranged in satisfactory order and proportions. (Perhaps "casual" is not the precise word; as a matter of fact, when she prances down Michigan Boulevard in a stiff off-the-lake breeze, you can hear eyeballs popping for fifty yards around.)

Yet Gerda gets periodic spells of hysteria about her weight. When these strike, she immediately embarks on a diet which even St. Simeon Stylites would have considered extreme. These regimens—which she clips out of women's magazines—run largely to mineral oil, chopped grapefruit rind, and seaweed. She sticks with them, on the average, for three days. Then, abandoning the project as abruptly as she took it up, she gorges herself for a week on chocolate malts, fudge cake, and ice cream éclairs. Her case, astonishingly enough, seems to be by no means unique.

This research group also will seek the reasons why seventy-eight women out of every hundred, when unprotected by a male, will gravitate at lunchtime into restaurants which feature (a) chintz, (b) triangular sandwiches with the crusts cut off and stuffed with a colloidal compound of tuna fish and peanut butter, (c) mayonnaise or whipped cream (or both) smeared over every other item on the menu.

Feminine logistics also will be put on the agenda, if the Fund can find a new project director; the man originally assigned to it cut his throat after the first week. Although it has long been known that the movement of two or more females from Point A to Point B is an undertaking of manic complexity, the principles on which such hegiras operate have never been discovered. A pilot study has, however, isolated a few rudimentary facts:

1. The take-off is always preceded by a minimum of seven phone conversations. At least five of these deal with what the other women in the party are going to wear.

2. The hours spent on pretrip phone calls increase in geometric ratio with the number of women traveling.

3. The number of bags each woman will try to take, unless forcibly restrained, can be determined by multiplying by two the number of days she expects to be away. These impedimenta will contain at least five dresses which she doesn't expect to wear, but thinks she ought to take along just in case. Upon arrival it will be found, in eighty-three cases out of a hundred, that they do *not* contain either a toothbrush or a shower cap.

4. Seventy-two per cent of all females studied made frantic efforts to board the train, ship, or plane twenty minutes before its scheduled departure.

5. It has never yet occurred to any woman so far investigated that she will have to pay her cab fare, until the cab in which she is riding actually stops at its destination. She then registers surprise and begins to scrabble for change among the compacts, shopping lists, safety pins, cigarettes, keys, hairnets, and other detritus in her purse. The resulting delays were responsible for 47 per cent of all traffic jams in New York City in 1957.

6. The commotion involved in getting a single slip of a girl off to college, camp, or boarding school is roughly equivalent to the movement of an artillery battalion, with full equipment, from Fort Sill to its port of embarkation.

7. The Fund is indebted to Mr. John Gardner of the Carnegie Corporation for the observation that women, when traveling, ignore all those conventions of considerate behavior on which our civilization is so precariously based.

When boarding a commuting train, for example, men seldom shove, gouge, or trip each other, and by unspoken agreement the man nearest the car door gets in first. This procedure is ignored, however, by any woman who happens to be on the platform —particularly if she is a little old lady with an umbrella and a low center of gravity.

"She flails her way through the crowd like a Notre Dame halfback," Mr. Gardner has reported, "and she will by God get aboard that train first no matter how many men she mangles in doing it. This same woman, under different—and stationary —circumstances often turns out to be mannerly, sometimes even demure."

8. The chaos which is so characteristic of women-in-motion results, in large part, from the fact that they seldom know where they are *and they don't care.*

The man used as a control in this study was Mr. William Caperton of Clayton, New Mexico. It was found that he—like most males with normal reflexes—showed acute signs of discomfort whenever he was temporarily disoriented; these symptoms disappeared as soon as he found out which direction was north, the general layout of the terrain, and the distance to the next town.

By contrast, none of the women studied could identify any point of the compass; 23 per cent didn't know what "terrain" meant; 57 per cent couldn't read a map and didn't want to learn; and 19 per cent had forgotten what address they were bound for. Moreover, in no case did this terrifying lack of essential data cause the slightest indication of distress.

"What of it?" one of them said when a Fund investigator pointed out that she was, for all practical purposes, lost. "I let men worry about those things. I got more important matters on my mind."

If its money lasts long enough, the Fund hopes to find out what they are.

August, 1958

ABOUT THE AUTHOR

John Fischer was born in Texhoma, Oklahoma, in 1910. He was graduated from the University of Oklahoma in 1932, and studied economics, politics and philosophy at Oxford on a Rhodes Scholarship from 1933 to 1935. He began newspaper work in high school with the Amarillo *Globe-News*, and later worked for several papers in Oklahoma and New Mexico. During vacations from Oxford he worked for the United Press in England and Germany, and on his return to the U.S. he joined the Associated Press in Washington, covering the Senate, the Supreme Court, and various government departments.

In 1937 he went to work for the Department of Agriculture, serving in the Farm Security Administration and the Bureau of Agricultural Economics. In 1941 he transferred to the newly formed Board of Economic Warfare, where he helped organize an economic intelligence service. During 1943 and 1944 he served as chief representative of BEW and its successor agency, the Foreign Economic Administration, for India and Burma, and as an economic intelligence officer on the staff of General Joseph W. Stilwell.

In 1945 Mr. Fischer went to Russia as a member of a team of supervisors checking on the distribution of UNRRA supplies in the Ukraine. On his return he wrote *Why They Behave Like Russians*, published in 1947. His *Master Plan: U.S.A.*, a study of American foreign policy, was published in 1951.

Mr. Fischer joined the *Harper's Magazine* staff in 1944. Between 1947 and 1953 he was chief editor of the General Books Department of Harper & Brothers, returning to the Magazine as editor-in-chief in 1953.

Mr. Fischer has written articles for a number of magazines and since 1955 has been the chief contributor to "The Editor's Easy Chair," a monthly feature of *Harper's Magazine*.